Soccer Diplomacy

Soccer Diplomacy

International Relations and Football since 1914

Edited by Heather L. Dichter

Scholarly publisher for the Commonwealth,
serving Bellarmine University, Berea College, Centre
College of Kentucky, Eastern Kentucky University,
The Filson Historical Society, Georgetown College,
Kentucky Historical Society, Kentucky State University,
Morehead State University, Murray State University,
Northern Kentucky University, Transylvania University,
University of Kentucky, University of Louisville,
and Western Kentucky University.

Editorial and Sales Offices: The University Press of Kentucky
663 South Limestone Street, Lexington, Kentucky 40508-4008
www.kentuckypress.com

Library of Congress Cataloging-in-Publication Data

Names: Dichter, Heather, editor.
Title: Soccer diplomacy : international relations and football since 1914 /
Edited by Heather L. Dichter.
Description: Lexington : University Press of Kentucky, [2020] |
Series: Studies in conflict, diplomacy, and peace | Includes index.
Identifiers: LCCN 2020013205 | ISBN 9780813179513 (hardcover) |
ISBN 9780813179537 (pdf) | ISBN 9780813179544 (epub)
Subjects: LCSH: Soccer—Political aspects. | Sports—International cooperation. |
Fédération internationale de football association.
Classification: LCC GV943.9.P65 S63 2020 | DDC 796.334—dc23
LC record available at https://lccn.loc.gov/2020013205

This book is printed on acid-free paper meeting
the requirements of the American National Standard
for Permanence in Paper for Printed Library Materials.

Manufactured in the United States of America.

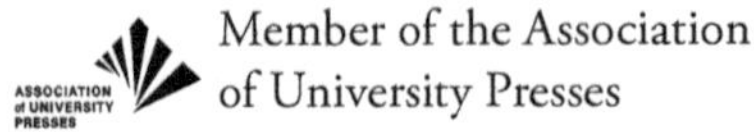

Contents

Abbreviations

AFC	Asian Football Confederation
ANC	African National Congress
ASF	Australian Soccer Federation
ATO	Allied Travel Office
BNDES	Banco Nacional de Desenvolvimento Econômico e Social
BRT	Bus Rapid Transit
CAF	Confédération Africaine de Football
CEF	Caixa Econômica Federal
CFI	Comité français interfédéral
CFU	Caribbean Football Union
CONCACAF	Central American and the Caribbean Federation
CONIFA	Confederation of Independent Football Associations
CONMEBOL	South American Football Confederation
CSTN	Caribbean Sport Television Network
DND	Delegación Nacional de Deportes (National Sports Delegation)
EA	Department of External Affairs
EEC	European Economic Community
FA	Football Association
FASA	Football Association of Southern Africa
FCO	Foreign and Commonwealth Office

FET de las JONS	Falange Española Tradicionalista y de las Juntas de Ofensiva Nacional Sindicalista (Traditionalist Spanish Phalanx of the Committees of the National Syndicalist Offensive)
FFF	French Football Federation
FFV	Football Federation of Vietnam
FIFA	Fédération Internationale de Football Association
FRG	Federal Republic of Germany
GDR	German Democratic Republic
IOC	International Olympic Committee
ISF	international sport federations
KSÍ	Football Association of Iceland
NAFU	North American Football Union
NATO	North Atlantic Treaty Organization
NCFE	National Council for Free Europe
NFL	National Football League
NGO	nongovernmental organization
OCB	Operations Coordinating Board
PAC	Political Advisers Committee (in NATO)
PSDB	Brazilian Social Democracy Party
RFEF	Real Federación Española de Fútbol (Royal Spanish Football Federation)
SAAFA	South African African Football Association
SABFU	South African Bantu Football Association
SACA	South African Cricket Association
SACFA	South African Coloured Football Association
SACOS	South African Council of Sport
SAFA	South African Football Association
SAIFA	South African Indian Football Association
SARB	South African Rugby Board
SASF	South African Soccer Federation

SOFE	Service des œuvres françaises à l'étranger
SPUJ	Soccer for Peace and Understanding in Jordan
SBS	Special Broadcasting Service
TTD	Temporary Travel Document
TTFA	Trinidad and Tobago Football Association
UEFA	Union of European Football Associations
UFEES	Union of Free Eastern European Sportsmen
UN	United Nations
USIA	United States Information Agency
USSFA	United States Soccer Football Association

Introduction

Heather L. Dichter

Soccer, football, fútbol, Fußball, or voetbal—however the sport of association football is known locally, it is a universal language to millions of people across the globe. International soccer's governing body, Fédération Internationale de Football Association (FIFA), has over two hundred member states—more than the United Nations. Soccer is often used as a marker of international legitimacy. One of the earliest acts that newly independent countries seek to accomplish on the international stage is to join FIFA. Ghana's independence in 1957 set off a wave of African decolonization, and the country's application for FIFA membership shortly thereafter began a pattern, continuing to South Sudan and Kosovo most recently. South Sudan even marked its independence in 2011 with a soccer match, pitting its new national team against a Kenyan club.[1] Although only a limited number of teams (soon to be increased to forty-eight) actually compete in the World Cup, nearly every member of FIFA participates in the qualification process. Not surprisingly, FIFA's World Cup is the most watched single-sport event in the world.

This book explores the nexus of the world's most popular sport and diplomacy, examining the historical interactions of soccer in three dimensions. The first is the use of soccer as a tool of nation-state–based diplomacy. In these cases, soccer serves the purposes of public diplomacy just as other forms of culture or exchange, or the simple action of holding (or preventing) a match, can serve the aims of a government. The second steps away from the state altogether and looks at the diplomacy of soccer as a non-state actor, often through the actions of soccer organizations themselves. The third dimension brings these two together to explore the relationship between soccer and a variety of diplomatic actors in the subnational, national, and transnational context. These ideas provide the guiding themes for the chapters contained herein, with the chapters using whichever term—soccer or football—is most appropriate to the area and countries examined. States sought to communicate their political goals through the diplomacy of international soccer games, tournaments, and tours. In other instances the sport served as a form of representation of identity and national policy. Finally, the many problems of recent soccer diplomacy have required—and continue to need—negotiation. This negotiation happens at many levels among and between diplomats and soccer elites within FIFA, continental federations, and national governing bodies, as well as local organizers of events.

The popularity of soccer across the globe, combined with this near-universal participation in the sport at the international level, makes examination of the intersection of soccer and diplomacy important. This single sport—more than the Olympics, regional multisport competitions, any other sport, or even any other type of activity—reveals much about international relations, states' attempts to influence foreign views (soft power), and regional power relations. For decades many states have sought to use the sport to demonstrate their position within the international community. Even with the very first FIFA World Cup, host Uruguay wanted to portray itself as a modern state to the rest of the world by constructing a ninety-thousand-seat stadium and using the event as part of the country's centennial celebrations. This use of the event for broader diplomatic purposes continued with the second World Cup, held in Italy in 1934, which contributed to "an image of Italian sporting prowess encouraged and manipulated by the Fascist regime." Later hosts have also sought to use subsequent iterations of this event to demonstrate their own visions to the world. South Africa, host of the 2010 World Cup, wanted to use the mega-event to prove its place as an advanced country on the African continent no longer burdened by its apartheid past. Soccer tournaments also force more people to pay attention to global affairs in regions they might otherwise ignore. For instance, when tensions among Gulf states arose in 2017, with the majority of the states aligning themselves with Saudi Arabia against Qatar, news stories raised questions about Qatar's ability to remain as host of the 2022 World Cup with such economic sanctions and flight restrictions within the region. With such global prominence, soccer can—and does—reach the masses, and, increasingly throughout the twentieth and twenty-first centuries, governments have attempted to harness the power of soccer to achieve their diplomatic aims, whether they are targeted to a specific or global audience or directly to a foreign government.[2]

Although the worlds of sport and diplomacy have coexisted since the late nineteenth century, scholars have been examining the complex relationship between soccer and diplomacy for only about twenty-five years. Analyses and studies of soccer abound, but scholarly publications have focused almost exclusively on the role of the game in national, sociological, and cultural contexts. Peter Beck's seminal *Scoring for Britain*, published in 1999, was not only an early historical monograph on sport and diplomacy, but also soccer and diplomacy. Since then individual articles have addressed this intersection, or it has been included as a small part—but by no means the full argument—of other monographs. In his conclusion of *Diplomatic Games*, the previous volume on sport and diplomacy I coedited with Andrew Johns, Thomas Zeiler noted within that book "the lack of attention to soccer is mystifying, particularly because the sport has been at the center of some diplomatic intrigues, national identities, business ties, and corporate globalization." This book provides a start to rectifying that criticism and brings together many new strands of research to reveal the extensive and lengthy relationships between soccer and diplomacy. With chapters that span both a temporal and geographical breadth, this volume demonstrates the extent to which, and the variety of ways in which, soccer has been—and continues to be—used for diplomatic purposes by numerous individuals, organizations, and governments.[3]

Indeed, the repeated uses of the game by so many states across the globe on every continent (save Antarctica, although no one would be surprised to learn the national scientific delegations have played against each other on the ice for continental pride) reveals how integral the sport is to international relations. No one denies the centrality of the game to national identity or culture in several countries. The "football war" between El Salvador and Honduras in 1969 is often used as the example of diplomatic tensions manifesting themselves within the sport as the two states played in a World Cup qualifying match. Yet this event is the aberration—it resulted in actual armed conflict—in contrast to the decades of governments using matches and tournaments, as well as friendly tours by national teams, to complement the work of political diplomats. Soccer has therefore long had a close relationship with international affairs.

Sport and diplomacy have also been mutually intertwined in transnational networks of governance and competition—not just on the field of play—and the nongovernmental bodies controlling the sport play an important role in the relationship between soccer and diplomacy, even if formal links were slower to develop. The emergence of international governing bodies to organize events and regulate sport in the late nineteenth and early twentieth centuries coincided with the development of international organizations in general, many of them organized along nongovernmental lines. The growth of national sport governing bodies along with the increase in athletes competing overseas led to the creation of international sport organizations in the 1880s and 1890s. Pierre de Coubertin's idea for the modern Olympic Games and the International Olympic Committee (IOC) itself to oversee this event contributed to the rapid expansion of international sport federations. FIFA, founded in 1904, was one of fourteen international federations formed before the First World War. Even with soccer's broad global acceptance by the end of the nineteenth century, it is still challenging to identify soccer and diplomacy before 1914. While the sport, alongside other traditionally British sports such as rugby and cricket, was firmly established by the late nineteenth century, diplomats did not embrace the opportunities provided by sport until the interwar period, as Barbara Keys has demonstrated for the United States, Germany, and the Soviet Union. It is not surprising to see European powers such as France and Spain using soccer in the interwar period, and the first three World Cup hosts each hoped organizing the event would benefit their countries. As seen in many of the chapters, at later points in the twentieth century lesser soccer countries also used the sport for diplomatic purposes, and surely others were doing so earlier as well.[4]

As soccer has pursued a goal of global engagement to consolidate its position as the world's preeminent sport in the past century, it has increasingly had to reckon or negotiate with the nation-state. Simultaneously, as state sovereignty has been challenged by the constituent and much-debated forces of globalization, so have long-standing characteristics of soccer's operation—most notably in a contested relationship among the national, regional, and international levels. The size and scope of the FIFA World Cup as a mega-event and other international soccer tournaments as second-order mega-events forces many government departments to engage with the sport when a country is selected to be the host. From finances to security to infrastructure, not to mention the presence of political leaders at opening or championship matches, governments frequently must address soccer. Tournaments organized at the continental level but involving professional clubs, such as the UEFA European Cup (now Champions League) often force clubs, governments, and national governing bodies to confront these issues. Real Madrid in the 1950s and 1960s under the Franco regime illustrates those complex negotiations, as seen in this book. The creation of regional soccer federations also has had a clear political purpose to assert the wishes of entire blocs of states, as seen with the FIFA presidential elections in 2015, with Joseph "Sepp" Blatter's short-lived reelection, and again in 2016, with the selection of his successor.[5]

Over the past century any number of states have sought to conduct diplomacy via soccer games, tournaments, and the sport's governance structures, including the international governing body, FIFA, itself. National governments have variously drawn on soccer as a tool to communicate with their own publics and those beyond their borders, as a means to establish and/or enhance national prestige, or simply bask in the reflective glory of their soccer players as ambassadors. Governments have particularly utilized soccer within the two related dimensions of public diplomacy and soft power. Joseph S. Nye initially articulated the concept of soft power, stating it "rests on the ability to shape the preferences of others," that is, the ability to attract others to a particular course of action. Later scholars drew on this concept and further elaborated the idea of public diplomacy. Nicholas Cull argues that public diplomacy is "an international actor's attempt to manage the international environment through engagement with a foreign public." Jan Melissen has a different emphasis in stating public diplomacy to be "the relationship between diplomats and the foreign publics with whom they work."[6] Exchanges or foreign tours have a close relationship with the deployment of soft power, and historians have examined the use of museum exhibits, plays, films, and vacation destinations within public diplomacy programs.[7] Sport exchanges fall within this realm as well, and the frequent use of soccer at many levels and by states of varying skill illustrates its value.[8]

Official competitions, primarily in the form of tournaments, play a central role in this diplomatic use of soccer, particularly through its visibility on the world stage. As events that take weeks—or years, if one includes the qualification for the World Cup—tournaments provide an extended period of time for a country or an idea to be on display. FIFA and its regional bodies, such as CONCACAF and UEFA, have pursued promotional strategies that have increased their revenues tremendously through sponsorship and broadcast contracts. The global viewing audience of tournaments now reaches more than half of the world's population, according to FIFA's reports on the 2018 World Cup. Even smaller continental or regional tournaments are able to draw spectators from further abroad, especially with the help of online streaming. Interest in these events has always come from within the participating states, but modern technology enables an even larger audience beyond those traditional boundaries, making participating in, and especially hosting, international soccer tournaments a particularly valuable way for a state to convey a message to a broad audience. While FIFA's World Cup (for men) commands by far the largest audience, FIFA's other tournaments (for youth players or women) and regional tournaments also provide comparable opportunities for diplomacy. Continental tournaments may even provide greater opportunities for diplomacy because the majority of states never qualify for the World Cup at a basic level, but also because for many countries regional relations are more pressing. Almost every chapter in this volume deals with diplomacy related to an international tournament, from bidding for events to hosting them, from sending teams to tournaments to diplomatic reports about events, including how one's country represented the state.[9]

The growth of soccer into a multibillion-dollar (or pound or euro) business has increasingly shaped the ways in which soccer is used within and by diplomacy. The potential for large revenues contributed to the ending of apartheid in South African soccer, the negotiating tactics of Jack Warner, and the changing of Brazilian laws—all issues addressed in chapters of this book. That money increasingly factored into the more recent events covered in chapters of this volume is not surprising. The power of the global game has led more countries, people, and soccer federations to seek to use the sport for advantages and influence. Although the costs associated with hosting major soccer tournaments have grown astronomically, especially with respect to security and venue construction or renovation, countries nonetheless still clamor to host FIFA tournaments for perceived value in terms of tourist money and soft power. Germany's federal tourism office supported the 2006 World Cup, whose slogan was "a time to make friends," and found that perceptions of Germans by foreign visitors had improved as a result of the event. Participation in the major tournaments, especially the World Cup, brings financial rewards for each country's football association; the accompanying international prestige contributes in many instances to government support for these actions.[10]

The global nature of soccer is readily visible in the content of this book. Chapters cover corners of the world that are renowned for the game—Amsterdam, Barcelona, and Rio de Janeiro—and those less known for soccer—Trinidad and Tobago, Vietnam, and Iceland (although the small European island garnered significant attention during its surprising and successful 2016

Euro run and qualification for and participation in the 2018 World Cup, including a draw with Argentina). Even countries such as the United States, Australia, and South Africa, where soccer competes with other sports domestically—often other more popular versions of "football"—attempt to use the global game to their advantage. The plethora of states using soccer for diplomatic purposes demonstrates the importance at all levels of the sport (at the grassroots level, during insignificant friendly matches, and at the pinnacle of the sport, the World Cup) and across a variety of diplomatic relationships and positions within the international community. Seemingly unimportant soccer matches—between the sport's minnows, at second-order international tournaments, or simple friendlies—can indeed be significant. Diplomacy within sport happens along a spectrum at mega-events such as the Olympic Games and the World Cup down to the person-to-person level, where sport forms the basis of a transaction. In fact, the inclusion of these other countries that may appear to lack status and events that do not capture a global audience demonstrates the broad scope of the sport within diplomacy.

Soccer is perhaps the one international sport whose regional bodies have such unprecedented strength as to warrant simultaneous attention as part of FIFA and in their own right. The majority of sports within the Olympic movement rely on distribution of Olympic television and sponsorship revenues, and the media power of that quadrennial event, in order to survive. Soccer is a noticeable exception, particularly with the rules limiting the age of competitors for the men's Olympic competition. Designed to prevent the Olympic tournament from eclipsing FIFA's cash cow, the World Cup, these regulations have also contributed to the success of the continental federations' football tournaments. The growth in power of these continental federations is evident in this volume, from UEFA's marginal impact on NATO in the early 1960s to the recent actions on the part of CONCACEF within the international community. Today the continental soccer tournaments generate significant spectatorship, media coverage, and sponsorship, and as major international sporting events they attract regional if not global attention, including as venues for diplomacy alongside the soccer games themselves. Continental federations are indeed an area ripe for future research, with the chapters in this book and a recent special issue of *Sport in History* on international and continental federations providing a starting point.[11]

This volume on the history of soccer and diplomacy is multidisciplinary in approach. While most of the contributions come from a history background, this book includes scholars from other disciplines, particularly with the examination of more recent examples of soccer's use within diplomacy. For these case studies the traditional archival materials from foreign ministries are not yet available and likely will remain embargoed for a few decades; in the meantime, scholars should not ignore these examples until the archives are open. The use of different sources, particularly public statements from political leaders, including their support for bringing international soccer tournaments to their countries, lends credence to the idea that the concepts seen in previous decades are still being used today—and, at times, even more obviously.

Following this introduction the book begins with a theoretical chapter on soccer and diplomacy from Sarah Snyder. Coming from outside the subdiscipline of sport history, Snyder expands on the benefit of incorporating soccer within traditional diplomatic history. As a scholar of human rights history, Snyder recognizes the value of newer strands of historical inquiry and how their combination with diplomacy studies can produce fruitful and greater understandings of the international system and global interactions. Ten chapters then explore a variety of intersections of soccer and diplomacy from around the world, largely in chronological order. Many of the major global concerns of the past century appear in this book: the rise of fascism, the Cold War, the Vietnam War, apartheid, the rise of the BRICS states (Brazil, Russia, India, China, and South Africa), and corruption. That soccer factors into the diplomacy surrounding all of these issues reveals the power of this sport.

In the interwar period the European—and soccer—powers began to incorporate the game in their diplomatic strategies. Paul Dietschy demonstrates in chapter 3 how the French Third Republic, as a democratic state, established a concept of football diplomacy that was in contrast to the use of the sport by its fascist and Nazi neighbors. The 1920 creation of a Sport and Tourism section within the foreign ministry led to French diplomats taking a clear interest in Les Bleus games as well as other international matches. Whereas World War II interrupted the French state's concerted use of soccer in its diplomatic endeavors, Spain had four decades to develop its football diplomacy under the Franco regime. In chapter 4 Juan Antonio Simón explores soccer's role in the foreign policy of Franco's Spain, including both the national team and Real Madrid's participation in UEFA's European Cup. Both interwar France and Francoist Spain used soccer matches across the continent to help promote their agendas abroad, and their hosting of tournaments—the 1938 World Cup in

France and the 1964 European Nations Cup in Spain—sought to demonstrate each country's strengths to a global audience.

The Cold War created a situation ripe for the use of the game of soccer. In chapter 5 George Kioussis examines reciprocal tours by national teams from the United States and Iceland in the 1950s and the hopes for these matches to improve Icelandic opinions of the United States following problems with the Keflavik airbase. Here two not very prominent soccer countries used a series of friendly matches between states on the same side of the Cold War to cement their relationship. Brenda Elsey, in chapter 6, shows how Chile exploited Cold War divisions to win the vote in FIFA to host the 1962 World Cup. The country then used this event to help shape the country's image abroad, an effort championed by soccer officials more so than the government. The Cold War also caused problems with the playing of soccer matches, as my own contribution demonstrates in chapter 7. In fact, the military alliance that is NATO quite frequently addressed the political complications of FIFA and UEFA's recognition of East Germany in the 1960s. The nature of the competitions, and the increasing tensions in the Cold War, had an impact on when East German teams were granted permission to travel to competitions in NATO member states and when they were refused entry.

Several chapters chart the ways in which soccer was a conduit for relations between states and non-state bodies and how soccer players consciously and subconsciously played out the role of diplomat. In chapter 8, Erik Nielsen traces the place of an Australian tour of Vietnam in the midst of the Vietnam War both at the time and as a contested site of Australian memory. Both the Australian government and soccer federation supported this trip, but any expected diplomatic or soccer benefits to be gained from this tour did not materialize as a result of the challenges of playing in a tournament in a war zone. In chapter 9, Chris Bolsmann considers one of the most infamous and misunderstood examples of sport and diplomacy, in an examination of apartheid South Africa's relationship with FIFA, and he expands on the established knowledge of how the IOC dealt with the country. In what Bolsmann calls a failed sports diplomacy, South Africa attempted to circumvent its pariah status in international sport through small modifications in the structure and composition of the domestic governing bodies for soccer. The continental federation, from its earliest years, stood up to the apartheid state, hindering South Africa's ability to achieve any change via soccer.

Soccer and diplomacy in the twenty-first century can be characterized by negotiation, particularly among national and international governing bodies, individuals, and governments, with money and prestige factoring prominently in these endeavors. Roy McCree explores the relationship between FIFA and the regional federation CONCACAF through the corrupt actions of a leading soccer executive from the small island nation of Trinidad and Tobago. Jack Warner negotiated as a politician, Trinidad and Tobago soccer official, CONCACAF official, and FIFA executive committee member to bring the 2001 Junior World Cup to the island nation and to reap financial benefits. He later used these same roles to gain personally from the 2006 and 2018 World Cup selection process, perhaps bringing the island country more into the public eye than the country's October 2017 defeat of the United States, which then qualified Trinidad and Tobago for the 2018 World Cup and kept the Americans home that summer. On a different level, in chapter 11 Euclides de Freitas Couto and Alan Castellano Valente look at the relationship between FIFA and one particular state, Brazil, through the country's efforts to host the 2014 World Cup. Presidents Lula and Rousseff sought to promote a Brazilian national identity by organizing this mega-event, although FIFA tested the state's sovereignty in those preparations by demanding changes to national laws to meet sponsor obligations—actions that required careful negotiations. These chapters on more recent events reveal the challenges of bidding for and organizing mega-events, particularly with the corruption and political difficulties that now often accompany such endeavors.

The book's final chapter, from soccer and diplomacy pioneer Peter Beck, offers concluding remarks on all of the chapters contained herein. The overarching question that emerged from the chapters in this volume is the extent to which it is possible to speak of "soccer diplomacy," and how this may or may not be differentiated from a broader sport diplomacy. Beck takes a broad look at how soccer has been used in diplomacy over the past century and how the field has advanced since his groundbreaking monograph on England, football, and diplomacy appeared twenty years ago. What this book therefore provides is a global understanding of the myriad ways the game of soccer is used within diplomacy, made apparent by both the numerous countries included within these studies and the national backgrounds of the authors.

This volume considers thirteen countries' involvement in the game of soccer across six continents, yet even with this global breadth there is still much more research to be done regarding countries or tournaments that could have been included. With major tournaments that gain global media coverage in three consecutive years—FIFA World Cup, FIFA Women's World Cup, UEFA's European Championship—soccer is increasingly a site for visible and frequent diplomacy. With the 2018 World Cup in Russia and 2022 in Qatar, the world's biggest single-sport mega-event will surely provide much fodder for future scholarship. The poisoning of a former Russian spy and his daughter on British soil in March 2018 led to British prime minister Theresa May publicly stating that no government ministers or members of the royal family would attend the World Cup in Russia. Several other governments followed suit (although the United States did not need to make a proclamation because the country failed to qualify for the tournament). Balkan politics made a frequent appearance during the tournament in Russia. In Switzerland's 2–1 victory over Serbia, two Swiss players of Albanian–Kosovar heritage made an Albanian nationalist symbol after scoring goals, actions that prompted FIFA to launch a disciplinary proceeding and fine the athletes. Croatia's Domagoj Vida, who had played professionally in the Ukraine from 2013 to 2018, appeared in a short online video saying "glory to Ukraine" after he led his team to a quarterfinal victory over Russia—a statement that clearly referenced the 2014 Russian annexation of the Crimea. The increased tensions within Middle Eastern politics, culminating in the Saudi-led blockade of Qatar, which began in the summer of 2017, raised further questions about and complications for the 2022 World Cup. England, original home of the codified laws and organization of the game, plays a minor role in this volume, primarily in its losing effort to win the right to host the 2018 World Cup. The separate control of the sport in the four home nations places the game somewhat at odds with the UK Foreign Office. Nonetheless, the country's vast colonial empire, hosting of the first globally live-televised World Cup, and global fandom and the financial worth of its professional teams are all ripe areas for expanding scholarly research in terms of diplomacy. Similar comments can be made for the other major soccer states of Europe.[12]

The African continent—whose sport history as a whole needs more study—can also provide many future projects. Soccer has clearly been used as a symbol of independence, particularly following decolonization, and the rise of the continental federation helped force change within FIFA. Outside of these European–African diplomatic relationships (often between European states and their former colonies) or the isolation of apartheid states, an examination of how the sport has been used within continental diplomacy will surely shed light on relations across the vast continent. Much media attention in 2014 focused on several African states' difficulties qualifying for the 2015 African Cup of Nations because of the deadly Ebola virus outbreak, along with Morocco's refusal to host the tournament over fears of further spreading the disease from the thousands of traveling spectators. The diplomacy behind these events—from the bid process for hosting through the negative treatment of Ebola-hit states as well as Morocco, whom the Confederation of African Football expelled for its actions, through Equatorial Guinea's ultimate organizing of the event with short notice—surely has much to reveal. Additionally, the intersection of global health with mega-events or second-order events is another area for soccer and diplomacy scholarship, one that can also provide valuable interdisciplinary discussions in the classroom. The global pandemic caused by the novel coronavirus (COVID-19) forced the cancellation or postponement of numerous sporting events, including the 2020 European Championship, further expanding this area.[13]

One notable and lamentable absence from this volume is the Women's World Cup or women's soccer as a whole. The Women's World Cup has only recently begun to be a site of academic scholarship, but none of these works consider its place within diplomacy. The women's game has grown tremendously in the past thirty years, but it has remained marginal to the diplomatic sphere. The 2011 event saw a global outpouring of support for eventual winner Japan four months after a devastating tsunami hit the country. During the decades when women's sport was largely an afterthought for the international sport community, it was rarely, if ever, used within diplomacy. The State Department occasionally included female star athletes such as Althea Gibson within postwar goodwill foreign tours, but on the whole sport diplomacy has—like both sport and diplomacy separately—been the realm of men as diplomats, athletes, and sport leaders. Scholarly investigations of the more recent use of women's soccer within diplomatic endeavors might be hindered by the closure rules regarding access to diplomatic records held in national archives, but other materials can be used to begin examining this topic. Class, gender, religion, race, and health—areas that diplomatic historians have been studying for quite some time—have only been addressed briefly in this volume.[14]

Throughout the past century governments have long used soccer within their diplomatic efforts, and soccer organizations have similarly sought to play a role within international diplomacy. As the chapters in this book have demonstrated, across the globe, power and influence on the international stage can be gained or wielded through the game of soccer. By bringing together such geographical and temporal diversity of research in one place, this volume also aims to spur additional research into soccer and diplomacy, expanding scholarship to match the global reach of the game, and to include all facets of the game. The perceived value of international soccer will contribute to the sport's continued use within diplomacy at all levels of the game: men's, women's, and youth tournaments, club matches, international friendlies, and person-to-person exchanges. Just as the FA and its foundation's current Grow the Game scheme seeks to expand participation in the sport, particularly for women and disability teams, this diplomatic growth of soccer will enable an exciting expansion for diplomatic scholars to grow the game as well.

Notes

1. Paul Darby, "'Let Us Rally around the Flag': Football, Nation-Building, and Pan-Africanism in Kwame Knrumah's Ghana," *Journal of African History* 54, no. 2 (2013): 221–246; Dario Brentin and Loïc Tregoures, "Entering through the Sport's Door? Kosovo's Sport Diplomatic Endeavours towards International Recognition," *Diplomacy & Statecraft* 27, no. 2 (2016): 360–378; "South Sudan Pound to Be Launched Next Week," BBC News, July 11, 2011, http://www.bbc.com/news/world-africa-14110475 (accessed November 27, 2016).

2. Alan Tomlinson and Christopher Young, "Culture, Politics, and Spectacle in the Global Sports Event—An Introduction," in *National Identity and Global Sports Events: Culture, Politics, and Spectacle in the Olympics and the Football World Cup*, ed. Alan Tomlinson and Christopher Young (Albany: State University of New York Press, 2005), 5; David Goldblatt, *The Ball Is Round: A Global History of Football* (London: Penguin, 2006), 248–250; Robert S. C. Gordon and John London, "Italy 1934: Football and Fascism," in *National Identity and Global Sports Events: Culture, Politics, and Spectacle in the Olympics and the Football World Cup*, ed. Alan Tomlinson and Christopher Young (Albany: State University of New York Press, 2006), 42; Janis van der Westhuizen and Kamilla Swart, "Bread or Circuses? The 2010 World Cup and South Africa's Quest for Marketing Power," *International Journal of the History of Sport* 28, no. 1 (2011): 168–180; Sabelo J. Ndlovu-Gatsheni, "The World Cup, Vuvuzelas, Flag-Waving Patriots and the Burden of Building South Africa," *Third World Quarterly* 32, no. 2 (2011): 279–293; Ben Rumsby, "Qatar 2022 World Cup Row Erupts after Report Warns Tournament May Be Held Elsewhere," *Telegraph*, October 6, 2017, https://www.telegraph.co.uk/football/2017/10/06/qatar-2022-world-cup-threat-report-warns-increased-political/ (accessed February 21, 2019).

3. Richard Guilianotti and Roland Robertson, *Globalization & Football* (Los Angeles: Sage, 2009); Laurent Dubois, *Soccer Empire: The World Cup and the Future of France* (Berkeley: University of California Press, 2010); Peter Alegi, *Laduma! Soccer, Politics and Society in South Africa* (Scottsville, South Africa: University of KwaZulu-Natal Press, 2004); Ian Syson, "Fronting Up: Australian Soccer and the First World War," *International Journal of the History of Sport* 31, no. 18 (2014): 2345–2361; Amir Ben-Porat, "Nation Building, Soccer and the Military in Israel," *International Journal of the History of Sport* 17, no. 4 (2000): 123–140; Liz Crolley and David Hand, *Football, Europe and the Press* (London: Routledge, 2002); Kausik Bandyopadhyay and Boria Majumdar, *A Social History of Indian Football: Striving to Score* (London: Routledge, 2006); Jamie Cleland, *A Sociology of Football in a Global Context* (London: Routledge, 2015); Daniel Kilvington, *British Asians, Exclusion and the Football Industry* (London: Routledge, 2016); John Hughson and Fiona Skillen, ed., *Football in Southeastern Europe: From Ethnic Homogenization to Reconciliation* (London: Routledge, 2014); Tom Gibbons, *English National Identity and Football Fan Culture: Who Are Ya?* (London: Routledge, 2014); Andrei S. Markovits and Steven L. Hellerman, *Offside: Soccer & American Exceptionalism* (Princeton: Princeton University Press, 2001); Alan Tomlinson and Christopher Young, *German Football: History, Culture, Society* (London: Routledge, 2006); Jayne Cauldwell, ed., *Women's Football in the UK: Continuing with Gender Analyses* (London: Routledge, 2012); Richard Giulianotti, "Built by the Two Varelas: The Rise and Fall of Football Culture and National Identity in Uruguay," *Culture, Sport, Society* 2, no. 3 (1999): 134–154; Peter Beck, *Scoring for Britain: International Football and International Politics, 1900–1939* (London: Frank Cass, 1999); Peter Gold, "Sport as a Political Tool: The Case of Spain and Gibraltar," *Sports Historian* 22, no. 2 (2002): 164–177; Raanan Rein and Efraim Davidi, "Sport, Politics and Exile: Protests in Israel during the World Cup (Argentina, 1978)," *International Journal of the History of Sport* 26, no. 5 (2009): 673–692; Sifiso Mxolisi Ndlovu, "Sports as Cultural Diplomacy: The 2010 FIFA World Cup in South Africa's Foreign Policy," *Soccer & Society* 11, no. 1–2 (2010): 144–153; Heather L. Dichter, "Kicking Around International Sport: West Germany's Return to the International Community through Football," *International Journal of the History of Sport* 30, no. 17 (2013): 2031–2051; John Horne and Wolfram Manzenreiter, ed., *Japan, Korea and the 2002 World Cup* (London: Routledge, 2002); Robert Edelman, *Spartak Moscow: A History of the People's Team in the Workers' State* (Ithaca: Cornell University Press, 2009); Brenda Elsey, *Citizens & Sportsmen: Fútbal & Politics in 20th-Century Chile* (Austin: University of Texas Press, 2011); Alan McDougall, *The People's Game: Football, State and Society in East Germany* (Cambridge, Cambridge University Press, 2014); Thomas W. Zeiler, "Conclusion: Fields of Dreams and Diplomacy," in *Diplomatic Games: Sport, Statecraft and International Relations since 1945*, ed. Heather L. Dichter and Andrew L. Johns (Lexington: University Press of Kentucky, 2014), 442.

4. Jeremi Suri, "Non-Governmental Organizations and Non-State Actors," in *Palgrave Advances in International History*, ed. Patrick Finney (Basingstoke: Palgrave Mac-

millan, 2005); Jean-Loup Chappelet and Brenda Kübler-Mabbott, *The International Olympic Committee and the Olympic System: The Governance of World Sport* (London: Routledge, 2008); Barbara Keys, *Globalizing Sport: National Rivalry and International Community in the 1930s* (Cambridge, MA: Harvard University Press, 2006).

5. David Black, "Dreaming Big: The Pursuit of 'Second Order' Games as a Strategic Response to Globalization," *Sport in Society* 11, no. 4 (2008): 467–480; Paul Darby, "Football, Colonial Doctrine and Indigenous Resistance: Mapping the Political Persona of FIFA's African Constituency," *Culture, Sport, Society* 3, no. 1 (2000): 78; Ben Weinberg, "'The Future Is Asia'? The Role of the Asian Football Confederation in the Governance and Development of Football in Asia," *International Journal of the History of Sport* 29, no. 4 (2012): 535–552.

6. Joseph S. Nye Jr.,"Soft Power," *Foreign Policy* 80 (1990): 153–171; Nicholas J. Cull, *The Cold War and the United States Information Agency American Propaganda and Public Diplomacy, 1945–1989* (Cambridge: Cambridge University Press, 2009), 12; Jan Melissen, ed., *The New Public Diplomacy—Soft Power in International Relations* (New York: Palgrave, 2005), xix.

7. Christopher Endy, *Cold War Holidays: American Tourism in France* (Chapel Hill: University of North Carolina Press, 2004); James R. Vaughan, "'A Certain Idea of Britain': British Cultural Diplomacy in the Middle East, 1945–57," *Contemporary British History* 19, no. 2 (2005): 151–168; Jessica C. E. Gienow-Hecht and Mark C. Donfried, ed., *Searching for a Cultural Diplomacy* (New York: Berghahn, 2010); Michael David-Fox, *Showcasing the Great Experiment: Cultural Diplomacy and Western Visitors to the Soviet Union, 1921–1941* (Oxford: Oxford University Press, 2011); Anders Bo Rasmussen, "Educational Exchange as a Cold War Weapon: American Influence on Danish Journalists after World War II," *American Studies in Scandinavia* 44, no. 2 (2012): 5–27; Alessandra Bitumi "Building Bridges across the Atlantic: The European Union Visitors Program. A Case Study for Public Diplomacy and the Transatlantic Relationship in the 1970s," *International History Review* 35, no. 5 (2013): 925–942; Neal M. Rosendorf, *Franco Sells Spain to America: Hollywood, Tourism and Public Relations as Postwar Spanish Soft Power* (Basingstoke: Palgrave Macmillan, 2014); Graham Carr, "'No Political Significance of Any Kind': Glenn Gould's Tour of the Soviet Union and the Culture of the Cold War," *Canadian Historical Review* 95, no. 1 (2014): 1–29; Gail Dexter Lord and Ngaire Blankenberg, ed., *Cities, Museums and Soft Power* (Washington, DC: AAM Press, 2015); Clare Croft, *Dancers as Diplomats: American Choreography in Cultural Exchange* (New York: Oxford University Press, 2015); Molly Bettie, "Ambassadors Unaware: The Fulbright Program and American Public Diplomacy," *Journal of Transatlantic Studies* 13, no. 4 (2015): 358–372; Andrei Kozovoi, "A Foot in the Door: The Lacy–Zarubin Agreement and Soviet-American Film Diplomacy during the Khrushchev Era, 1953–1963," *Historical Journal of Film, Radio & Television* 36, no. 1 (2016): 21–39.

8. Damion Thomas, "Playing the 'Race Card': U.S. Foreign Policy and the Integration of Sports," in *East Plays West: Sport and the Cold War*, ed. Stephen Wagg and David L. Andrews (London: Routledge, 2007), 207–221; Kausik Bandyopadhyay,

"Feel Good, Goodwill and India's Friendship Tour of Pakistan, 2004: Cricket, Politics and Diplomacy in Twenty-First-Century India," *International Journal of the History of Sport* 25, no. 12 (2008): 1654–1670; Damion L. Thomas, *Globetrotting: African American Athletes and Cold War Politics* (Urbana: University of Illinois Press, 2012); Kevin B. Witherspoon, "Going 'to the Fountainhead': Black American Athletes as Cultural Ambassadors in Africa, 1970–1971," *International Journal of the History of Sport* 30, no. 13 (2013): 1508–1522; Kevin B. Witherspoon, "'Fuzz Kids' and 'Musclemen': The US-Soviet Basketball Rivalry," in *Diplomatic Games: Sport, Statecraft, and International Relations since 1945*, ed. Heather L. Dichter and Andrew L. Johns (Lexington: University Press of Kentucky 2014), 297–326.

9. Alan Tomlinson, *FIFA (Fédération Internationale de Football Association): The Men, the Myths and the Money* (London: Routledge, 2014), 87–120; FIFA.com, "More Than Half the World Watched Record-Breaking 2018 World Cup," December 21, 2018, https://www.fifa.com/worldcup/news/more-than-half-the-world-watched-record-breaking-2018-world-cup (accessed 21 February 2019).

10. German National Tourism Board, "'A time to make friends™' The 2006 FIFA World Cup™ and Its Effect on the Image and Economy of Germany," https://www.germany.travel/media/en/pdf/dzt_marktforschung/Fazit_der_FIFA_WM_2006_PDF.pdf (accessed August 9, 2016).

11. *Sport in History* 37, no. 3 (2017), edited by Grégory Quin and Philippe Vonnard.

12. Britain's obsession with football has led to some previous work on the 1966 World Cup, hosted by England, but much more work can still be done with respect to Britain and diplomacy. "World Cup 2018: Ministers & Royal Family Will Not Go to Russia," BBC News, March 14, 2018, https://www.bbc.co.uk/sport/football/43404915 (accessed May 8, 2018); James Montague, "Switzerland Beats Serbia in a Game Tinged with History and Politics," *New York Times*, June 22, 2018, https://www.nytimes.com/2018/06/22/sports/world-cup/switzerland-shaqiri-serbia.html (accessed July 27, 2018); Sid Lowe, "Switzerland's Xhaka and Shaqiri Charged by Fifa over Serbia Goal Celebrations," *Guardian*, June 23, 2018, https://www.theguardian.com/football/2018/jun/23/xhaka-and-shaqiri-goal-celebrations-bring-balkan-politics-to-world-cup (accessed July 27, 2018); Samuel Lovett, "World Cup 2018: Croatia Defender Avoids Match Ban over Post-Match Celebrations after Russia Win," *Independent*, July 8, 2018, https://www.independent.co.uk/sport/football/world-cup/croatia-russia-domagoj-vida-celebrations-ukraine-independence-video-latest-watch-a8437146.html (accessed July 27, 2018). For the use of sport—and especially soccer—in Croatia, see Dario Brentin, "'A Lofty Battle for the Nation': The Social Toles of Sport in Tudjman's Croatia," *Sport in Society* 16, no. 8 (2013): 993–1008; John Duerden, "A Soccer Tournament Breaks Through the Boycott of Qatar," *New York Times*, January 30, 2018, https://www.nytimes.com/2018/01/30/sports/soccer/afc-champions-league-saudi-qatar-boycott.html (accessed May 8, 2018); Martin Polley, "The Diplomatic Background to the 1966 Football World Cup," *Sports Historian* 18, no. 2 (1998): 1–18.

13. A conversation with a microbiology colleague teaching a class on infectious diseases led to her incorporating a project that addressed the broader implications of a mass outbreak of Ebola on Sierra Leone's society, particularly with respect to the playing of soccer. Paul Darby, "Football, Colonial Doctrine and Indigenous Resistance: Mapping the Political Persona of FIFA's African Constituency," *Culture, Sport, Society* 3, no. 1 (2000): 61–87; Ian Hughes and Piers Edwards, "Nations Cup 2015: Seychelles Forced to Forfeit," BBC News, July 31, 2014, http://www.bbc.co.uk/sport/football/28583563 (accessed August 24, 2017); John Bennett, "Ebola Affecting Sierra Leone team—Michael Lahoud," BBC News, July 31, 2014, http://www.bbc.co.uk/sport/football/29621447 (accessed August 24, 2017); "Morocco Ruled Out as Africa Cup Host over Ebola Turmoil," France24, November 12, 2014, http://www.france24.com/en/20141111-morocco-not-host-2015-africa-cup-nations-CAF-disqualified (accessed August 24, 2017); Kari Brossard Stoos and Heather Dichter, "Will Coronavirus Cancel the Olympics and Other Big Sporting Events?" *Washington Post,* March 5, 2020, https://www.washingtonpost.com/outlook/2020/03/05/will-coronavirus-cancel-olympics-other-big-sporting-events/ (accessed March 28, 2020); "Euro 2020 postponed until next summer," *BBC Sport,* March 18, 2020, https://www.bbc.com/sport/football/51909518 (accessed March 29, 2020).

14. Cassandra Ogunniyi, "Perceptions of the African Women's Championships: Female Footballers as Anomalies, "*Sport in Society* 17, no. 3 (2014): 537–549; Kelly Knez, Tansin Benn, and Sara Alkhaldi, "World Cup Football as a Catalyst for Change: Exploring the Lives of Women in Qatar's First National Football Team—A Case Study," *International Journal of the History of Sport* 31, no. 14 (2014): 1755–1773; Eileen Narcotta-Welp, "A Black Fly in White Milk: The 1999 Womens World Cup, Briana Scurry, and the Politics of Inclusion," *Journal of Sport History* 42, no. 3 (2015): 382–393; Gertrud Pfister, "Sportswomen in the German Popular Press: A Study Carried Out in the Context of the 2011 Women's Football World Cup," *Soccer & Society* 16, no. 5/6 (2015): 639–656; Barbara Ravel and Marc Gareau, "'French Football Needs More Women Like Adriana'? Examining the Media Coverage of France's Women's National Football Team for the 2011 World Cup and the 2012 Olympic Games," *International Review for the Sociology of Sport* 51, no. 7 (2016): 833–847; Carrie Dunn, *Football and the Women's World Cup: Organisation, Media and Fandom* (Basingstoke: Palgrave Macmillan, 2016); Ashley Brown, "Swinging for the State Department: American Women Tennis Players in Diplomatic Goodwill Tours, 1941–59," *Journal of Sport History* 42, no. 3 (2015): 289–309.

Playing on the Same Team

What International and Sport Historians Can Learn from Each Other

Sarah B. Snyder

I first began thinking about how sport intersected with my research and teaching when I read works by Thomas Zeiler about a late nineteenth-century world baseball tour and by Simon Stevens on English activists who organized a boycott of traveling South African teams. Their research demonstrated how athletes could serve as informal ambassadors overseas, how the business of sport could expand a state's influence abroad, and how a country tied to its identity as a sporting power could be targeted within that sphere for odious domestic practices. It was not until I read a piece by historian Brenda Elsey several years ago that I thought about how soccer per se might intersect with my own research agenda. As Elsey reveals in "'As the World Is My Witness': Transnational Chilean Solidarity and Popular Culture," Chile's place in the 1974 World Cup rested on the Soviet team's refusal to play in Chile's National Stadium, the site of summary executions, torture, and indefinite detention in the wake of the 1973 military coup. By forfeiting the game, the Soviets failed to qualify for the tournament. Yet, the team's protest signaled to a broad audience, one potentially traditionally unconcerned with high politics, the Soviet Union's censure of Chile's human rights violations. The Soviet Union achieved a diplomatic objective or, to use a pun, a goal by refusing to take the field in Santiago; it made Soviet soccer players actors in a broad, international campaign against the junta in Chile. Without Elsey's work and that of her colleagues, some of it collected in this volume, international historians would miss important perspectives on and sources for their research.[1]

Elsey is a contributor to this volume, which is fitting as *Soccer Diplomacy: International Relations and Football since 1914* demonstrates the many ways in which diplomatic or international historians will benefit from engaging sport, and specifically soccer, in their teaching and research. Thus far, there has been limited scholarship on the intersection between soccer and diplomacy. Yet, this edited collection demonstrates the varied ways in which football has been used for diplomatic ends. Within that history, the chapter authors show how the dynamics of competition on the pitch (or the field in American English) mirrored and transcended East–West or Cold War competition in the second half of the twentieth century. The contributions that follow also highlight how states have utilized football as a signal to the international community of a new status—using soccer as a rite of passage or power. These chapters, mirroring broader themes in diplomatic history, raise important questions about the unintended consequences of such diplomatic initiatives, including how efforts at diplomacy via soccer have failed or even backfired.

There are different models for thinking about how sport and diplomacy, or soccer and diplomacy, fit together. Euclides de Freitas Couto and Alan Castellano Valente have framed two options as the influence of international sport on diplomacy or the impact of diplomacy on international soccer. But certainly there are others. For example, international sporting events can offer opportunities for bilateral or multilateral negotiations, such as when German chancellor Angela Merkel and Chinese president Xi Jinping watched a Chinese–German youth soccer game together on July 5, 2017. We might term such encounters diplomacy through sport or even diplomacy during sport. In addition, soccer can serve as a type of people-to-people or grassroots diplomacy wherein diplomatic goals are accomplished through low-level or non-state interactions. Finally, soccer can serve diplomatic means through a projection of soft power abroad.

For those used to studying the history of diplomacy, much about soccer will seem familiar. For example, the structure of international soccer lends itself well to international relations scholars' preference for utilizing three levels of analysis: the international, national, and individual. Similarly, in many ways, the structure of the Fédération Internationale de Football Association (FIFA) is akin to the United Nations General Assembly, granting each member one vote. Given the significant number of postcolonial states in FIFA, it would be interesting to examine to what extent this arrangement grew out of frustration with other institutions, such as the United Nations Security

Council, that entrenched the power of former empires. Furthermore, international soccer and international organizations face similar challenges in terms of recognition of political and sport entities. To address one aspect of these dilemmas, CONIFA (Confederation of Independent Football Associations) exists. CONIFA, as opposed to FIFA, hosts a kind of alternative World Cup in which teams such as Western Armenia, Tibet, and Northern Cyprus compete.

The boundaries that have heretofore separated scholars of soccer and diplomacy in its many forms are artificial. At the time of the 1978 World Cup, which was held in Argentina at the height of the military junta's repression, soccer enthusiasts claimed that soccer was the domain of sports and not of politics.[2] Yet the two spheres have rarely been wholly distinct, a conclusion many of the chapters in this volume highlight. In one of the most egregious examples of such a blurring between diplomacy and soccer, in the late 1960s conflict between Central American neighbors El Salvador and Honduras erupted over competition for a place in the 1970 World Cup and escalated into cross-border military conflict, all of which have been collectively termed the "soccer war."

In another connection between the historical subfields, a number of authors in this collection demonstrate the extent to which countries can exercise soft power through soccer. For example, soccer competitions (and sport more broadly) can facilitate international connections at times of political isolation. In such instances, winning competitions is secondary. In one case, highlighted in this volume, a popular team was used as a vehicle to advance political interests, showing that sporting relations can occur when formal diplomatic relations are nonexistent or damaged. These contacts, fueled by soccer, function in much the same way as some world's fairs have in the past or as "ping pong diplomacy" did between the United States and the People's Republic of China in the early 1970s.[3]

Hosting sporting events, especially mega-events such as the Olympics and the World Cup, enables countries to enhance their soft power, in part by engaging in "place branding."[4] This is a particularly appealing opportunity for countries with less traditional power, such as Qatar. Qatar's bid to host the 2022 World Cup seemed to fit perfectly into a broader campaign to change its regional and international profile. Powerful regional sporting associations such as Central American and the Caribbean Federation (CONCACAF) also enable smaller Caribbean or Central American powers to play roles outsized to their traditional place in the world. International soccer competitions can bring foreign policy or high politics to smaller countries less engaged in traditional power politics. In an intervention that will be appreciated by scholars focused on the diplomacy of small states, examining the realm of soccer shows that diplomatic gains can be made even by weak teams. Thus the obstacles smaller states encounter in other spheres, such as fielding successful teams and exerting their influence internationally, should garner their interest.

Hosting mega-events can mobilize domestic opposition. For example, Brazil has faced considerable economic, social, political, and cultural costs as a result of hosting the 2014 World Cup, including the destruction of urban neighborhoods and an increase in the polarization of Brazilian politics. In this case, the domestic political dynamic became so fraught that potentially any effort to tout the World Cup potentially strengthened foes of the government. Increasingly, citizens in prospective host cities and countries are asking whether they want to bear the burdens and costs of such an event. Strikingly, the residents of Boston mobilized forcefully against a bid, joining other cities such as Rome, Hamburg, and Budapest in declaring they would not host the 2024 Olympics.[5]

Yet, at the same time, Brazil undertook a significant campaign to intersect increasingly with a globalized world economy. In those respects, hosting the World Cup may have been advantageous as it amplified a dramatic increase in diplomatic engagement by Brazil's leaders. Such analysis reveals a complicated web in which causation is difficult to discern. What is clear is that hosting a mega-event is not necessarily a crowning achievement for an upwardly mobile power.

The mixed record of Brazil's World Cup was not without precedent. As this volume shows, examining the 1962 Chile World Cup might have made proponents of hosting a World Cup cautious. In these cases and others, host countries have come to realize, potentially belatedly, that they cannot always control conditions during the event. In the case of Chile, this dynamic created negative rather than positive impressions, such as those shared by Italian journalists who criticized manifestations of urban poverty in Chile and even the physical attributes of women there. Interestingly, Chileans have positive memories of the World Cup even if it was regarded as disappointing by external observers.

Diplomatic historians have for some time engaged with development as a principal way that the United States and other wealthy countries have sought to improve the lives of foreign citizens, exert their influence internationally, and advance a particular political agenda. Scholars have also been interested in new types of expertise conveyed through novel types of experts such as Peace Corps volunteers and community development specialists. Examining soccer through a diplomatic lens similarly enables us to understand more about technical education in sport and grassroots diplomacy at the other end of the spectrum. The United States has offered training to soccer coaches, in part to convey soft skills in addition to dribbling and scoring. Such programs aim to enhance bilateral relations. US efforts have also aimed explicitly at developing leadership among coaches as well as fostering female empowerment and ethnic coexistence. In these instances, American soccer coaches served as diplomats, advancing US objectives through technical drills and other training.[6]

More broadly, the volume fits into efforts to illuminate the power of lower-level actors in diplomatic initiatives. This work implicitly builds upon the efforts of scholars such as Akira Iriye and Petra Goedde, who have sought to illuminate the historical role of non-state actors in diplomacy.[7] This volume helps answer the question, Can we talk about soccer as a form of diplomacy? International historians will benefit from efforts to see footballers, their coaches, and fans as possible actors in international relations. As this literature expands, we will be able to ask, In what ways is diplomacy conducted via soccer distinct, beyond the exchange of striped pants for multicolored jerseys? In other words, what does "soccer diplomacy" mean, and what can it add to the history of international relations?

Historians of foreign relations have examined how non-state actors, whether Zeiler's baseball players, Brian Rouleau's mariners, Richard Ivan Jobs's European backpackers, or Whitney Walton's American exchange students in France, have influenced international relations in a range of geographic and chronological contexts. Current or former footballers often serve as informal diplomats, and some countries, such as the United States, formally train their athletes as "ambassadors." Most notably, David Beckham served as an ambassador for Great Britain's effort to host the 2018 World Cup; in this case, the desired effect, being selected as the host country, was not achieved.[8]

In other instances, the effects of framing soccer players as representatives of a country have been damaging; foreign tours by soccer teams can even create or reinforce negative stereotypes. Misbehavior by football fans, or more colloquially hooligans, can have similar effects. Repeated incidents of racial, xenophobic, and homophobic abuse show that soccer has its own "ugly" ambassadors. In many ways, soccer and other sports can facilitate expressions of ethno-nationalist stereotypes, inhibiting productive forms of diplomacy.[9]

More could be done in this volume and elsewhere to examine soccer and diplomacy from the perspective of lower-level actors in order to supply, as sports studies scholar Wray Vamplew writes, "its own version of 'history from below.'" In the ways that international historians have increasingly utilized the records of NGOs, sport historians could examine archives relating to team boosters or undertake oral histories to highlight new types of voices in their work. Such a shift would echo much of the work being done by international historians to reveal the significance of lower-level and non-state actors.[10]

The role of corruption as a factor in affiliation, international tours, and, most clearly, the awarding of mega-events such as the World Cup underlies a number of these chapters but is rarely addressed explicitly.[11] Both international historians and historians of sport and soccer more specifically should directly confront the degree to which corruption and opportunities for personal enrichment more broadly drive interference with diplomatic or sport initiatives. Efforts to secure soccer matches, and particularly large-scale league, national, regional, and international soccer tournaments, also intersect with the study of diplomacy and other types of international relations. For example, countries are increasingly collaborating militarily to ensure the safety of athletes and spectators at such events. Scholars are beginning to examine such cooperation; its story warrants telling.[12]

Using the framework of the influence of international sport on diplomacy, soccer diplomacy, or sport diplomacy more broadly, can shift public opinion internationally on significant foreign policy questions. These findings echo research done by Penny von Eschen, Yale Richmond, and others on how cultural exchanges have directly and indirectly shaped international relations.[13] International historians would benefit from expanding their work in the cultural sphere to include sport and soccer. In particular, future scholarship might address the ways in which soccer diplomacy should be seen as a subset of cultural or public diplomacy and the ways in which it is distinct.

When considering the impact of diplomacy or international relations on soccer, however, one should not always assume a positive influence. Indeed, contributors in this volume show that international relations can inhibit sports such as soccer in a range of ways. For example, there can be considerable obstacles, including diplomatic, to travel by athletes. Diplomats could impede sport competitions both in the prohibition or regulation of athletic teams outside a country and by barring the entry of foreign teams for sporting competitions. Granting visas or other types of permission could even rise to the level of top-level diplomats. A willingness, in some cases, to consider limits on national expressions such as flags and/or anthems suggests that the significance of participating in international sport competition can trump even national identity.

Soccer has intersected with and been shaped by major international events, such as the Second Indochina War (or Vietnam War in US terminology) and the anti-apartheid movement. Integrating the soccer component brings new dimensions, even to very well-developed literatures. Of interest to scholars of European integration and other international historians should be the ways that soccer has connected at multiple points with efforts to foster solidarity among North Atlantic Treaty Organization (NATO) allies. It is also a sphere in which historical developments and past events such as European colonialism and World War II continue to resonate. For example, the experience of cohosting the 2002 World Cup led to postwar reconciliation between South Korea and Japan. Subsequently the two states, which had not submitted a joint bid, have moved closer together diplomatically and culturally in the wake of the tournament.[14] Soccer, then, is shaping international relations in multiple and unexpected ways that diplomatic historians should consider.

Beyond these models of different patterns of interplay between sport and diplomacy, this volume offers other avenues of inquiry. For example, international or diplomatic historians particularly attentive to questions of race will benefit from the fascinating discussion of soccer in South Africa in this volume. Considerable work, including Stevens's, has shown how anti-apartheid activists targeted the racially discriminatory system by excluding South Africa from international sports competitions and boycotting South African sports teams when they toured internationally. Yet, much as Jamie Miller has turned the attention of international historians to how the apartheid regime sought to maintain power, we should also recognize the ways in which white South Africans made attempts to work around such restrictions, including by fielding two teams in international soccer competitions—one white and one black.[15] In the words of the Football Association of Southern Africa (FASA), for 1966 World Cup qualification, it intended to play a "non-European" team when facing a "non-white" country and a white team against a white country.[16]

FASA's efforts to both maintain its racially segregationist system and compete in high-level international sport competitions illuminate different aspects of South African identity and officials' conceptions of South Africa's place in the world.

Within international history, scholars have paid considerable attention in recent years to European integration.[17] For those interested in the dynamics of Europe or other regions, the examination of regional soccer organizations in this volume will offer a new avenue through which to explore those relationships. To that end, utilizing the records and interworkings of Union of European Football Associations (UEFA), Asian Football Confederation (AFC), and CONCACAF, as contributors to this volume do, could be illuminating. Specifically, examining the affiliation decisions of particular countries, such as Australia's move from the Oceania Football Confederation to the AFC, raises questions about national and regional identity and whether such decisions are driven by sporting, diplomatic, or economic factors.

National and subnational identity, a frequent concern for international historians, is also revealed in scholarship on soccer. For example, participation in or rooting for national soccer teams as well as hosting soccer mega-events can forge a stronger national identity among immigrant groups and effectively integrate diverse groups into the broader whole. Within Chile during the 1962 World Cup, passion for soccer drew Italian, Spanish, Czechoslovakian, and Yugoslavian immigrants into a broader cultural experience. Yet, Great Britain's efforts to field soccer teams for the Olympics (which recognizes Great Britain, as opposed to FIFA, in which England, Northern Ireland, Scotland, and Wales are each separate teams) show that soccer does not inevitably bring disparate groups together. The national football associations' resistance to the participation of their soccer players on British Olympic teams demonstrates that soccer, and sport more broadly, has yet to overcome long-standing regional and political divisions.

The study of soccer, which today is less national and/or international than ever, also fits into the transnational turn within international history, in which international historians have increasingly analyzed the flow of people, ideas, and goods across borders. Such an approach has given rise to a growing body of literature on migration and transnational protests, to offer just two examples. J. Simon Rofe has shown that being a supporter of a soccer team, such as Manchester United, can be an identity that transcends national boundaries. As one measure, as of July 2010, Manchester United's Facebook page had 34 million followers. Only months earlier, the population of Manchester was counted at 483,000 and Great Britain's as a whole was 61.8 million. The deep levels of support for other teams in that country suggest many of Manchester United's Facebook fans come from beyond Britain's borders. In part, this shared transnational identity is possible because soccer, like sport more broadly, is based on myth.[18]

Using the most recent edition of Frank Costigliola and Michael J. Hogan's *Explaining the History of American Foreign Relations* as one measure, United States–centered international historians or historians of US foreign relations are currently most concerned with questions of political economy, development, domestic politics, the influence of non-state actors, nationalism, nation branding, and memory. Many of those themes are highlighted in the contributions in this volume. Considerable opportunities exist for historians of soccer and sport more broadly to integrate into their work questions of gender, emotions, the environment, and religion, all issues of increasing interest to international historians. For example, scholars such as Frank Costigliola, Barbara J. Keys, and Andrew J. Rotter have become increasingly focused on the influence of emotion and/or the senses on international relations. Given the extent to which soccer is also a game of high emotion and sensory experience, it might offer opportunities for further expansion of these scholarly trends. Similarly, for many players, political leaders, and fans, soccer is not "just" a game. Therefore the symbolic value with which soccer losses and victories are imbued might also interest international historians.[19]

In Heather Dichter's assessment, sport historians and, by extension, soccer historians and diplomatic historians have too often worked in their respective archives—those of sporting organizations or foreign ministries—and have not sufficiently brought those materials together.[20] This volume represents an integration of these two subfields of history, and the rich resources examined here highlight myriad opportunities for future research and collaboration. The contributions to this volume utilize records in six languages (English, French, German, Icelandic, Portuguese, and Spanish) and draw upon the archival collections of a range of regional soccer bodies, foreign ministries, and NATO; and beyond bridging two research traditions, these chapters demonstrate the interconnectedness of these often formerly separate concerns.

Finally, historians of US foreign relations, or more broadly international historians, will benefit from this volume and other efforts to integrate soccer and diplomacy as they help to provincialize the United States. Given the historic lack of popular support for professional soccer within the United States, historians who focus more of their attention there may have overlooked the broader popularity and power of the sport elsewhere in the world. In addition, United States–centered historians may have underemphasized the significance of international organizations such as sporting bodies that are headquartered beyond the United States' borders. Indeed, more countries are members of FIFA than of the United Nations. Drawing upon the work of sport and soccer historians could adjust such blind spots. At the same time, historians of soccer and sport more broadly might benefit from interaction and collaboration with international historians, as the former seek to move beyond a focus on single country or bilateral relationship and to situate their accounts in broader histories of the period. If historians of international relations and sport work to bridge the borders of their subfields, scholars in each will benefit from new approaches to old questions, new archival collections to mine, and new audiences for their work.[21]

Notes

The author appreciates the feedback of J. Simon Rofe, Heather L. Dichter, and Matthew Jones.

1. Thomas W. Zeiler, *Ambassadors in Pinstripes: The Spalding World Baseball Tour and the Birth of the American Empire* (Lanham, MD: Rowman & Littlefield, 2006); and Simon Stevens, "Why South Africa: The Politics of Anti-Apartheid Activism in Britain in the Long 1970s," in *The Breakthrough: Human Rights in the 1970s*, ed. Jan Eckel and Samuel Moyn (Philadelphia: University of Pennsylvania Press, 2014), 210–215; Brenda Elsey, "'As the World Is My Witness': Transnational Chilean Solidarity and Popular Culture," in *Human Rights and Transnational Solidarity in Cold War Latin America*, ed. Jessica Stites Mor (Madison: University of Wisconsin Press, 2013), 177–178.

2. Patrick William Kelly, *Sovereign Emergencies: Latin America and the Making of Global Human Rights Politics* (New York: Cambridge University Press, 2018), 237.

3. See Juan Antonio Simón's chapter on Real Madrid's contributions to Franco-era Spain's international diplomacy; Joseph S. Nye Jr., *Soft Power: The Means to Success in World Politics* (New York: Public Affairs, 2004). For more on the influence of world's fairs amid international tension, see Marco Duranti, *The Conservative Human Rights Revolution: European Identity, Transnational Politics, and the Origins of the European Convention* (New York: Oxford University Press, 2017), 82–93.

4. Stuart Murray and Geoffrey Allen Pigman, "Mapping the Relationship between International Sport and Diplomacy," *Sport in Society* 17, no. 9 (2014): 1109.

5. Hayden Bird, "The Life and Death of Boston's Olympic Bid," August 4, 2016, https://www.boston.com/sports/sports-news/2016/08/04/the-life-and-death-of-bostons-olympic-bid (accessed August 15, 2017). For work on earlier local defeats of Olympics bids, see Mark S. Foster, "Colorado's Defeat of the 1976 Winter Olympics," *Colorado Magazine* 53, no. 2 (1976): 163–186.

6. See for example, Nick Cullather, *Hungry World: America's Cold War Battle with Poverty in Asia* (Cambridge: Harvard University Press, 2010); Michael E. Latham, *Modernization as Ideology: American Social Science as "Nation Building" in the Kennedy Era* (Chapel Hill: University of North Carolina Press, 2000); David Ekbladh, *The Great American Mission: Modernization and the Construction of an American World Order* (Princeton: Princeton University Press, 2011); Elizabeth Cobbs Hoffman, *All You Need Is Love: The Peace Corps and the Spirit of the 1960s* (Cambridge: Harvard University Press, 2000); and Daniel Immerwahr, *Thinking Small: The United States and the Lure of Community Development* (Cambridge: Harvard University Press, 2015).

7. Akira Iriye, "The Transnationalization of Humanity" and Petra Goedde, "Challenging Cultural Norms" in *Global Interdependence: The World after 1945*, ed. Akira Iriye (Cambridge: Belknap Press of Harvard University Press, 2014).

8. Zeiler, *Ambassadors in Pinstripes*; Brian Rouleau, *With Sails Whitening Every Sea: Mariners and the Making of an American Maritime Empire* (Ithaca: Cornell University Press, 2014); Richard Ivan Jobs, *Backpack Ambassadors: How Youth Travel Integrated Europe* (Chicago: University of Chicago Press, 2017); and Whitney Walton, "Internationalism and the Junior Year Abroad: American Students in France in the 1920s and 1930s," *Diplomatic History* 29, no. 2 (April 2005): 255–278; J. Simon Rofe, "Introduction: Establishing the Field of Play," in *Sport and Diplomacy: Games within Games*, ed. J. Simon Rofe (Manchester: Manchester University Press, 2018), 3.

9. See, for example, "Racist Serb Fans Torment Brazilian Footballer Everton Luiz," http://www.bbc.com/news/world-europe-39028982 (accessed July 27, 2017). See also Eugene Burdick and William J. Lederer, *The Ugly American* (New York: Norton, 1958).

10. Wray Vamplew, "The History of Sport in the International Scenery: An Overview," *Revista Tempo* 17, no. 34 (2012), doi:10.5533/TEM-1980–542X-2013173402; Barbara J. Keys, "Nonstate Actors," in *Explaining the History of American Foreign Relations*, 3rd ed., ed. Frank Costigliola and Michael J. Hogan (New York: Cambridge University Press, 2016), 119–134.

11. One notable exception is Heather L. Dichter, "Corruption in the 1960s?: Rethinking the Origins of Unethical Bidding Tactics," *International Journal of the History of Sport* 33, no. 6–7 (2016): 666–682.

12. Richard Giulianotti and Francisco Klauser, ed., "Special Issue: Security and Surveillance at Sport Mega Events," *Urban Studies* 48, no. 15 (November 2011): 3157–3366.

13. See, for example, Penny M. Von Eschen, *Satchmo Blows Up the World: Jazz Ambassadors Play the Cold War* (Cambridge: Harvard University Press, 2004); and

Yale Richmond, *Cultural Exchange and the Cold War: Raising the Iron Curtain* (State College: Penn State University Press, 2004).

14. Wolfram Manzenreiter, "Football Diplomacy, Post-Colonialism and Japan's Quest for Normal State Status," *Sport in Society* 11, no. 4 (2008): 419–420.

15. Jamie Miller, *An African Volk: The Apartheid Regime and Its Search for Survival* (New York: Oxford University Press, 2016).

16. Chris Bolsmann, "Apartheid Football, FIFA and Failed Sports Diplomacy."

17. See, for example, several key works by N. Piers Ludlow, *Dealing with Britain: The Six and the First UK Membership Application* (New York: Cambridge University Press, 1997); *The European Community and the Crises of the 1960s: Negotiating the Gaullist Challenge* (New York: Routledge: 2006); and *Roy Jenkins and the European Commission Presidency, 1976–1980: At the Heart of Europe* (New York: Palgrave, 2016).

18. J. Simon Rofe, "Sport and Diplomacy: A Global Diplomacy Framework," *Diplomacy & Statecraft* 27, no. 2 (2016): 222; Sarah B. Snyder, "Bringing the Transnational In: Writing Human Rights into the International History of the Cold War," *Diplomacy & Statecraft* 24, no. 1 (March 2013): 100–116; Meredith Oyen, *The Diplomacy of Migration: Transnational Lives and the Making of U.S.-Chinese Relations in the Cold War* (Ithaca: Cornell University Press, 2015); Martin Klimke, *The Other Alliance: Student Protest in East Germany & the United States in the Global Sixties* (Princeton: Princeton University Press, 2010); J. Simon Rofe, "It is a Squad Game: Manchester United as a Diplomatic Non-State Actor in International Affairs," *Sport in Society* 17, no. 9 (2014): 1143; and "UK Population Estimates: How Many People Live in Each Local Authority?" https://www.theguardian.com/news/datablog/2010/sep/21/uk-population-local-authority (accessed July 26, 2017); and Robert Redeker, "Sport as an Opiate of International Relations: The Myth and Illusion of Sport as a Tool of Foreign Diplomacy," *Sport in Society* 11, no. 4 (2008): 497.

19. Costigliola and Hogan, ed., *Explaining the History of American Foreign Relations*; Frank Costigliola, "'Unceasing Pressure for Penetration': Gender, Pathology, and Emotion in George Kennan's Formation of the Cold War," *Journal of American History* 83, no. 4 (March 1997): 1309–1339; Barbara J. Keys, *Reclaiming American Virtue: The Human Rights Revolution of the 1970s* (Cambridge: Harvard University Press, 2014); and Andrew J. Rotter, "Empires of the Senses: How Seeing, Hearing, Smelling, Tasting, and Touching Shaped Imperial Encounters," *Diplomatic History* 35, no. 1 (January 2011): 3–19.

20. Heather L. Dichter, "Diplomatic and International History: Athletes and Ambassadors," *International Journal of the History of Sport* 32, no. 15 (2015): 1741–1744.

21. For a similar approach regarding the history of human rights, see Mark Philip Bradley, *The World Reimagined: Americans and Human Rights in the Twentieth Century* (New York: Cambridge University Press, 2016), 9; Wolfram Manzenreiter, "Football Diplomacy, Post-Colonialism and Japan's Quest for Normal State Status," *Sport in Society* 11, no. 4 (2008): 414.

Creating Football Diplomacy in the French Third Republic, 1914–1939

Paul Dietschy

In his masterwork *La Décadence: 1932–1939*, published in 1979, the French historian Jean-Baptiste Duroselle evokes the place occupied by sport in the relations between France and other countries. He stresses the importance of major international sporting events such as the Olympic Games, Tour de France, and FIFA World Cup. He saw a change in the 1930s: the regiments that had won the First World War received less applause from the French crowds when they paraded on July 14 than did Tour de France's champions and main pack of riders that same month. Yet, Duroselle seems to consider sport diplomacy only from the point of view of the 1936 Berlin Olympic Games. Although he had encouraged works on sport as an indicator of public opinion and what Pierre Renouvin called "*forces profondes*" (deep forces), research on sport history was very limited or even nonexistent when he mentioned sport as a topic to be studied.[1]

Over the past forty years this gap has been filled by a great number of works. Perhaps compared to works on the social or cultural role of sport, in French academic literature the question of sport diplomacy has been somewhat neglected or restricted to Olympic matters. If football has also aroused the interest of historians, the period from 1914 to 1939 is crucial to define what could be termed soccer diplomacy. In 1920 the French Ministry of Foreign Affairs created a special service for sport diplomacy: the *section sport et tourisme* of the Service des œuvres françaises à l'étranger (SOFE). Association football should have taken a central place in such a diplomatic service. One year before SOFE's foundation, a unique football association had been created in France. Soccer was the most popular sport in France, and in 1921 the Fédération Internationale de Football Association (FIFA) elected the Frenchman Jules Rimet as president. Yet, the invention of a soccer diplomacy faced many difficulties, including the distance between the social background of the diplomatic milieu and the popular culture of football, the French national team's low level of performance, and the lack of state subsidies available to organize sporting events such as World Cup; meanwhile, fascist powers spent lavishly to build huge stadiums even as they subverted international sport.[2]

Football matches did not express the hegemony and the power that France had attained at the end of the First World War. Yet, the French foreign ministry created a soccer diplomacy and contributed to spreading French influence despite the weakness of French football and French decline in the 1930s. The aim of this chapter is to expose and explain the contradiction and the paradox of this kind of soccer diplomacy. On one hand, French diplomats began to understand that soccer matches and competitions were a new and sometimes efficient way to spread propaganda or to analyze the evolution of international relations in the interwar period. On the other hand, despite the dynamism of SOFE at its beginning, the government gave little financial help to the French FA, especially when France organized the World Cup in 1938. Although the French state supported football within international relations in the 1930s by creating a specific branch of the foreign ministry that was focused on sport, international matches, and major events such as the 1938 FIFA World Cup, the results reveal the limits of the ambitions of this kind of soccer diplomacy.

Inventing Soccer and Sport Diplomacy

On the eve of World War I, French political milieus and the government paid attention to physical exercises only as they were useful as a preparation for soldiers' drill. Officials and ministers, therefore, attended gymnastics, shooting, and military training federation festivals but not rugby or association football matches. The situation changed during and immediately after the First World War with the invention of sport diplomacy, in which soccer took an ambivalent place.

During the First World War, French military teams played against their allied counterparts; and officials of the Comité Français Interfédéral (CFI), the organization that gave birth to the French FA two years later, wanted to use football tours abroad as a means to spread propaganda in neutral countries. In January 1917 CFI officials proposed that French Foreign Affairs plan a tour by a French football team from Spain to the United States, passing through Uruguay, Paraguay, Chile, and Canada. The purpose of such a *tournée* was to fight the image of a "bleeding France" that was prevalent after the Battle of Verdun. By playing games against teams in the Americas, the French would "make propaganda" and display "despite war, to Neutrals, the French race's vitality." However, the French War Office refused to grant the necessary leave to the players enlisted in the French army, answering that "public opinion wouldn't understand that a vigorous youth's elite, would be shielded from the honor to serve at the forefront, at this critical time." However, it was only a matter of time before this idea for a football trip became a reality. In the fall of 1919, the consul general of France in Stockholm invited a military team. "After a German football team's tour in Sweden," he "had requested the French government to dispatch a football team in order to balance German influence." It is doubtful that the three defeats (1–7 against AIK, 1–3 against a Stockholm selection, and 2–3 against the Swedish national team) convinced the Scandinavian public of the merit of the French national team. Nevertheless, *Football Association*, the official weekly of the brand-new French Football Association, insisted that the Swedish reception showed a "touching liberality and cordiality."[3]

Despite the human losses of the First World War and the destruction of the northeastern part of the country, France was, in the aftermath of the conflict, the most influential power in continental Europe. In this new diplomatic position, sport occupied a peculiar place. SOFE, the propaganda service of the Quai d'Orsay, established a new department called *section sport et tourisme* in 1920. Thus, the French Republic invented—more than eight years before the USSR or Fascist Italy conceived similar ideas—a kind of sport diplomacy that coincided with a period during which most international sport federations had French presidents and were headquartered in Paris. Although FIFA's secretary was based first in Amsterdam and then in Zurich, and despite the fact that French football was not part of the European soccer elite, its president was French.

According to the Ministry of Foreign Affairs' 1920 budget report to the Chamber of Deputies, the creation of this Sport and Tourism section aimed first to combat the perception of a destroyed and disorganized country, to which Anglo-Saxon tourists came only to visit the battlefields. Moreover, it insisted that it was essential that France not "lose this prestige given by the supreme sport which is war in the eyes of the athletic world, predominant in numerous countries as America, England and Scandinavian countries." They stressed the necessity "to create opportunities for our sport clubs and for our athletic values that have been closed for a lack of subsidy." SOFE had three goals: to strengthen French influence within the International Olympic Committee (IOC), increase the number of sporting events with foreigners, and spread cinematic propaganda by broadcasting images of national champions.[4]

Since the first task of SOFE was to secure French influence within the IOC, any emphasis to be given to football remained unspecified. The famous French playwright Jean Giraudoux (a former amateur football player) led the new Sport and Tourism section. During the 1920s association football became the most popular sport in France, even though it could not be considered the "national game" as it was coming to be in other European countries. Nonetheless, by the beginning of the 1920s, association football was given greater consideration by French diplomats because the game permitted the development of linkages with British sport organizations. In a note certainly written in 1920–1921, SOFE explained that the Football Association had withdrawn from FIFA because the English wanted to apply a double boycott: against the federations from the former central powers (Austria, Germany, Hungary, and Bulgaria) and against neutral football associations that continued to play against the former. The French felt that it was necessary to maintain links with the British and, at the same time, to replace them at the head of FIFA.[5]

In a post–Great War era marked by confrontational relationships between France and Germany, football offered the opportunity to compete against German propaganda in a very sensitive area for French diplomacy: the Balkans and Yugoslavia. After learning from the French ambassador in Belgrade that the Germans planned to play matches against Croatian clubs, the French Ministry of Foreign Affairs asked the French FA to send a representative team. Since it seemed to be difficult to gather a civilian team to play matches in Ljubljana, Zagreb, and Sarajevo in June 1921 because of the timing (at the end of the official season), the French Ministry of Foreign Affairs had to ask the war office to grant leave for the military players. In addition, the Quai d'Orsay offered 25,000 francs to the French FA for this tour—a considerable sum that amounted to more than 10 percent of the global budget of the Sport and

Tourism section. The French FA, not surprisingly, felt this payment was worth it. Even though the military authorities refused to allow the football players under arms to wear the French *bleu horizon* uniform, whose prestige was "universal," the French FA considered the tour a success, with six matches played in Ljubljana, Zagreb, and Belgrade (two victories, two draws, and two defeats). The feelings of the crowd may have differed greatly from the officials' discourse in some Germanophile places like Slovenia or Croatia. While the spectators enthusiastically celebrated the Croatian team's victory (4–1), Doctor Milovan Zoricic, state councillor, affirmed in his speech that "Zagreb was proud to welcome the valorous sons of the powerful France." Even with two losses, the outcome of the tour "exceeded the expectations of the propaganda service of the French Foreign Office" as Clément Simon, the French ambassador in Belgrade, commented in the FFA's official publication.[6]

The French diplomatic service remained aware of the political implications of international football matches during the 1930s. A decade earlier the main concern was the gap between political prestige won on the battlefields of the First World War and the defeats experienced by the French football national team. During the interwar period, Les Bleus played 118 international matches: they lost 70 games, won 35, and tied in 13. It is not surprising, with such a record, that in February 1929 Fernand Pila, SOFE's director from 1926 to 1933, wrote to Jules Rimet to congratulate the French players who had just beaten the formidable Hungarian team (3–0). He explained that his department followed "with interest all the events that are likely to increase, abroad, the good name, of our French youth." Especially in Hungary, after the Trianon Treaty (1920), resentment toward France was very high and lingered throughout the first half of the decade. Less than two years before the French victory, the Hungarian national team had crushed the French team 13–1, a clear demonstration of Hungary's continued hostility toward the wartime victor.[7]

French diplomacy was innovative in the aftermath of the Great War in its use of sport diplomacy led by a special service (SOFE) and supported by state credits, which helped to organize football matches or tours abroad. Because of its growing importance, soccer played a major role, even though the performance of the French football teams did not match the French diplomatic position. Nonetheless, the aim of this sport diplomacy was to develop new forms of contact and exchange through football, as a means for the rapprochement of people.

The Football Pitch: A Barometer of France's Bilateral Relations

French ambassadors in the 1930s frequently mentioned international football matches in their diplomatic correspondence. Some of them recognized that sport had become a barometer of international relations, and in some cases the French Foreign Office instructed its embassies to provide accounts of certain sporting events that would interest SOFE or demonstrate France's influence.

The first FIFA World Cup in Uruguay provided one such case. Aristide Briand, the minister of foreign affairs, requested that the French ambassador in Montevideo, Gaston Velten, report to the Quai d'Orsay about the way Uruguayan spectators received and supported the French team during the 1930 World Cup. First, Velten emphasized that Rimet displayed such diplomatic qualities as tact, finesse, and impartiality, adding that it was "excellent for [French] prestige that the great event which has captivated the entire country for a month has been organized under the presidency of one of our compatriots." Another positive point Velten noted was that the "solid gold Cup, the work of a French artist" had been presented to the winning team from the host country while a military band played the "Marseillaise," as the public sang along. Velten reported that, although the French team had won one game and lost two, resulting in the elimination of Les Bleus at the end of the first round, "their way of playing had been considered particularly praiseworthy, in particular during the game they played against the sport and historical rival of Uruguay: Argentina." The crowd, impressed by "their bravery and the Argentineans' inability to beat them," was "seized by a growing enthusiasm," and spectators applauded and constantly encouraged the French players by shouting: "France, France! Come on, the French." In conclusion, Velten said that the participation of the French national team had broadened the Uruguayan public's image of France. They no longer saw France as only the country of great intellectuals or poets, such as Jules Supervielle (born in Montevideo in 1884). It was therefore important, Velten commented, "to be able to intervene in good style, wherever possible, with sporting people. Aside from our intellectual expansion, there is a range of action that it would be regrettable to neglect." His statement shows the ambivalent place sport held in French diplomacy. Even as the French ambassador recognized the potential of soccer as a propaganda tool in a country that was passionate about the sport, such as

Uruguay, at the same time he sounded as though he were only then discovering this concept. However, although Velten had been stationed in Montevideo for only two years, the service had been created ten years earlier.[8]

Soccer propaganda was easy to spread in Uruguay in 1930 because France was one of just four European associations that crossed the Atlantic to participate in the first World Cup. As in other South American countries, the Uruguayan elite were Francophone and Francophile. The diplomatic aspect of football matches, however, had to be handled more delicately when the opponent was a more traditional enemy. By 1922 the French national team had played against all of the country's neighbors except Germany. The special relationship that developed between Aristide Briand and German politician Gustav Stresemann contributed to changing this lack of a football relationship. SOFE supported all sporting events that included both French and German teams. In April 1929, as the Paris Football League prepared for a representative team to play matches in Berlin and Leipzig, Fernand Pila, then the head of SOFE, commented that he wanted "the team that would go to Germany [to] leave the best impression of our vitality and of our sports quality." Despite the rapprochement between Paris and Berlin, it was important to display a certain degree of strength in football and not to endure a beating in the capital of the former enemy.[9]

Such an aim was certainly included in the organization of the first game between the French and German national teams. Finally, after what Rimet called "years of talks and diplomatic consultations," the first France–Germany international match took place at the Olympic Colombes Stadium in the Parisian suburb on March 15, 1931. Despite an escalation of tensions between the two countries—the creation of a customs union between Austria and Germany was announced one day before the game—the match was a huge success. The result, a 1–0 victory for France as a result of a German own goal, satisfied the French press and public opinion. The sizable crowd included fifteen thousand German supporters as well as several government officials, including Fernand Bouisson, president of the Chamber of Deputies, and Leopold von Hoesch, the German ambassador to France. According to the popular daily *Le Petit Parisien*, "Never, maybe except the final of the 1924 Olympic Games, had a football match gathered such an amazing crowd." Although "a special train had brought 750 policemen to maintain order" that morning, the police had very little to do because the sixty thousand spectators (with another ten thousand people standing outside the stadium) maintained great discipline during the game. The

French government was pleased by the calm atmosphere, and particularly by the fact that the arrival of the largest number of Germans since the 1914 invasion did not lead to any nationalistic incident.[10]

Two years later, in a very different political climate, the two teams played a revenge match in the Grünewald stadium in Berlin. In a drawing in the weekly *Football* (Figure 1), a suitcase-carrying French ball character greets a football-kicking German ball character, whose legs rotate to form a swastika shape, saying "Oh! you are so altered!!" The image portrays the clear change in the spirit of the international matches between France and Germany. This match between two federations was not played with the goal of improving relationships; instead, two ways of playing football were contrasted. The French FA and players were contending with a regime that wanted to politicize sport and that had begun by expelling Jewish and socialist members of the Deutscher Fussball-Bund. On the eve of the game, the French ambassador to Germany, André François-Poncet, officially received the French delegation. In his comments, the French press noted, François-Poncet "emphasized why it was appropriate that the match was played in that moment." The ambassador advised them that as a new, openly anti-French government had come to power in Germany, a shift in the relations between the countries was required and that, in their performance, French players should prove that France wanted to maintain good relationships with its eastern neighbor but remained strong against every aggressive action from Adolf Hitler's government. The French players clearly heard the ambassador since they managed a timely equalizer and scored two goals in two minutes for the final 3–3 result. The French players and the two thousand French supporters at the match might not have fully realized the change of atmosphere that day because they felt they were able "to circulate freely, to be able to know about everything, to 'participate in Germany's life, so to speak.'" The Nazi Party's official newspaper, *Der Völkischer Beobachter*, reported that Jules Rimet had even praised "the calm and order that reigned in Germany." This statement did not mean that Rimet, president of the French FA and of FIFA, had become a supporter of the Nazi regime, but it expressed his relief because he had feared that the political change would provoke an anti-French manifestation. Divergent views were rare in France, with the exception of Jean-Bernard Lévy, chairman of Racing Club de Paris, who refused to play a match against SSV Nuremberg "after the anti-Jewish actions of 1 April 1933 and the exclusion of Jews from most of German sports organizations." The "calm and order"

Cartoon from *Football*, March 16, 1933.

proved that football could bridge the gap between two peoples who had been at war twenty years earlier.[11]

Even though France and Germany played two additional matches against each other before the start of the Second World War, France's soccer diplomacy played an even greater role in its relationship with Fascist Italy. During the 1930s Fascist Italy sought to use football for ideological propaganda. Even though, Benito Mussolini was not initially thrilled by the prospect of organizing the second FIFA World Cup in Italy in June 1934, he quickly recognized the advantages it offered. By personally attending games, Il Duce could address the crowd, just as he did in the Piazza Venezia, and be seen by many foreign journalists. The 275 foreign journalists—including 27 from France—praised the modernity of the stadium and the efficiency of the event's organization. Ten thousand French supporters also admired the brand-new Mussolini stadium, where Les Bleus, once again, were eliminated in the first round, although at least this time with honor since they lost 2–3 to the Austrian *wunderteam* after extra time. At the end of the competition, Jules Rimet was very satisfied with the event; he excused the passionate and chauvinistic behavior of the Italian public, declaring that "the Italians were at home and, therefore, their enthusiasm was legitimate." Rimet, like many of his contemporaries, always tried to separate sport and politics. In his memoirs Rimet described

Mussolini as cold and distant, but he did not hide his enthusiasm for Giorgio Vaccaro, the Fascist president of the Italian Football Association: "We don't have to value in the general Vaccaro the political figure. But the sportsman belongs to us."[12]

Some French papers were less enthusiastic than Rimet. If *Le Miroir des Sports* criticized the behavior of some French players who, unshaven, "sang a defeatist Italian song, derogatory toward the regime" and asked that they behave with more dignity because they were, to some extent, the ambassadors "of the physical qualities of our race," other papers, such as *L'Auto*, criticized the chauvinistic atmosphere, the referees, and the violence displayed by Luis Monti, the fighting Argentinian center-half *azzurro. Football* even described a Mussolini who, at the final's half-time, "painfully eager to see the cruel Monti produce new victims, informed him that he should have another attitude during the rest of the match." Even though the French press was rather complimentary, the Italian journalists showed themselves very sensitive to criticism. Journalist Renato Casalbore railed against his French colleagues in a column of *La Gazzetta del Popolo*: "Who are they? What do they represent? What is French football in the international football's hierarchy?" Thus, by winning the World Cup, Italy was now a sporting power that could reverse the traditional roles and display the same condescension toward the French that they had typically displayed toward Italy.[13]

Such a quarrel did not escape the notice of French diplomacy. Former journalist Jean Herbette, the French ambassador to Spain, wrote to the minister of foreign affairs about the press coverage in Spain that followed the two quarterfinal matches between Italy and Spain. After a first draw, 0–0, Italy narrowly won the second game, 1–0. The Spanish press denounced what they termed a plot planned by the Swiss referee, calling him "Italy's twelfth man." Herbette believed that the reaction of the Spanish press showed "the vehemence of national feeling in Spain and the very great place occupied by sport in the life of this country." He also concluded that "the organizers should have done better to choose referees whose neutrality and authority were indisputable and to take precautions against the public patriotic exaltation." Finally, Herbette wrote back to Paris that "good international understanding has nothing to win from tremendous sport competitions."[14]

Herbette was not the first French diplomat to report on the tensions provoked by Italian football teams. In July 1932, home and away Mitropa Cup matches between Slavia Prague and Juventus Turin went horribly wrong, prompting Léon Noël, the French ambassador in Prague, to report, "This match was marked by numerous incidents: one Italian player punched a Czechoslovakian player, another one punched the referee in the face. The public tackled the Italian team and the members of the Italian legation who were attending the match couldn't leave the room of the stadium where they had been placed for safety until 21h30 and under police protection." Noël was well aware of the role physical exercises played in nation building; one of his own first official appearances in Prague was at a huge Sokol parade in which both the Czechoslovakian prime minister and home minister participated. Noël provided a balanced account of the events, assigning shared blame to the Czechoslovakian public's "xenophobia" and the fact that "the Italian players lost their composure and self control"; still, the affair necessitated close observation. Czechoslovakia was part of the Little Entente, the French alliance system in Central Europe, which also included Romania and Yugoslavia. Mussolini's Italy aimed to become the hegemonic power in this area. Czechoslovakian and Italian teams participated in the International and Mitropa Cups, two football competitions created in 1927, with the Austrian, Czechoslovak, Hungarian, and Italian national teams competing in the former and their club teams for the latter. Because the teams met regularly in football, the risk of inflaming public opinion on both sides was multiplied.[15]

Football matches attracted huge crowds during the interwar period and quickly became a new way of expressing national feelings. French diplomats discovered the game's utility, as illustrated by the 1930 World Cup organized in Uruguay or the shift of bilateral relations between France and Germany after Hitler became chancellor in January 1933. In a Europe where tensions were growing, French diplomats reported incidents created by international football matches back to the Quai d'Orsay as real and important diplomatic matters.

The 1938 World Cup and Its Aftermath

On August 14, 1936, in Berlin, at the end of the FIFA Congress and the Olympic Games, the French bid to host the next FIFA World Cup received nineteen votes to Argentina's three and Germany's lone vote. France faced many challenges in organizing the 1938 World Cup. Uruguay, for the World Cup in 1930, and Nazi Germany, for the Olympic Games in 1936, had each provided stadiums that could accommodate more than one hundred thousand spectators. The 1934 World Cup had been played in the futuristic stadiums of Fascist Italy. In October 1936 the organizers from the French FA asked the French government to build a hundred-thousand-seat stadium so that France could be equal to these other countries. The Popular Front government member with oversight of such matters, the health minister, rejected this proposal and called it "a monstrous heresy." Because the left-wing government, which had established the first national sport policy in France, preferred that public money be spent to increase the number of people who actually participated in sport, funding for programs that promoted sport for all took precedence over financing the organization of the World Cup. On November 1936, Jules Rimet had to inform his colleagues on FIFA's executive committee "that a formal guarantee that the Stade de Colombes will be enlarged and modernized has not been given." This news prompted responses from both German and Italian representatives. Germany's Peco Bauwens declared that "if France resigns, Germany is ready to take over the organization of the 1938 World Cup," adding that the offer was, of course, made "not in a spirit of competition against the FFFA, but solely in a desire to help FIFA." The Italian member followed, stating: "I support these words and make the same declaration on behalf of Italy." Eventually the Racing Club de France, which owned the Colombes Stadium, improved the venue and made it more comfortable for spectators, only five months before the opening of the competition. The French government ultimately granted one million francs for these renovations; to cover the rest, the French FA agreed to pay 1,300,000 francs (approximately $400,000), the same amount as the Racing Club de France. These renovations expanded the stadium's capacity by one thousand seats, to sixty-five thousand. In February 1938, one journalist predicted: "And whatever the success of the third World Cup, one thing is certain: that the small number and low capacity of our stadiums will not be nearly sufficient for the interest which this contest deserves or to meet the continued and incessant growth in the popularity of football." Though true, this statement was harsh. The nine cities hosting World Cup matches offered a range of venues, from the most basic (Fort-Carré stadium in Antibes) to modern Italian-inspired stadiums (Bordeaux and Marseilles). Additionally, while the official program for the 1934 World Cup had contained numerous images and plans of the stadiums hosting the competition, the official program of the French edition, the *Revue de la Coupe du Monde de Football 1938*, merely alluded to the stadiums. Instead, the 1938 program concentrated on the gastronomy, the culture, and the tourist attractions of the host cities. France was already the country of the Michelin guide, whose first issue was published in 1900. The foreigners who could travel to France to follow their team were very few and certainly belonged to the middle or upper middle class, and this program emphasized the country's greatest strength: its culture.[16]

Even though the French organizers had to suffer from the state's parsimony, they could rely on the symbolic presence of the Third Republic's representatives. The importance of this football competition did not register as much with the French government, which in 1938 had bigger diplomatic and military problems to deal with. Although in the 1960s, the FIFA World Cup began to acquire importance, in the 1930s it did not compare with the Olympic Games, which gathered, as in Berlin, the who's who of diplomatic and aristocratic milieus. Additionally, the 1938 World Cup used the protocol of the French FA cup final, with the French president invited to award the trophy to the winning team. The FFFA received permission from the Ministry of Foreign Affairs for the final draw to be held in the prestigious Salon de l'Horloge in the Palais du Quai d'Orsay. To the French press, this venue was no demonstration of power and force. On the contrary the press was keen to point out that "on Saturday, the final draw for the World Cup will take place in the very room where not long ago, the pact renouncing war was signed," alluding to the Kellogg–Briand pact of 1928. Even though the French public openly supported Switzerland against Germany and booed the Italian team during part of its match in Marseilles, the competition did not result in any diplomatic incidents. Although Italy won the 1938 World Cup, *Le Temps*, the unofficial organ of the Quai d'Orsay, still felt able to praise the "success both from a sporting point of view and in organizational terms" of the competition and the "perfect behavior" of the French crowds. After the victory of the *azzurri* in the quarterfinal against Les Bleus, the Italian weekly *Il Calcio Illustrato* even conceded that "it must be handed to them, the French 'working class': they are good losers . . . on the sport field at least. In the field of politics, not so much—that is the problem." The 1938 World Cup final saw Italy defeat Hungary 4–2, and the Italian captain, Giuseppe Meazza, made a Fascist salute toward the official stand before being presented with the World Cup trophy by the French president. This gesture did not elicit any commentary in a time when raised arms and fists were a common part of the political vocabulary.[17]

However, this lack of reaction to the Italian's actions was surprising in a period of increased tensions between France and Italy. A few months later,

André François-Poncet, then French ambassador in Rome, visited the Camera delle Corporazioni e dei Fasci, the Fascist Chamber of Deputies, on November 29, 1938, and "was greeted with raucous cries of 'Savoy,' 'Nice,' 'Corsica' and 'Djibouti,'" jeers orchestrated by the chief of Italy's National Fascist Party. Just a few days later France and Italy played an international match in Naples. The Italian press had made some ironic and racist comments about the composition of the French team. A journalist in *La Stampa* attempted to explain that the Italian public was curious to see the black and Moroccan Larbi Ben Barek play football, but added that the Italian people congratulated themselves on not having "among azzurri, men made of . . . chocolate." Throughout the game, which the French team lost 0–1, the Neapolitan public booed the French team. The Italian officials and players tried to explain that the public's behavior had nothing to do with the recent diplomatic incident. The French players were given gifts by the Italian FA; and some members of the Italian team, particularly those players from the northern part of the country, attempted to dismiss the spectators' actions by blaming it on regional differences: "The Neapolitan public has not booed the French team but the visiting team," indeed, "football doesn't make sense for them." French journalists spread the story that even Bruno Mussolini, the Duce's son, was shocked by the public and called it *porcheria* (a dirty trick).[18]

The 1938 World Cup and its aftermath clearly revealed the weakness of French sport diplomacy. Because it lacked the financial means and because it had a different sport philosophy, the left-wing Popular Front government refused to give the French FA the money to build a hundred-thousand-seat stadium, which would have equaled Montevideo's Centenary stadium or been more prestigious than the Italian stadium. The government, however, gave a limited amount to make the Colombes stadium more comfortable and lent symbolic spaces, such as the Salon de l'Horloge at the Quai d'Orsay, for some official meetings. By these minimal efforts, the French state showed that the era of great soccer diplomatic ambition was over. In a way, totalitarian countries had won not only on the football pitch (at least Italy) but also on the political propaganda front. Although there was no diplomatic incident during the 1938 World Cup, the Third Republic exposed some weaknesses in comparison to the totalitarian states.

At the end of World War I, French football officials had begun to invent a sport diplomacy. While football games played between military teams emphasized war brotherhood, football tours in neutral countries were designed to spread the image of a France full of vitality and to struggle against German propaganda and the negative portrayal the Anglo-Saxon press had drawn of France as a bled-to-death country. This purpose was central to the mission of the Sport and Tourism section of SOFE, and football was one of the sports used for this new sport diplomacy. The rather rich French FA did not need the additional financial support that other federations required; and, although the numerous defeats suffered by the French national team did not constitute the best propaganda, France's many losses did not prevent French football officials from occupying high positions in the international football world. Perhaps in the 1920s French political hegemony was balanced by the weakness of French football.

From a solely diplomatic point of view, soccer illustrated the short rapprochement between France and Germany, and French diplomats integrated it within their analysis of public opinion and international relations, especially when it came to central Europe. Some ambassadors found that football was a way of reaching other milieus than the elite. France had long promoted its culture to foreign publics to attract tourism to the country, and it seemed that playing French football games abroad and hosting the 1938 World Cup could work in a similar fashion. However, the French state—marked by strong instability throughout the 1930s—did not provide much support to the French federation when FIFA chose France to host the 1938 World Cup. Either due to ideology under the Popular Front or indifference toward a competition seen as less prestigious than the Olympic Games, the government provided minimal help for the event's organization. Even though it was certainly conscious of the sport challenge launched by totalitarian states, the French government nevertheless wanted to confine its action to sport neutrality or even to share with the British some illusions about the appeasement policy. Jean Zay, who as education minister from 1936 to 1939 was responsible for physical education and sport, perceived that more than political propaganda was at stake. Defeats in international sport acutely revealed the bodily weakness of the French youth, which required, according to Zay in March 1939, the "reorganization of sports, physical education and military training." Yet this sentiment came a bit too late, as the dramatic events of the spring of 1940 revealed.[19]

Football, as the most popular sport in France, became a tool that the government used to spread French propaganda in South America and Europe even though the performance of the French teams did not meet high French expectations. The French diplomatic corps considered football incidents to be a good barometer of international relations, especially in Central Europe. Unlike Fascist Italy, which placed a tremendous emphasis on its World Cup, the French state did not perceive much difference between regular international matches and the FIFA World Cup, even when it hosted the quadrennial event. The Olympic Games were considered to be a real diplomatic moment, especially the 1936 games in Berlin, but the French state viewed the World Cup as a world championship, not as an actual mega-event. This perception lasted in France until the 1990s when the country bid for, hosted, and then won the 1998 World Cup.

Notes

1. In English "deep forces," i.e., all the parameters (public opinion, economic and military power, national feeling, among others) that influence the statesman's decisions and international relations. Jean-Baptiste Duroselle, *Politique étrangère de la France. La décadence 1932–1939* (Paris: Imprimerie nationale, 1979), 184–185; Marcel Spivak, *Education physique, sport et nationalisme en France du Second Empire au Front populaire: un aspect original de la défense nationale* (PhD diss., Paris I University, 1983) thèse d'Etat d'histoire contemporaine, sous la direction de Jean-Baptiste Duroselle, tome 1, Paris, université de Paris I, 1983; Jean-Baptiste Duroselle and Pierre Renouvin, *Introduction à l'histoire des relations internationales*, 4th ed. (Paris: Armand, Colin, 1992), 5–282.

2. Pierre Milza, Francis Jéquier, and Philippe Tétart, *Le pouvoir des anneaux. Les Jeux Olympiques à la lumière de la politique 1896–2004* (Paris: Vuibert, 2004); Florence Carpentier, *Le Comité international olympique en crises. La présidence de Henri de Baillet-Latour, 1925–1940* (Paris: L'Harmattan, 2004); Thierry Terret, ed., *Les paris des Jeux Olympiques de 1924* (Biarritz: Atlantica, 2008); Patrick Clastres, "Neutralité politique, compromissions avec le régime nazi, continuité olympique. Les présidents successifs du CIO (1925–1972) au défi des Jeux de Berlin," in *Sport, Corps et Sociétés de masse. Le Projet d'un homme nouveau*, ed. Georges Bensoussan, Paul Dietschy, Caroline François, and Hubert Strouk (Paris: Armand Colin, 2012), 211–228; Alfred Wahl, "La Fédération Internationale de Football Association (1903–1930)," in *Sports et relations internationales. Actes du Colloque de Metz-Verdun septembre 1993*, ed. Pierre Arnaud and Alfred Wahl (Metz: Publications du Centre de Recherche Histoire et Civilisation de l'Université de Metz, 1994), 31–45; Paul Dietschy, Yvan Gastaut, and Stéphane Mourlane, *Histoire politique des coupes du monde de football* (Paris: Vuibert, 2006).

3. Letter, Henry Delaunay to Foreign Affairs Ministry, January 22, 1917, CFI box, Fédération Française de Football (FFF) Archives, Paris, France; letter, General

Margot, Infantry's director to Henri Delaunay, February 4, 1917, FFF; Maurice Pefferkorn, *Le football association. Théorie et pratique du jeu du football* (Paris: Flammarion, 1921), 294; "Notre équipe militaire en Suède," *Le Football Association. Organe Officiel de la Fédération Française de Football Association (3.F.A.)*, October 4, 1919, 2.

4. Report to the Chamber of Deputies on Foreign Affairs Ministry—financial year 1920, Service Affaires culturelles (SAC), sous-série Œuvres françaises à l'étranger (SOFE), box 85, Archives du Ministère des Affaires étrangères (AMAE), La Courneuve, Département de la Seine-Saint-Denis, France; Pierre Arnaud, "Des jeux de la victoire aux jeux de la paix? (1919–1924)," in *Sports et relations internationales*, 133–155.

5. Note on sport propaganda abroad, n.d., SAC, SOFE, box 85, AMAE.

6. Letter, Minister of Foreign Affairs to Minister of War, May 20, 1920, SAC, SOFE, box 85, AMAE; letter, Minister of Foreign Affairs to Jules Rimet, May 31, 1921, SAC, SOFE, box 85, AMAE; "La 3 F.A. en Yougo-Slavie," *Football Association*, June 17, 1921, 1008; "Le Football français en Yougo-Slavie," *Football Association*, July 8, 1921, 1055; "Après le retour de Yougo-Slavie," *Football Association*, July 15, 1921, 1071.

7. Letter, Fernand Pila to Jules Rimet, February 27, 1929, SAC, SOFE, box 87, AMAE.

8. Letter, Gaston Velten to Aristide Briand, July 31, 1930, Uruguay, 25 Political and commercial correspondence (CPCOM) 9, AMAE.

9. Belgium, Romania, and Yugoslavia were the other three European teams. Letter, Fernand Pila to the physical education Under State Secretary, April 23, 1929, SAC, SOFE, box 87, AMAE.

10. Quoted by Marc Barreaud and Alain Colzy, "Les rencontres de football France-Allemagne, de leur origine à 1970: déroulement, environnement et perception," in *Sports et relations internationales*, 117; "Le match de football Allemagne-France gagné par nos joueurs," *Le Petit Parisien*, March 16, 1931, 1.

11. *Football*, March 16, 1933; "Le match France-Allemagne de football," *L'Auto*, March 19, 1933, 1; Marc Barreaud and Alain Colzy, "Les rencontres de football France-Allemagne, de leur origine à 1970: déroulement, environnement et perception," in *Sports et relations internationales*, 118; Quoted by Hans Joachim Teichler, "Étapes des relations sportives franco-allemandes de 1933 à 1943," in *Le Sport et l'éducation physique en France et en Allemagne. Contribution à une approche socio-historique des relations entre les deux pays*, ed. Jean-Michel Delaplace, Gerhard Treutlein, and Giselher Spitzer (Clermont-Ferrand: AFRAPS, 1994), 62.

12. *Coppa del Mondo. Cronistoria del II Campionato di Calcio* (Rome: FIGC, 1936), 222; "Les impressions d'Italie de M. Jules Rimet," *L'Auto*, June 14, 1934, 4; Jules Rimet, *La fabuleuse histoire de la Coupe du Monde* (Geneva: Editions René Kister, 1954), 99.

13. "Impressions sur l'Italie sportive, de Turin à Florence," *Le Miroir des sports*, June 5, 1934, 370; "La vérité est-elle en marche?" *Football*, June 21, 1934, 3; "Noie

della celebrità. Giudizi degli scontenti sul Campionato del mondo," *La Gazzetta del Popolo*, June 13, 1934, 4.

14. Letter Jean Herbette to Louis Barthou, June 2, 1934, Cultural Affairs, Z, Spain, box 237, AMAE.

15. Letter, Léon Noël to Edouard Herriot, July 11, 1932, Z, Czechoslovakia, box 864, file 11, AMAE; Léon Noël, *La Tchécoslovaquie d'avant Munich* (Paris: Publications de la Sorbonne, 1982), 22.

16. Minutes of the 23rd Congress held at Berlin on August 13–14, 1936, Congress Serie, digitized material, FIFA, Zurich, Switzerland; quoted by Joan Tumblety, "La Coupe du monde de football de 1938 en France. Émergence du sport-spectacle et indifférence de l'État," *Vingtième Siècle. Revue d'histoire* 93 (January–March 2007), 143; minutes of the meeting of the Executive Committee held in Frankfurt, November 28, 1936, Executive Committee box 1936–1936, FIFA; "Une bien grande épreuve pour nos petits stades," *Excelsior*, February 11, 1938, 4; *Programma ufficiale del campionato mondiale di calcio edito a cura della FIGC* (Milan: 1934), 50–64.

17. "Là où fut signé naguère le pacte qui mettait la guerre 'hors la loi,'" *Football*, March 2, 1938; "La Coupe du monde de football," *Le Temps*, June 21, 1938, 5; "Tre ore a Colombes fra i 'popolari,'" *Il Calcio Illustrato*, June 9, 1938; Philippe Burrin, "Poings levés et bras tendus. La contagion des symboles au temps du Front populaire," *Vingtième Siècle. Revue d'histoire* 11 (1986), 5–20.

18. Davide Rodogno, *Fascism's European Empire: Italian Occupation during the Second World War* (Cambridge: Cambridge University Press, 2006), 20; "Il negro tricolore," *La Stampa*, November 17, 1938, 4; "'Ce n'est pas l'équipe de France mais l'équipe visiteuse qui a été sifflée' disent les joueurs italiens," *L'Auto*, December 5, 1938, 1; "Porcheria!" *Le Miroir des Sports*, December 13, 1938, 15.

19. Paul Dietschy and Patrick Clastres, *Sport, société et culture en France du XIXe siècle à nos jours* (Paris: Hachette, 2006), 127.

Football, Diplomacy, and International Relations during Francoism, 1937–1975

Juan Antonio Simón

In March 1969 the Spanish ambassador in Tunis, Alfonso de la Serna, informed the Ministry of Foreign Affairs that an international football tournament had been organized in May, in which clubs like Inter Milan, Benfica, and Dynamo Moscow were to participate. The ambassador wrote to inform the minister about the significance that the presence of Real Madrid in this tournament could have, emphasizing that it could be "a positive element and a stimulating factor" of the diplomatic relations between Spain and the Maghreb countries. As Alfonso de la Serna highlighted the importance this tournament could have at a diplomatic level, he added that it would be necessary to counsel Real Madrid to reduce the amount of money it typically earned in international friendly matches.[1] This example perfectly illustrates the importance of football to Francisco's dictatorship as a means to transform the international image of Francoism and to spur new diplomatic strategies.

Although the history of sport is less frequently studied in Spain than in countries such as Great Britain, the United States, and France, in recent years the analysis of sport during Francoism has been an area of interest for historians. What is more, football—a social phenomenon since the 1930s—has formed a large part of these studies.[2] In fact, the Franco government used football as a tool to legitimize its political regime abroad in an effort to end the isolation Spain suffered after the Second World War and to improve its international image. The Ministry of Foreign Affairs developed this strategy and implemented a public diplomacy scheme through sport. These actions demonstrate that sport, foreign policy, and diplomacy were strongly connected during the dictatorship, as evidenced by the extensive football-related documentation found in the Ministry of Foreign Affairs archives. The Franco government's actions and foreign policy affected the country's standing (or lack thereof) within the international community in general, and these same positions impacted Spain's ability to play football matches with other countries in FIFA and UEFA.

The political–sporting structure created by the regime and the protocol put in place by the Ministry of Foreign Affairs gave special allowances to Spanish clubs expected to play international matches. In particular, Real Madrid members played a role as "ambassadors" of Franco's Spain following their victories in the first five editions of the European Cup. Real Madrid and the Ministry of Foreign Affairs maintained a close, mutually beneficial relationship in a period when Spain's main foreign policy objective was to end its international isolation. The 1960s were a turning point in shifting strategy to use football at the international level; from this point, there was a focus on a greater degree of openness and the progressive normalization of sporting relations with communist countries, especially the Soviet Union. The attitude of the Franco government shifted with regard to the Spanish national team's participation in the first two editions of the European Nations Cup. Together, these actions demonstrate how central the sport of football was to Spain's relations under Franco with the international community. The Ministry of Foreign Affairs increasingly understood the important role football could play within Spanish foreign policy and directed their ambassadors to take maximum advantage of matches abroad. Additionally, the Ministry of Foreign Affairs recognized the importance of organizing major sporting events for the international image of the country, even as other government ministers feared that such activities could weaken internal security and incur significant economic costs.

Foreign Policy under Francoism: From Belligerence to Isolationism

The ideological rapprochement of Franco with Adolf Hitler and Benito Mussolini directly affected Spain's foreign policy, particularly from the beginning of the Second World War, and had an immediate impact in the context of football. Spanish encounters with club and national teams from Germany, Italy, and Portugal symbolized the new authoritarian fraternity of the 1930s.

The diplomatic transition of Francoism—from alliance with the Axis powers, to isolation after the end of the Second World War, and then to gradual inclusion in the Western bloc with the beginning of the Cold War at the end of the 1940s—had a direct impact on football in Spain. Through these transitions, the sport of football remained subordinate to the political and propagandistic interests of the Franco regime and totally lost its independence.

Franco's agreement with the Rome–Berlin Axis became clear in July 1936 with the beginning of the military coup against the legitimate government of the Second Republic. From 1937 on, Franco's diplomats sought for legitimization at an international level, while they simultaneously attempted to isolate the republican leadership by any available means. Football had been a mainstream sport in Spain since the 1930s, but during the Civil War it became a tool for political propaganda and an instrument for maintaining a facade of normality on the home front. The Basque Country (Euzkadi) used its national side's international tour through France, Czechoslovakia, Poland, the Soviet Union, and South America in 1937 to garner international support for the fight against the forces of the right in the Civil War. With the start of the Second World War, the regime declared its complete neutrality with regard to the conflict, more out of necessity than choice, given the state the country found itself in following the Civil War. In reality, it was a collaborative neutrality that allowed Hitler to rely on a logistical base and the provision of raw materials in Spain. The fall of Mussolini and Fascism in July 1943 hastened the repositioning of Spain toward neutrality, but Francoism was not able to hide the ideological proximity it had maintained with undemocratic powers. After 1945 Franco tried to eliminate the ministers most closely linked to Nazism and Fascism from his government in order to form his new ultra-Catholic and profoundly anticommunist government. Franco instead oriented Spain's foreign policy toward Portugal and Ibero-America and toward the development of the concept of *Hispanidad* (Spanishness); at the same time he sought to form closer links with Arab countries. Spain's process of defascization was also made explicit in the world of football, with the abolition of the Fascist salute and the reinstatement of the traditional red shirt for the national side in 1945.[3]

Germany's defeat in May 1945 started a long period of international isolation for Spain, which was formalized on June 19 when the United Nations (UN) approved, without opposition, a Mexican proposal to ban Francoist Spain from joining the new international body. At the Potsdam Conference the leaders from the war's great powers, in a joint declaration, confirmed Francoist Spain's condemnation to international ostracism because of its links with the Axis countries. As the Cold War unfolded, however, the diplomatic siege against Francoism weakened. In 1948 France opened its borders with Spain and also signed a trade deal with its neighbor, similar to the one Spain had made with Great Britain in June that year. These circumstances had an immediate impact in the world of football. In January 1949 the new Latin Cup project included Spanish clubs alongside clubs from France, Italy, and Portugal, an act that represented a new diplomatic victory for Francoism in the field of sport. The complete rehabilitation of Francoism waited for another four years: in August 1953, the concordat was signed with the Vatican and, above all, in September of the same year, the Pact of Madrid was signed with the United States. Eventually, in 1955, Spain joined the UN, an act that had an important political and symbolic underlying message for the country: Spain had formally returned from international exclusion.[4]

With the arrival of Fernando Castiella as minister for foreign affairs in February 1957, Spain's foreign policy developed a clear Western and European tendency, which immediately influenced the international relations of Spanish football clubs. Castiella's successor, Gregorio López-Bravo, continued to lead Spanish foreign policy in this direction into the next decade.[5] The start of the 1960s was marked by a process of social and economic modernization reflected by an opening up to the rest of the world and an increase in Spain's presence abroad. A key part of this process was the application to join the European Economic Community (EEC) in 1962, through which the regime wanted to present an image of normalcy abroad. Although Spain had to wait until June 1970 to sign a preferential arrangement with the EEC, the application itself reflected a Western and European outlook.

The renegotiation of agreements with the United States in 1963 fell in line with these strategies, as did the strengthening of bilateral relations with France and West Germany and the initiation of policies that promoted diplomatic rapprochement with the newly independent African nations. Within this new diplomatic strategy, and in conjunction with its impact upon Spanish clubs and the national side's international sporting relationships with Iron Curtain countries, the first meeting between Spanish and Soviet Union ambassadors took place in Paris in 1958. This meeting had the clear intention of laying the foundations for future collaborations between the two countries; the cooperative relationship ultimately materialized between 1963 and

1964 and was consolidated in 1967 when Spain allowed Soviet ships use of its ports. Thus, Spanish foreign policy completed the shift from its first phase of clear ideological alignment with the Axis powers, to international isolation, and, after the Cold War started, to gradual integration into the Western bloc, with a direct impact on football in Spain.[6]

Francoism's Sporting Diplomacy and Its Impact on Football

After the end of the Civil War in 1939, one of Francoism's prime objectives was to transform physical activity and sport into a "matter of the State," following the model that had been developed by Fascist Italy in the 1920s. The task of building what could be defined as "New Spain's" sporting sector fell to the sole political party, the Falange Española Tradicionalista y de las Juntas de Ofensiva Nacional Sindicalista (Traditionalist Spanish Phalanx of the Committees of the National Syndicalist Offensive; FET de las JONS). Sport, and more specifically football, played a significant role in garnering favor and strengthening foreign policy strategy.[7] From the outset, Franco's government used sport as a tool for ideological propaganda and for inculcating Spanish youth with the values imposed by the dictatorship. After 1939 the Ministry of Foreign Affairs became the central body to evaluate whether or not the participation of football clubs in international competitions was advantageous and valuable for the Franco regime.

From the first years of Francoism, football quickly became an outlet for social tensions, a way of channeling them in a less conflictual direction. Spain's connection with the Axis nations during the Second World War left the country isolated on the international stage by the 1940s, and football was practically the only tool left for international communication. During Spain's political isolation, the simple acts of staging international football matches became triumphs that Franco's propaganda machine amplified to represent victory over their foreign diplomatic restrictions. The government valued these matches far beyond their measure on a sporting level. As a result, international contact for Spanish football teams during this period was limited primarily to matches against "friendly countries," such as Portugal, Germany, and Italy.[8]

At the same time, however, Franco signed a decree on February 22, 1941, that reorganized the former National Sports Council and created the new Delegación Nacional de Deportes (National Sports Delegation; DND) of the

FET de las JONS. This decree tasked the new institution with controlling all areas related to physical education and sport in Spain. The regime tried to apply the same concepts that Hitler and Mussolini had implemented in their respective countries. Sport—now under the control of a new body with immense power—lost all hope of independence; the Franco government had absolute control over all aspects of sport.[9]

In September 1937 the Francoist national zone created the Spanish Football Federation, with its headquarters in San Sebastián; the executive committee was presided over by Lieutenant Colonel Julián Troncoso Sagredo, with Luciano Urquijo as secretary. From the beginning they began conversations with FIFA to become the official representative of Spanish football at the international level. At FIFA's executive committee in Paris on November 6–7, 1937—in the middle of the Spanish Civil War—the international body decided to recognize the two football federations existing at that time in Spain: the Spanish Federation of Football situated in Barcelona (the republican area) and the recently created Federation located in San Sebastian (Francoist area). With the end of the Civil War in 1939 and the victory of Francoism, FIFA finally recognized the Federation in San Sebastian as its only interlocutor in Spain.[10]

While the new national football federation under Franco attempted to gain FIFA recognition, the country continued to play international matches and ascribe importance to them. When the Spanish national side played Portugal in Lisbon on January 30, 1938 (Spain lost 1–0), the newspaper *La Nueva España* commented on the game's role as a tool for international legitimacy. In the middle of a civil war, "winning or losing a match is not important"; the true importance, in the opinion of the journalist, lay in other factors: "Right now, international football matches serve to extend bonds of friendship with neighboring countries. Even to promote a feeling of patriotic fervor. To give an impression of what Spain is, what our temperament and our spirit are."[11] This match, in fact, followed one that Spain had played on November 28, 1937, against Portugal in Vigo, and two additional friendlies that the countries had played in February 1938 in the North African cities of Melilla and Tetuán. FIFA, however, did not recognize these matches because it had previously made clear that the selected teams of these two federations could not organize international matches:

> After having heard the delegates of the Spanish Federation sited in Barcelona and the delegates of a federation created in San Sebastian,

> the Executive Committee, taking into account the present-day situation which does not allow one single federation to efficiently direct football in the whole Spanish territory, decides, in a provisional way, that the affiliated associations can compete with the clubs of both organization which direct the football in Spain as well as of the national selected teams, excluding the possibility that these last matches have international character or use.[12]

The *Real Federación Española de Fútbol* (Royal Spanish Football Federation, RFEF) repeatedly tried to break out of the footballing isolation that it had suffered since 1945 by attempting to set up international friendlies with England and France. However, neither of these countries' governments was prepared to break the diplomatic boycott imposed by the UN on Spain. Spain therefore had to wait until 1949 for its first match against France and even longer—at the 1950 World Cup—before playing the English for the first time since the dictatorship began. Nonetheless, when the Franco-Spanish border opened in February 1948, that same month Jules Rimet mentioned, in a telegram to the RFEF, that the French Football Federation (FFF) felt "honored to initiate the renewal of communications by sending this message of friendship to the Spanish Federation." Armando Muñoz Calero, in his role as RFEF president, replied to Rimet, thanking him for the telegram and reiterating that there was a "sporting fraternity" between the two countries. This new international context coincided with the beginning of the Cold War and, as already mentioned, Francoism's gradual emergence from the isolation Spain had suffered since the start of the Second World War.[13]

Also in 1948, the DND consulted the Ministry of Foreign Affairs regarding how they should respond to invitations received by football clubs requesting their participation in international matches. Aware that government policy forbade the playing of football matches against teams from countries with which Spain did not have good diplomatic relations, the DND suggested that the ministry consider a compromise: "Prevent the Spanish national team from playing against countries who are not declared allies, but allow local matches, those which are club vs club, as well as our involvement in the Latin Cup, which owing to its racial nature, we are not isolated from."[14]

The ministry responded in July 1948, devising a set of rules for participation in international football matches that made clear the significant role football could have as a propaganda tool. These new rules demonstrated the extreme importance that the government attributed to Spanish clubs competing at an international level in order to present an image of fictitious normality. Yet, the government forbade the national side to play "matches in which they ran an evident risk of losing." In the case of countries such as Portugal, Ireland, Switzerland, the Netherlands, Sweden, Greece, and Egypt, with whom Spain maintained friendly diplomatic relations at the end of the 1940s, RFEF usually arranged matches without problem. However, the ministry made it clear that, given the quality of British players, clubs must be prepared to play against rivals such as England, Scotland, and Wales without embarrassment. The Ministry of Foreign Affairs also urged RFEF to ensure Spain's participation in matches with "the best national teams, making sure that the foreign rival is of the same ranking, and the team was as well-prepared as possible and, naturally, after rigorous enquiry." Also, the directive strictly forbade sporting relations with Eastern European communist countries, not surprising considering those countries' support of the Soviet efforts to remove Spain from all international federations and the Olympic movement.[15]

Carrying out this "rigorous enquiry" entailed a complex bureaucratized process implemented by Francoism for the application of permission for football clubs that wished to play matches outside of Spain or invite foreign clubs to visit. The federations, including RFEF, had to apply to the DND in either their own name or that of the clubs dependent on them, for permission to take part in an international sporting activity, either within the national territory or abroad. The DND, in turn, had to consult, through the secretary general of the National Movement, the Ministry of Foreign Affairs. The ministry evaluated the importance of the match, the dates on which it would take place, the financial compensation the clubs would receive, the opponent, and the possible diplomatic obstacles that could arise between the two countries. On the basis of their evaluation, they accepted or refused the applications from football clubs; in some instances, they consulted Franco's government to reach a decision. With permission granted, the Ministry of Foreign Affairs immediately contacted the ambassadors and diplomatic representatives in the cities where the matches were to take place, to arrange for the football club's visit to be completely under the ministry's control while abroad.

In this way Franco's state directly controlled the international relations of the football teams so as to avoid meetings that could interfere with the regime's diplomatic strategy and accept those that could promote its diplomatic interests. The ministry required all club and national team trips to pass through this administrative process to compete outside of Spain. For example, the secretary general of the National Movement at the Ministry of Foreign Affairs in 1969 requested permission for Athletic de Bilbao to play against Glasgow Celtic in Scotland at the end of March in the Inter-Cities Fairs Cup. Similarly, the Spanish ambassador in London commented on having received the necessary permission from RFEF to participate in the 1966 World Cup in England.[16]

European Cup and Real Madrid and 1950s Foreign Propaganda

Real Madrid's victories in the first five European Cup tournaments (1955–1960) coincided with the signing of the Treaty of Rome in 1957 and the creation of the EEC. In this political context the international victories of a Spanish club favored Franco's attempts to break Spain's isolation and improve diplomatic relations with Europe. Real Madrid's victories facilitated a process of domestic cohesion, while the rest of the world viewed the club as an example of a new cosmopolitan and triumphant Spain. The Francoist regime did not hesitate to take advantage of Real Madrid's popularity to further its own political interests. At the same time, the club's management, aware that the relationship could be mutually beneficial, were careful during these years not to create situations that could possibly compromise the regime's image abroad.[17] The Ministry of Foreign Affairs and its ambassadors recognized the international success of Real Madrid and sought to utilize it for the country's benefit. In a period when the external image of Francoism had deteriorated tremendously, the triumphs of the Spanish team in the European Cup actually served as the best propaganda for Franco outside of the country.

In December 1954 Gabriel Hanot, president of the French sporting newspaper *L'Équipe*, proposed the creation of a European interclub competition, which Real Madrid supported from its inception. The decision on whether the Spanish club could participate in this competition—which included teams from the Communist bloc—lay in the hands of the Ministry for Foreign Affairs and, as a last resort, Franco's own government. The Spanish ambassador in Paris informed the ministry that, even though teams from the other side of the Iron Curtain were also taking part, he saw Real Madrid's participation in the competition in a positive light, given that "their absence could provoke unfavorable comments" against Franco's regime in popular international opinion.[18]

The same ambassador continued to praise the behavior of Santiago Bernabéu, president of the club, and Raimundo Saporta, treasurer and later vice president, in the Paris meeting that developed the rules of the European Cup. The ambassador pointed out to the ministry that "it would be damaging if we were the ones who refused to play against teams from Russian satellite states."[19] Spain demonstrated its growing support for this new competition in May by hosting the executive committee meeting of the European Champion Clubs' Cup in Madrid. FIFA ultimately approved the competition as long as it was under the direction of UEFA. Meanwhile, the government gave Real Madrid permission to take part in the European Cup, fearing the image a Spanish refusal would project. Additionally, should the scenario of getting through to the final against a communist country arise, Spain could appeal to play on neutral territory.

The competition quickly put the diplomatic flexibility of Franco's government to the test when Real Madrid had to face Partizan Belgrade in the quarterfinals of the first European Cup. The political weight of the match was extremely significant given that diplomatic relations between the two countries were nonexistent. Marshall Josip Broz Tito's regime had, since the 1950s, maintained an intense campaign of criticism against the Francoist dictatorship in international meetings; meanwhile, Spain had become a safe haven for the Ustaše Croatians ruled by Ante Pavelić, a German and Italian collaborator during the Second World War. Real Madrid began to fear that this match would not take place, but Saporta's assurances to the political and sporting Francoist authorities secured the government's approval of Real Madrid's participation. The two clubs even signed an agreement, under the supervision of UEFA, in which they stated "that the significance of these matches would not go beyond a sporting level, but nevertheless, this reinstatement of sporting relations between the two nations was a great achievement for the progress of the competition."[20]

The media highlighted the role of Real Madrid as a diplomatic actor, frequently quoting actual diplomats on the importance of the club's matches as a way to improve the international image of the regime. In December 1968, *ABC* journalist Juan Hernández Petit famously asked Fernándo María Castiella, minister for foreign affairs, about Real Madrid's "diplomatic" work and the "implications on a national level." Castiella responded: "Real Madrid, in addition, demonstrate a style of sportsmanship in their own right and they know how to travel the world with the utmost decorum in the name of Spain.

Their players act like true ambassadors, and their actions contribute to the prestige of our homeland. I myself, while overjoyed with their victories, feel a closer connection with the team when, despite their best endeavors, they lose a match." The ambassador to Italy acknowledged that the club was "one of the best instruments, perhaps the best and most important in recent times, for affirming our popularity abroad." The minister-secretary general of the National Movement, José Solís, made a similar reflection in October 1968, when he acknowledged to the Real Madrid players that "you have done much more than many embassies scattered throughout the four corners of the earth. People who hated us now understand us, thanks to you, for you have broken down many walls."[21]

Real Madrid always tried to maintain close relations with members of the Ministry of Foreign Affairs, through a channel that also linked Raimundo Saporta with Ramón Sedó, director general of foreign policy, and with the minister for foreign affairs himself, Fernando María Castiella.[22] As the foreign ministry supported Real Madrid and allowed the club to participate in the newly created European Cup, the image of the Franco regime began to be rehabilitated abroad. Domestic newspapers also highlighted this diplomatic work of the football club, further reinforcing the important role given to the sport under Franco.

Football as a Political and Diplomatic Tool in the 1960s

The arrival of Fernando María Castiella as foreign minister in February 1957 began a new phase in Spanish foreign policy, which was immediately reflected in the international relations of the football clubs and the Spanish national side. The sporting policy the FET had tried to implement since the end of the Civil War—using sport to promote physical activity in Spanish society—had demonstrably failed. Several factors contributed to this failure. The Falangist faction lost the prominence it had previously enjoyed in Franco's government, which by the 1960s placed trust in other factions of Francoism, such as representatives from the army and the Catholic church. Equally important was the lack of a clear and determined direction from Franco's political organization, and the unavoidable economic investment that a project of this magnitude required. At the same time, and consistent with the new foreign policy that from the mid-1960s sought to strengthen relations with other European powers, the Ministry of Foreign Affairs implemented a clear change in direction regarding the sporting policies of Francoism, henceforth orienting itself with improving the international image of the country. Franco's foreign policy evolved, moving away from the radical prohibition against Spanish clubs playing against teams from communist countries, in particular the Soviet Union. By the end of the 1950s and early 1960s, the international propaganda benefits that organizing large international sporting events such as the Olympic Games or the FIFA World Cup could bring to the Franco regime—and the necessity to finally normalize sporting relations with the Soviet Union, as the rest of Western Europe had already done—had become evident. In this way, the diplomacy of sport served as a counterpoint to the fierce criticism that was leveled against Francoism's repressive policies by the European countries most opposed to Franco and by the Far Left international media.[23]

The new era of Francoist foreign policy—from the appointment of Castiella as minister of foreign affairs and its reflection in sporting relations—is highlighted in a March 1957 letter from the national head of FET's Foreign Service, Sergio Cifuentes, to the director general of cultural relations at the Ministry of Foreign Affairs. Cifuentes reported that some French sporting newspapers, like *L'Équipe*, had "started a campaign designed to unite the efforts of Western European countries, for the improvement of sport, forming a bloc which would allow better sporting performance, in all disciplines, and which would make it possible to reduce the huge difference that exists between the countries of Europe, the United States, and the Soviet Union." His letter mentioned that this project was consistent with the first economic agreements reached among Germany, France, Italy, Belgium, the Netherlands, and Luxembourg. The Portuguese press criticized this move for leaving out other Western European countries, prompting France to invite countries such as Portugal, Spain, Switzerland, and Austria into this new "sporting community of the West." When FET's Foreign Service asked the ministry what it thought about Spain joining this new European sporting project, it responded with total support for Spain's inclusion.[24]

The ministry, particularly the DND and the secretary general of the National Movement, uncompromisingly demanded that sporting bodies update the ministry continuously about the movements of sport clubs outside of Spain and that they follow the protocols established for such trips. A lengthy report in February 1959 from the ministry to the secretary general of the National Movement articulates this organization's preoccupation with maintaining control over sporting activities outside of Spain. The Spanish ambassador to Rome had learned through the press that a match between the Spanish and Italian national sides had been scheduled in the capital on February 28, an event about which he had not been informed at any point. The ministry used this example to then launch into the rationale behind its demand to be informed "with sufficient warning of when an international sporting event of any sort involving Spain is to take place." First, the report underlined the political nature of football as one of the reasons making it essential for the diplomatic sector to be kept apprised of these trips. They acknowledged that the DND usually consulted the ministry about sporting encounters involving Spanish clubs or the national side with other countries "subject to Soviet influence"; however, the ministry was not always properly informed "about the organization of sporting activities which affect our country and other countries of the free world." The ministry highlighted the fundamental importance of knowing about sporting exchanges with "friendly countries" so that it was "able to express its opinion about them, within the general frame of our international relations," and the necessity for the secretary general of the National Movement to inform the ministry with "decent warning, and always before the organizers of the proposed sporting activities have made firm agreements abroad, which—for purely international political reasons—may then have to be rescinded, with the resulting losses, economic and otherwise."[25]

The second consideration articulated for the need for diplomatic forewarning about Spanish athletes traveling abroad or the arrival of foreign teams in Spain was that it enabled the ministry to find the most efficient solutions to "any administrative issues that should be resolved by our diplomatic representatives." Diplomatic representatives could also "work together to assist in the organization and overall success" of these competitions. Finally, the ministry highlighted the duties of the diplomatic sector to use Spanish sporting victories as a foreign propaganda tool:

> In many instances it is in Spain's interest to throw a greater spotlight on those sporting activities and competitions which take place abroad and in which our sportsmen and women take part. In these cases, the Spanish diplomatic corps should in some way contribute to emphasizing our presence outside of Spain. As Your Excellency is aware, all of our diplomatic representatives abroad have always had the honor of welcoming our sports stars when they have travelled

> abroad. However, these warm receptions should not be reduced to mere social gatherings; they should, like any other event organized in honor of our sportsmen and women in which the diplomatic mission takes part, be organized well in advance, always highlighting as much as possible our sporting activities abroad, as is already the case in other fields and activities.

Thus, the ministry—and more specifically its Dirección General de Política Exterior (executive management of foreign policy)—demanded that the secretary general of the National Movement take appropriate measures to ensure that the cooperation that existed between the two bodies, with regard to "the issues which affect our relations with countries on the other side of the 'Iron Curtain,'" would also extend to "all other countries and to all the different sporting activities that Spain would take part in abroad." The Spanish Ministry of Foreign Affairs was thus clearly interested in keeping under its control all sporting relations at the international level in order to use them as a propaganda tool for Franco's regime.[26]

In contrast with the prestige Spanish clubs gained internationally, the Spanish national team had not had much sporting success. Fourth place in the 1950 World Cup in Brazil and victory in the 1964 European Nations Cup were the only moments from the national side's success that merited celebrations of national pride. In fact, disappointment became the general rule regarding the national team's results during Francoism. Spain did not qualify for the World Cup in 1954 and 1958, played poorly in 1962 and 1966, and again failed to qualify in 1970 and 1974.

Yet although the Spanish national side did not perform to the standard that Franco's government would have liked, the state did not pass up the opportunity to use its participation to its advantage in the same way as they had with the clubs. Indeed, the July 1959 correspondence between the president of the RFEF, Alfonso de la Fuente, and the foreign minister, Castiella, demonstrates this use in the wake of the national team's frequently poor performances. De la Fuente expressed his gratitude for the ministry granting the RFEF permission to organize various matches outside of Spain, highlighting the national side's 4–2 victory over Poland in Katowice in a qualifying match for the final phase of the first European Nations Cup. He acknowledged that this victory had been especially important for the "joy of seeing our flag, and, above all, of hearing our national anthem, in politically hostile lands like the

Iron Curtain." As the man in charge of Spanish football, he informed Castiella about the RFEF's intentions to organize a tour of various South American countries in July 1960. The Spanish team planned to play games against Peru, Chile, and Argentina, but he also suggested to Castiella the possibility of "gaining great sporting success and national prestige for Spain" by including a match in Mexico.[27]

The strained diplomatic relations between these two countries turned a proposed friendly match into an event with great diplomatic relevance. Mexico had never recognized Franco's Spain and had in fact helped and continued to recognize the Spanish Republican government in exile. Not until 1977, after a break of thirty-eight years and the arrival of democracy, did Mexico and Spain resume diplomatic relations. Despite the obvious obstacles that made it difficult for Franco's government to give this sort of match the go-ahead, the president of the RFEF was very aware of the diplomatic importance and the benefits for Spain's image abroad that this match could bring: "I understand the obstacles that might beset this idea—and not on the part of the Mexican Football Federation, who are always keen to play against us—but, on the other hand, I calculate that it would be immensely beneficial for our homeland if our national side were to play just once in Mexico, in an international friendly. Without doubt it would be an invaluable act of diplomatic and sporting ambassadorship." A few days later Castiella replied, stating that he still could not "definitively decide for or against the inclusion of Mexico amongst the countries to be visited." The minister reminded de la Fuente of the difficulties Real Madrid had previously incurred on their tour of Mexico and, above all, of "the anomalous situation of our relations with the Government of said country." As such, he advised "postponing any decision" for the moment, planning the tour with the matches already arranged and "leaving until the last minute, and not until after thorough examination, the inclusion of the match against the Mexican team." The Spanish team, failing to obtain the permission to play against Mexico, participated in matches only against Peru, Chile, and Argentina.[28]

In addition to friendly matches, the first two European Nations Cup tournaments demonstrate a turning point at the end of the 1950s in Francoism's use of football as a tool for domestic self-confidence and, above all, international propaganda, particularly in the regime's management of the national side's participation. Franco's government again showed its strong internal contradictions and discrepancies with regard to the political utilization of football in the first edition of this tournament. In May 1960 Spain convincingly beat Poland in the quarterfinal round with an aggregate score of 7–2. The draw next paired Spain with the Soviet Union on May 29 in Moscow and June 9 in Madrid. Elola Olaso, president of the DND since 1956, together with Foreign Minister Castiella and José Solís, minister for the secretary general of the National Movement, represented the faction most convinced of the benefits football could bring to Spain's new foreign policy interests. Opposing them was the most radical and uncompromising core of the government, led by Carrero Blanco and Camilo Alonso Vega, ministers of the Presidency and Interior, respectively; this group prioritized security and law enforcement over any other factor and did not hesitate to block any type of sporting venture that might cause issues for law enforcement.

Meanwhile, tickets for the match in Moscow had sold out, and at the end of April both coaches had presented their team lists for the games. The cabinet, however, finally decided on May 25 to deny permission for Spain to play the two matches against the Soviet Union. The best efforts of individuals in the political and sporting hierarchy who favored playing the matches and making the most of them for propaganda purposes could not stop the ban. News related to the withdrawal of the Spanish team was censored in the Spanish press, which published only a very short notice that the Spanish Federation had communicated to FIFA about the suspension of the football matches between the Spanish and Soviet national teams.[29]

From this point onward a radical change in the way Francoism understood the role of sport and football became evident. In 1963 Real Madrid's basketball team finally managed to receive government permission to play two matches against CSKA Moscow in the final of the European Cup. This concession was the first step toward the normalization of sporting relationships with the main ideological enemy of Francoism. The continuation of this process came the following year, with Spain hosting the final phase of the European Nations Cup. From the radical position that Spain had taken in 1960, with its refusal to allow the two matches against the Soviet Union, in just four years they had reversed course to agree to be the host country of the tournament, welcoming the Iron Curtain countries of Hungary and the Soviet Union. As Spain celebrated "twenty-five years of peace" under Franco, the final against the Soviet team in the Santiago Bernabéu became the ideal occasion to reinforce Franco's prestige nationally and show off Spain's policy of economic development and the boom in beach tourism to the rest of the world. This time, though some ministers expressed doubts about the possible consequences of hosting the tournament, Castiella and José Solís convinced the cabinet that Spain would enjoy political and economic benefits and also project a more tolerant and hospitable image of the country.[30]

The 120,000 spectators who witnessed the Spanish team's 2–1 victory over the Soviet team applauded Franco when he arrived at the stadium. The Spanish press emphasized the crowd's respectful reception of the Soviet team and the sporting spirit that flourished in the match, which was broadcast on television to around fifteen European countries.[31] For the newspaper *ABC*, the Spanish team's win constituted a victory for the Franco regime, a display of the cohesion of Spanish society under Franco's leadership, and at the same time the image of a modern country that had backed the liberalization of its economy with the creation of the Stabilization Plan in 1959:

> In front of the team from the U.S.S.R., whose red flag was raised atop the stadium, in front of six hundred journalists from around the world and in front of millions of Eurovision and Intervision TV viewers, a diverse crowd of 120,000 Spaniards of all ages and classes paid tribute on Sunday to their Head of State, in one of the longest, most fervent and resounding ovations ever witnessed in his long political life. It was a spontaneous and supportive gesture that the Spanish people presented to the world and more specifically to the Soviet Union. After twenty-eight years of peace, behind each round of applause an authentic and eloquent endorsement of the spirit of July 18th could be heard.[32]

In contrast to the Spanish team's forced withdrawal in 1960 and the related government-imposed media censorship, by 1964 Franco took advantage of the Spanish national team's triumph in the European Nations Cup. Francoism now relied on organizing major sporting events as a tool for consolidating identity and national prestige around Franco. The triumph of the national team strengthened domestic cohesion around the dictator's image. The mass media supported those efforts, directly relating football achievements with the success attributed to Francoism for the celebration of "twenty-five years of peace" following victory in the Civil War.

Football, as with any other aspect of Spanish society, was under the control of Franco's political authorities. Football was regularly exploited at home by the Franco regime, based on its integration into the social fabric and its aptitude for generating consensus and strengthening national identities. Similarly, this sport was also an important tool for improving the weak image of the dictatorship abroad. It was the Ministry of Foreign Affairs' task to develop this strategy, which it closely linked to the regime's foreign policy interests at each stage. While it is difficult to state unequivocally that football allowed Spain to open up new diplomatic relations with other countries, it did serve to enhance, improve, and strengthen Francoism's diplomatic relations abroad. As it strengthened their ideological stance alongside the Axis powers and, later, their alliance with the United States, in the end it helped pave the way toward joining the recently created European Economic Community (forerunner to the European Union).

The case of football under Francoism is by no means exceptional, particularly in a European context. There are several representative examples of the use of sport as a form of public diplomacy throughout the twentieth century: Mussolini's Italy in the 1930s, Britain in the 1930s (to improve its international image), and the German Democratic Republic from the 1950s onward. Spain's actions under Franco therefore mirrored a broader trend at the time. Football allowed Franco's Spain to break out of isolation and engage with the wider international community, as had been the case with Germany and games organized with Swiss teams in 1948. And, similar to the way the Franco regime used Real Madrid's success in the European Cup in the 1950s, the Salazar dictatorship in Portugal also used Benfica's success in the same tournament in the early 1960s. Spain attempted to use football in all its forms at the international level, with both the national team and club teams playing in friendly matches and tournaments, as well as hosting competitions inside Spain—all in an effort to rehabilitate the country after years of isolation.[33]

The Franco government, with all its limitations, tried to use sporting success and the organization of sporting events as a soft power strategy to influence opinions of the regime abroad. Following the success of the 1964 European Nations Cup, Spain sought to organize other sporting events. In December 1965 Madrid put forward its candidacy to host the 1972 Olympic Games (ultimately losing to Munich), but in July 1970 FIFA selected Spain as the host of the 1982 World Cup. These two instances further demonstrate the definitive change of how the Franco regime used sport within a global strategy of foreign policy. In the 1960s a group of ministers within Franco's government recognized the benefits that could come from hosting sporting events in the country, in contrast with a more radical group that placed security above any type of international opening. These conflicts contributed to the varied nature of how the Spanish government under Franco used sport as a tool of propaganda and diplomacy during this period. Sport, and specifically the success garnered on the football pitch, ultimately became one of the few elements the Franco regime could use to show a positive image of the country at the international level while favoring its foreign policy strategies.

Notes

1. Letter, Alfonso de la Serna to Spanish Ministry of Foreign Affairs, March 26, 1969, file R11206 E54, Spanish Ministry of Foreign Affairs Archive, Madrid, Spain (hereafter AMAE).

2. Angel Bahamonde, *El Real Madrid en la historia de España* (Madrid: Taurus, 2002); Eduardo González Calleja, "El Real Madrid, ¿'equipo de España'? Fútbol e identidades durante el franquismo," *Política y Sociedad* 51, no. 2 (2014): 275–296; Teresa González Aja, "La política deportiva en España durante la República y el Franquismo," in *Sport y autoritarismos: la utilización del deporte por el comunismo y el fascismo*, ed. Teresa González Aja (Madrid: Alianza, 2002), 169–202; Carlos Fernández Santander, *El fútbol durante la Guerra Civil y el franquismo* (Madrid: San Martín, 1990); Alejandro Viuda-Serrano, "Santiago Bernabéu y el Real Madrid: un análisis histórico del mito del fútbol. Política y deporte en la España franquista," *Agon International Journal of Sport Sciences* 3, no 1 (2013): 33–47; Xavier Pujadas, *Atletas y ciudadanos: historia social del deporte en España 1870–2010* (Madrid: Alianza, 2011); Bartolomé Escandell Bonet, Eduardo González Calleja, and Francisco Villacorta Baños, eds., *Historia del Real Madrid, 1902–2002. La entidad, los socios, el madridismo*, 2 vols. (Madrid: Everest/Fundación Real Madrid, 2002); Carlos García-Martí, "Reshaping Spanish Football Identity in the 1940s: From Fury to Tactics," *International Journal of the History of Sport* 33, no. 10 (2016): 1–17; Ramon Llopis-Goig, *Spanish Football and Social Change: Sociological Investigations* (Basingstoke: Palgrave Macmillan, 2015).

3. Andrés Domínguez Almansa and Xavier Pujadas i Martí, "Estadios y trincheras: Deporte y retaguardia en la Guerra Civil, 1936–1939," in *Atletas y ciudadanos: historia social del deporte en España 1870–2010*, ed. Xavier Pujadas i Martí (Madrid: Alianza, 2011), 169–201; Fernando Estomba Echepare, *Deporte, política y sociedad en vizcaya: afición y espectáculo en la Segunda República y la Guerra Civil* (PhD diss., Universidad del País Vasco, 2006); Matilde Eiroa San Francisco, "Urdiendo el tejido exterior para el Nuevo Estado: la política internacional del Primer Franquismo," *Historia y Comunicación Social* 6 (2001): 203–214; Montserrat Huguet, "La política exterior del fran-

quismo (1939–1975)," in *La política exterior de España (1800–2003)*, ed. J. C. Pereira (Barcelona: Ariel, 2003), 633–657; González Aja, "La política deportiva en España," 169–202; García-Martí, "Reshaping Spanish Football Identity."

4. Juan Manuel Fernández Fernández-Cuesta, "La información al servicio de la política exterior. La creación de la oficina de información diplomática, respuesta del franquismo al aislamiento internacional (1945–1950)," *Revista internacional de Historia de la Comunicación* 1, no. 1 (2013): 132–154; Rafael García Pérez, "España y la Segunda Guerra Mundial," in *La política exterior de España en el siglo XX*, ed. J. Tussell, J. Avilés, and R. Pardo (Madrid: UNED/Biblioteca Nueva, 2000), 301–321; Stanley G. Payne, *El franquismo: 1939–1950. La dura posguerra* (Madrid: Alianza, 2005); Juan Carlos Pereira Castañares, "De 'Centinela de Occidente' a la conspiración masónica-comunista. La política exterior del franquismo," in *En el combate por la historia. La república, la guerra civil y el franquismo*, ed. Ángel Viñas (Barcelona: Pasado y Presente, 2012), 659–678; "Acuerdos del Comité Directivo de la Federación Española," *Boletín oficial de la Delegación Nacional de Deportes de F.E.T. y de las J.O.N.S.* 70 (1949): 18–20; Bruno Bongiovanni, *Storia de la guerra fredda* (Roma y Bari: Laterza, 2004); John Lewis Gaddis, *La Guerra Fría* (Barcelona: RBA Editores, 2008); Ronald E. Powaski, *La guerra fría: Estados Unidos y la Unión Soviética, 1917–1991* (Barcelona: Crítica, 2000); Robert McMahon, *La Guerra Fría. Una breve introducción* (Madrid: Alianza, 2008); Juan Carlos Pereira Castañares and Pedro A. Martínez Lillo, "Política exterior, 1939–1975," in *Historia Contemporánea de España (siglo XX)*, ed. Javier Paredes (Barcelona: Ariel, 1998), 737.

5. Rosa Pardo Sanz, "La etapa Castiella y el final del Régimen, 1957–1975," in *La política exterior de España en el siglo XX*, ed. J. Tussell, J. Avilés, and R. Pardo (Madrid: UNED/Biblioteca Nueva, 2000), 341–369.

6. Stanley J. Payne, *El régimen de Franco, 1936–1975* (Madrid: Alianza, 1987); J. A. Martínez, (coord.), *Historia de España siglo XX, 1939–1996* (Madrid: Cátedra, 1999); A. Mateos and A. Soto, *El final del franquismo, 1959–1975* (Madrid: Historia 16, 1997); Juan Antonio Simón, "Jugando contra el enemigo: Raimundo Saporta y el primer viaje del equipo de baloncesto del Real Madrid CF a la Unión Soviética," *Revista Internacional de Ciencias del Deporte* 28 (2012): 109–126.

7. González Aja, "La política deportiva en España," 169–202.

8. Juan Antonio Simón, "De la furia espagnole au tiki-taka. Football et constructions identitaires en Espagne (1920–2015)," in *Le football des nations: des terrains de jeu aux communautés imagines*, ed. Fabien Archambault, Stéphane Beaud, and William Gasparini (Paris: Publications de la Sorbonne, 2016), 75–91.

9. Bahamonde, *El Real Madrid en la historia*, 185–187.

10. Juan Luis Franco, "1937, dos Federaciones Españolas de fútbol," *Iusport.com*, October 17, 2016, https://iusport.com/not/24326/1937-dos-federaciones-espanolas-de-futbol/ (accessed July 15, 2018).

11. U.V.E., "Comentario. En un compás de espera," *La Nueva España*, February 1, 1938, 9.

12. Process-Verbal de la Reunion du Comite Executif, November 6–7, 1937, Fédération Internationale de Football Association, Zurich, Switzerland (hereafter FIFA).

13. Duncan Shaw, *Fútbol y franquismo* (Madrid: Alianza, 1987), 165; "Acuerdos del Comité Directivo de la Federación Española," *Boletín oficial de la Delegación Nacional de Deportes de F.E.T. y de las J.O.N.S.* 59 (1948): 18–19.

14. "Normas para la celebración de encuentros internacionales de fútbol," July 1948, file R-2586, doc. 46, AMAE.

15. Ibid.; Jenifer Parks, "'Nothing but Trouble': The Soviet Union's Push to 'Democratise' International Sports during the Cold War, 1959–1962," *International Journal of the History of Sport* 30, no. 13 (2013): 1554–1567; Heather L. Dichter, "'We Have Allowed Our Decisions to Be Determined by Political Considerations': The Early Cold War in the International Ski Federation," *Sport in History* 37, no. 3 (2017): 290–308.

16. Letter, Secretary General of the National Movement to Ministry of Foreign Affairs, March 20, 1969, file R11206 E56, AMAE; letter, Ministry of Foreign Affairs to Spanish ambassador in London, January 21, 1966, file R8410 E17, AMAE.

17. Eduardo González Calleja, "El Real Madrid, ¿'Equipo del Régimen'? Fútbol y política durante el Franquismo," *Esporte e Sociedade* 14 (2010): 14–15; Bonet, Calleja, and Baños, eds., *Historia del Real Madrid, 1902–2002.*

18. Letter, Spanish ambassador in Paris to Ministry of Foreign Affairs, March 1954, file R-4833, doc. 50, AMAE.

19. Ibid.

20. Pal Kolsto, ed., *Strategies of Symbolic Nation-Building in South Eastern Europe* (London: Routledge, 2016); Bahamonde, *El Real Madrid en la historia*, 246; letter, Spanish ambassador, Paris to Ministry of Foreign Affairs, December 1955, file R-4833, doc. 50, AMAE.

21. Juan Hernández Petit, "El gol belga, fruto de la técnica flamenca y del candor español," *ABC,* December 12, 1968, 75–76; Shaw, *Fútbol y franquismo*, 44, 18.

22. Bonet, Calleja, and Baños, eds., *Historia del Real Madrid, 1902–2002*; Simón, "Jugando contra el enemigo."

23. Carles Santacana i Torres, "Espejo de un régimen. Transformación de las estructuras deportivas y su uso político y propagandístico, 1939–1961," in *Atletas y ciudadanos: historia social del deporte en España 1870–2010*, ed. Xavier Pujadas (Madrid: Alianza, 2011), 214; Juan Antonio Simón, "La diplomacia del balón: deporte y relaciones internacionales durante el franquismo," *História e Cultura* 4, no. 1 (2015): 165–189.

24. Letter, Sergio Cifuentes, FET's Foreign Service to Ministry of Foreign Affairs, March 8, 1957, file R4775, doc. 14, Archive of the Spanish Administration, Madrid, Spain (hereafter AGA).

25. Letter, Spanish ambassador in Rome to Ministry of Foreign Affairs, February 24, 1959, collection Spanish Ministry of Foreign Affairs 84/14066, doc. 54, AGA.

26. Ibid.

27. Letter, Alfonso de la Fuente to Castiella, July 2, 1959, file R5544, doc. 54, AGA.

28. Juan Carlos Pereira, "España en el mundo," in *Historia contemporánea de España, 1931–2017*, vol. 2, ed. Jordi Canal (Barcelona: Taurus, 2017), 321–369; letter, Alfonso de la Fuente to Castiella, July 2, 1959, file R5544, doc. 54, AGA.

29. Ramón Ramos, *¡Que vienen los rusos! España renuncia a la Eurocopa 1960 por decisión de Franco* (Comares: Granada, 2012); "El partido España-Rusia suspendido," *ABC*, May 26, 1960, 69.

30. Simón Sanjurjo, "Jugando contra el enemigo," 109–126; Ramos, *¡Que vienen los rusos!*, 157–159; letter, RFEF to Secretary General of the National Movement, July 29, 1964, file 82/18661, AGA.

31. Shaw, *Fútbol y franquismo*, 168–170.

32. "España gana la Copa de Europa de Naciones al vencer a la U.R.S.S. por 2–1," *ABC*, August 23, 1964, 55.

33. Simon Martin, *Football and Fascism: The National Game under Mussolini* (Oxford: Berg, 2004); Peter J. Beck, *Scoring for Britain: International Football and International Politics, 1900–1939* (London: Frank Cass, 1999); Heather L. Dichter, "'A Game of Political Ice Hockey': NATO Restrictions on East German Sport Travel in the Aftermath of the Berlin Wall," in *Diplomatic Games: Sport, Statecraft, and International Relations since 1945*, ed. Heather L. Dichter and Andrew L. Johns (Lexington: University Press of Kentucky, 2014), 19–51; Heather L. Dichter, "Kicking Around International Sport: West Germany's Return to the International Community through Football," *International Journal of the History of Sport* 30, no. 17 (2013): 2031–2051; Ricardo Serrado, *O Jogo de Salazar: a política e o futebol no Estado Novo* (Lisbon: Casa das Letras, 2009).

"The Finest Ambassadors"

American–Icelandic Football Exchange, 1955–1956

George N. Kioussis

On August 23, 1955, the United States national football team landed at the Keflavík air base on the southwest tip of Iceland. Conservative newspaper *Morgunblaðið* carried news of the group's arrival, running a pair of photographs on its back page the following morning. One showed the delegates, neatly dressed in matching blazers, emerging from their plane with broad smiles. The other showed American officials posing alongside, and interlocking arms with, Bragi Kristjánsson, president of the Olympic Committee of Iceland.[1] Although hardly atypical of reporting for such an occasion, the coverage would have pleased policymakers in Washington, who sponsored the three-match tour for the purposes of building goodwill.

The timing of the trip to the North Atlantic, and the Icelandic national team's visit to the United States the following year, was by no means a coincidence. Rather, the exchange occurred amid weakening diplomatic relations between the countries. The fallout was due in large part to the presence of American servicemen at Keflavík, where they were first stationed during the Second World War. Originally sent to help protect Icelandic sovereignty, the troops came under increased pressure from citizen groups that questioned their necessity and railed against the threat of American cultural influence. As the situation grew ever more tenuous, the administration of Dwight D. Eisenhower used football to deal with the base question specifically and the political realities of the region more broadly.

The American delegation arrives in Iceland for a three-match goodwill tour in August 1955. The trip was sponsored by the US Department of State. Courtesy of Sigmundur Ó. Steinarsson/KSÍ.

The inclusion of American footballers in the effort to win Icelandic hearts and minds was perhaps a nod to the diplomatic potential of what was quickly becoming the global sport par excellence. Yet though football lent itself to cultural initiatives by sheer virtue of its geographic reach, its role within American Cold War–era sport diplomacy has been relatively unexplored. The exchange with Iceland, thus, represents a useful case study for assessing the capacity of the global game to serve American policy ends—and at a time of mounting international tension. As became clear over the course of the two tours, football could cut across political lines and act as a vehicle for what FIFA president Jules Rimet called "le rapprochement des peuples."[2]

Furthermore, the reciprocal nature of the exchange with Iceland adds a new layer to the literature on sporting goodwill tours. While previous scholarly forays have shined a light on the deployment of American athlete-ambassadors, many of whom crossed the Iron Curtain, the direct, one-for-one nature of the Icelandic experiment provides a valuable lens for comparing the import and export of cultural representatives. Indeed, bringing people into the country posed unique challenges to American policymakers, as the reality that visitors experienced differed markedly from the curated image that Washington projected abroad. Although these and other mishaps did not sully the venture on the whole, they reflect a diplomatic machine that was still learning the contours of the cultural Cold War.

Cultural Diplomacy and the Eisenhower Administration

Upon taking the oath of office in January 1953, and with virtually his first words as president of the United States, Dwight D. Eisenhower painted a grim portrait of the rivalry between East and West. "We sense with all our faculties," he proclaimed, "that forces of good and evil are massed and armed and opposed as rarely before in history." Nearly two weeks later, he carried forward the leitmotif at his State of the Union address. He also promised to put into place a "new, positive foreign policy" so as to check the "calculated pressures of aggressive communism." In due course, this strategy came to emphasize the importance of public opinion. As historian Kenneth Osgood has chronicled, "Far from being a peripheral aspect of the U.S.-Soviet struggle, the competition for hearts and minds—the cold war of words and of deeds—was one of its principal battlegrounds."[3]

The Eisenhower administration put significant thought into designing a system to oversee all matters related to psychological strategy. In August 1953 it established the United States Information Agency (USIA) to convince the world that American policy goals were in concert with "their legitimate aspirations for freedom, progress, and peace." Although Washington did not shy away from psychological methods prior to that point, it was the formation of the USIA that, in Shawn Parry-Giles's estimation, elevated the role of propaganda within American statecraft. The new body was not left to its own devices, but rather worked alongside the Operations Coordinating Board (OCB), the State Department, and the Central Intelligence Agency. Collectively, the psychological apparatus organized cultural presentations, goodwill tours, people-to-people exchanges, and the like. The goal of such efforts, broadly speaking, was to improve relations with foreign citizenries, advertise the country's social, cultural, and economic progress, and sell "the American way."[4]

Sportsmen and women were folded into the government's cultural strategy. Over several decades, a diverse range of athlete-ambassadors was sent across the globe to help ease political tension and win hearts and minds. Eisenhower and his team recognized the diplomatic value of sport shortly into the president's first term, and the sport–statecraft nexus assumed its most public dimension in the early 1970s, when the exchange of table tennis players set the stage for Richard Nixon's visit to communist China.[5] Thus, the American–Icelandic football experiment was embedded in a broader diplomatic framework that evolved throughout the Cold War. At the same time, the deployment of the US national team to the North Atlantic in the summer of 1955 was a direct response to a geopolitical situation that was, from the perspective of Washington, careening toward crisis.

North Atlantic Geopolitics in the Early Cold War

The diplomatic relationship between the United States and Iceland took on new importance within the context of the Second World War. Until that point, trade between the countries was virtually nil and Washington had yet to station an envoy in Reykjavík. In 1941, however, the governments entered into a defense agreement that made the United States responsible for the island country's protection. Under the terms of the deal, American forces would take over for the British, who had previously occupied Iceland to keep it from falling into German hands. In 1942, construction was completed on the Keflavík air base and, by the following year, roughly fifty thousand soldiers were stationed in the North Atlantic.[6]

As that conflict came to a close, and as hot war turned into cold, Keflavík retained its strategic value. Its geographic position rendered it important to Washington's plans for a regional alliance. Moreover, it offered a useful defensive post against potential Soviet aggression and, if necessary, a launch pad for attacks. Accordingly, both the Harry Truman and Eisenhower administrations sought to procure a more permanent presence at the base. Their efforts, however, encountered several obstacles. Among the challenges was an Icelandic government that struggled to negotiate its traditional neutrality with the political exigencies of the early Cold War. A fractured domestic political scene complicated matters still further, as did the insular nature of the Icelandic populace. Tellingly, one American diplomat dubbed Iceland the "reluctant ally."[7]

It was not until May 1951 that the Icelandic government granted the United States the position it sought. The countries agreed, at the urging of NATO and against the backdrop of the Korean War, to a bilateral treaty that placed responsibility for the defense of Iceland in American hands. The pact, however, generated little enthusiasm among Icelandic citizens. "To them," notes historian Valur Ingimundarson, "the Defense Treaty was a result of rising international tensions, perhaps a necessity but not an occasion for celebration." Public sentiment did not become any more celebratory as American military personnel began to filter into the island country. Nationalists claimed that the servicemen posed a threat to Icelandic nationhood and culture, tapping into fears over fraternization between soldiers and local women. The sense of angst was such that Icelandic policymakers lobbied for social and racial restrictions to be placed on the defense force. In 1954 the base was cordoned off with fencing, and soldiers were, by and large, limited in their off-site movement. Furthermore, black servicemen were banned from Keflavík altogether.[8]

As the 1950s reached their midpoint, support for the defense force continued to ebb. A combination of domestic and international factors was to blame. First, the Soviet Union rekindled its economic ties with Iceland and became, within a short period of time, the island country's second largest trading partner. What is more, the emergence of the isolationist National Preservation Party lent further voice to those opposing the presence of American troops. Finally, the death of Joseph Stalin and the start of the Khrushchev "thaw" led many to hope that peace was on the horizon. For American policymakers long concerned that Iceland was susceptible to communist machinations, and fully aware of the allure of the Soviet charm offensive, the developments proved most worrying.[9]

In November 1953, G. Hayden Raynor, director of the Office of British Commonwealth and Northern European Affairs, penned a memorandum expressing his alarm over the "steadily deteriorating public attitude" toward the defense pact. He also offered a series of prescriptions for how Washington might address the state of affairs. Among the suggestions was a call to bolster what was, in his mind, a woefully inadequate informational campaign. "We have a tremendous public relations job in Iceland that we are trying to do with pennies," Raynor complained. "The Russians are making an all-out effort including the sending of concert artists and 'cultural' propagandists into Iceland in numbers, and these are being well received." In addition to the musicians that Raynor cited, Soviet ballerinas, chess players, and athletes descended upon the North Atlantic.[10]

Weeks after Raynor's memorandum circulated, Undersecretary of State Walter Bedell Smith sought to coordinate a meeting between the USIA and Edward B. Lawson, the American minister to Iceland, "with a view to reinforcing our information program." The line of thinking was also reflected in an OCB report, which stressed the need to "develop an increased understanding of American life, institutions, and culture." Although the document did not reference sport per se, an accompanying note made it clear that athletic personnel were to be included in the exchange of students, teachers, and musicians. In July 1954 calls for a more robust cultural strategy crystallized in NSC 5426, a National Security Council Statement of Policy on Iceland. The document laid renewed emphasis upon fostering foreign relations through "such means as exchanges of persons, particularly in the field of education and labor; stop-over visits by U.S. concert artists and leaders; and appropriate utilization of Americans of Icelandic origin." Accordingly, Washington dispatched a cadre of goodwill ambassadors to the North Atlantic, most notably Nobel Laureate William Faulkner and various classical musicians.[11]

A Valiant and Entertaining Start: The United States in Iceland, 1955

The government also turned to the United States national soccer team. From the perspective of Washington, the use of footballers made sense. Much as the internationalism of the modern Olympic movement could be co-opted for political ends, so, too, could the internationalism of the Fédération Internationale de Football Association. From the perspective of the United States Soccer Football Association (USSFA), the partnership was similarly appealing, as government-sponsored ventures offered a welcome opportunity to compete abroad. Thus, when the State Department reached out in the autumn of 1954 regarding a potential goodwill tour of Iceland, the overture met with much enthusiasm. "It is a great source of satisfaction," beamed James P. McGuire, an official with the national body, "that our Government has finally realized the value of soccer football as a medium of good will with other nations." McGuire also hinted that a successful journey to the North Atlantic could, on account of broader political tension, lay the foundation for similar efforts elsewhere.[12]

The men responsible for smoothing out the details with the State Department were USSFA president Edward Sullivan and executive secretary Joseph J. Barriskill. Barriskill impressed upon policymakers that though the federation was not concerned with making a profit, it "certainly should not be compelled to lose money." Washington agreed and, by the following spring, sent along a formal draft agreement for approval. In the end, the athlete-ambassadors would play three matches during the summer months—one of which would be a contest against the Icelandic national team—with the federal government footing the bill. Additional matters needed to be determined, including the selection of a squad. Although the USSFA was left to choose the players it preferred, the State Department stressed that only American citizens were eligible for the international fixture. To what extent, if any, the proviso was rooted in concerns about the trustworthiness of noncitizens is unclear. The national body did not appear to press the issue, however, settling upon an experienced group anchored by veterans Walter Bahr and Harry Keough.[13]

On August 22, a delegation of fifteen players and five officials departed from McGuire Airfield in New Jersey. By the time the group landed at Keflavík, it had become a prominent story. The local press devoted ample coverage to the Yankee tourists, publishing photographs of their arrival, overviews of the squad, and details of their training session. Journalists also reported on matters from the Icelandic end, as the national team concluded its preparations with a well-publicized *prova generale.* The buildup culminated on the morning of the Americans' first and most prestigious match, a friendly against the Icelandic national team. Several newspapers printed the expected tactical lineups, and *Tíminn* assured readers that the visiting squad was "undoubtedly the strongest that the United States could put together." If public interest was not sufficiently piqued, the local reception committee took out a series of newspaper advertisements. Although the text provided basic details about where and when the match would take place, the subtext served to convey a motif of sporting fraternity. One such advertisement featured an illustration of two footballers—in different, but generic uniforms—competing for the ball. The lack of overt national symbols, coupled with the coming together of players in a firm but fair challenge, suggested that political tension would be cast aside in the name of keen athletic rivalry.[14]

When the time came for a ball to be kicked, some ninety-five hundred spectators turned up to the Melavöllur in Reykjavík. Although modest on its

Í. S. Í. Landsleikurinn K. S. Í.

ÍSLAND — BANDARÍKIN

fer fram á Íþróttavellinum í kvöld kl. 7,30

Aðgöngumiðar seldir frá klukkan 1 í aðgöngumiðasölu Íþróttavallarins.

DÓMARI: LUDVIG JÖRKOV

Komið og sjáið bandaríska knattspyrrumenn í fyrsta sinn á Íslandi.

Móttökunefndin.

Icelandic newspapers of varying political persuasions advertised the Americans' three matches. This image, taken from *Morgunblaðið*, ran ahead of the first and most prestigious contest, a friendly against the Icelandic national team. *Morgunblaðið*, August 25, 1955. Courtesy of the Icelandic National Library (https://landsbokasafn.is).

own, the figure is far more impressive when one considers that it constituted roughly 6 percent of Iceland's total population. In keeping with the tour's underlying purpose, the occasion was draped in goodwill. The official match program, whose cover was decorated with interlocking Icelandic and American flags, helped set the tone for the evening. The sense of bonhomie was hardly limited to the pages of this publication. Indeed, the most significant gesture of goodwill was the temporary lifting of the base restriction on American servicemen. Those individuals who meandered to the stadium were treated to a *fête du football.* A brass band performed prior to kickoff, team captains exchanged courtesies, and the presence of Icelandic president Ásgeir Ásgeirsson added a dollop of political pomp. Following the proceedings, the Football Association of Iceland (KSÍ) hosted a gala for the visitors, giving delegates time to socialize with one another and invited dignitaries.[15]

The match itself generated a mixed reaction. Iceland edged the United States by three goals to two in a dramatic affair that was not settled until five minutes from time. Yet despite maintaining a close score line, the visitors did not appear to impress the local punditry. *Alþýðublaðið* acknowledged good individual performances, but noted that "this was not a question of 'supermen' on the field." *Vísir* suggested that within minutes, it became clear that the home support need not fear defeat. Curiously, the paper that seemed to offer the most charitable assessment was the communist *Þjóðviljinn.* Although it noted that the Americans were weaker than the opponents Iceland typically encountered, it commended the visitors for their competitive spirit and suggested that "the team played valiantly in all respects."[16]

Landsleikur í knattspyrnu

ÍSLAND - BANDARÍKIN

í Reykjavík 25. ágúst 1955.

A sense of sporting fraternity was underscored by the interlocking flags that adorned the program for the friendly between the Icelandic and American national teams. Courtesy of Sigmundur Ó. Steinarsson/KSÍ.

Whatever the merits of the American team, those at the Melavöllur delighted in the fray and reveled in the result. "The spectators used their vocal cords unsparingly," recounted *Verkamaðurinn*. "It will be a wonder if some of them are not hoarse today." Upon the referee's final whistle, spectators rushed onto the field to celebrate with the triumphant Icelandic players. The excitement trickled down to those following from afar, thanks to Sigurður Sigurðsson's radio commentary. "It was among the more entertaining games that I have 'listened to,'" glowed one audience member. "There is no denying that the pleasure was greater because our Icelandic boys had defeated the American superpower." The statement, and the scenes of exuberance following the match, seemed to reflect the unease many Icelandic citizens felt toward the United States. Yet while football provided a space for displays of nationalism, it channeled those sentiments into a nonbellicose form.[17]

Fans continued to turn up at the turnstiles for the remainder of the tour. The Americans' second match, a loss to current Icelandic champions Akranes by the odd goal in five, drew an estimated attendance of sixty-five hundred. The tour concluded with the visitors falling to a picked Reykjavík squad by a goal to nil. By that point, whatever questions remained about the visitors' athletic qualities were answered. *Tíminn* appeared to speak for many when it dubbed the Americans "among the weakest teams that have come here." In retrospect, the assessment may have been harsh. The tourists faced a taxing itinerary of three matches in six days—a challenge made still more daunting by the fact that the players were in the off-season and, thus, lacked match fitness. *Þjóðviljinn* acknowledged as much, noting that, by the end of the tour, "it is not unlikely that exhaustion had started to make its presence felt among the guests."[18]

If the Americans left something to be desired from a sporting perspective, they fared much better from an ambassadorial one. "The valiant and entertaining behavior of the team on the field will without a doubt live in memory for a long time," noted *Tíminn*. *Morgunblaðið* was even more fawning: "The Icelandic teams are naturally proud of their victories. But the American players also won a victory, if only of a different nature. They won their victories by displaying the best in fair play and sportsmanship ever shown by a visiting soccer team. It is first and foremost because of these qualities that their visit to Iceland, anno Domini 1955, will long be remembered." Although the level of flattery may reflect the newspaper's conservative sympathies, the communist *Þjóðviljinn* struck a similar tone. "This visit was an

The Icelandic and American captains, Ríkharður Jónsson (*left*) and Walter Bahr, exchange pennants and pleasantries prior to kickoff as match officials look on. Courtesy of Sigmundur Ó. Steinarsson/KSÍ.

entertaining episode in an eventful summer for football," it wrote. "These new guests were pleasant and courteous players and for this became popular with spectators." The global game lived up to its billing as a sport that could transcend political divide.[19]

Following the completion of the tour, Harold E. Howland, an official at the State Department, wrote the USSFA to register his delight: "The selection of the team has been most noteworthy; certainly no better aggregation could have been found anywhere. The way the fellows performed on and off the field—as players, as men, as Americans—is a great tribute to the U.S. Soccer [Football] Association and to everyone associated with this venture." The only apparent misgivings were voiced in a tract on American soccer governance by Eugene Held, who claimed that the performances generated "worldwide adverse criticism." Yet if the lackluster display mattered to Icelandic newspapermen and American football men, it did not seem to trouble policymakers in Washington. If anything, they appeared relieved that the goodwill-building purpose of the journey was not compromised by a strong showing on the pitch. Political currency and athletic success were, in this instance, not one and the same; and, when push came to shove, the former trumped the latter for those controlling the purse strings.[20]

An Amazing Wonderland: Iceland in the United States, 1956

Before the 1955 tour had concluded, the Icelandic press began to speculate about a reciprocal visit to the United States. Björgvin Schram, president of the KSÍ, wrote the USSFA to evince his desire for extending the footballing relationship into the future. “We are pleased to say that the players and the officials have, both on and off the field of play, been the finest ambassadors for American sports that could ever [have] been sent to us,” he began. “It is with great regret that we see your party leave our country and nothing would please us more than continued co-operation and friendship between our Associations and the football players of our two countries.” Schram’s effusiveness would have warmed the hearts of many American policymakers. It would also validate pre-tour suggestions that a successful trip to the North Atlantic would function as a springboard to similar ventures.[21]

In the summer of 1956, USSFA president Edward Sullivan confirmed that, “as a result of the direct contacts and good relations between the USSFA and the State Department,” the Icelandic national team would visit American shores in the autumn to play three matches. On October 5, a delegation that included players, administrators, and radio commentator Sigurður Sigurðsson left for the United States via American military transport. From the start, the trip would differ from the previous summer’s in two respects. First, the visitors would not face the American national team, which was preparing for a pre-Olympic training camp in Los Angeles and a subsequent state-sponsored goodwill tour of Asia. Second, Washington would not underwrite the entirety of the visit, leaving the USSFA to put up the funds for the “keep and entertainment” of their guests. The national body’s willingness to dip into its own coffers reflects the sense of duty it felt both to country and to sporting kin, if not a more calculated effort to increase the chance for future federal support. Yet despite the best efforts of America’s football men, the venture was not without its share of mishaps.[22]

When Iceland kicked off the tour against the Philadelphia Uhriks, only fifteen hundred spectators traveled to Twenty-Ninth and Cambria Streets to witness the teams finish on level terms. Neither the paltry crowd, nor the poor advance publicity, went unnoticed in the Icelandic press. The poor playing surface also proved irksome, as did the dubious officiating and—the presence of local dignitaries notwithstanding—insufficient pageantry. "There was no brass band to play the countries' national anthems," carped *Tíminn.* "It also would seem to be a matter of common courtesy to fly the flags of both countries while such a match is going on, not least on a 'goodwill tour.'" The city itself provided a more welcoming experience. The visitors were treated to a luncheon at John Wanamaker's department store and opening night of the Ice Capades, where they met with Catherine Machado and Ronnie Robertson, the show's headliners. A photograph of the Icelandic captain, Ríkharður Jónsson, posing alongside the duo graced the pages of the *Philadelphia Inquirer* the following day. Perhaps as a result, *Tíminn* held out hope that, going forward, "Uncle Sam will show nobility."[23]

Time proved the optimism well-founded. The tourists went sightseeing in Washington before traveling by rail to Maryland for their second match. In the Old Line State, the players garnered the attention that eluded them during their prior travels. The *Baltimore Sun* ran a series of articles in advance of the side's encounter with a local all-star aggregation, trumpeting Iceland as "one of the smoothest teams" to pass through the area. Organizers rolled out the red carpet, arranging a program that included a meeting with Mayor Thomas D'Alesandro and a scrimmage and dinner at the Naval Academy in Annapolis. They also invited President Eisenhower and the First Lady to attend the affair as guests, but the former sent his regrets because of a full schedule. Although Eisenhower's explanation was not in accordance with the contents of his appointment book, which showed that he had no commitments on the evening of the match, it is difficult to suggest that his absence reflected a sense of indifference. On the contrary, Washington afforded the event enough importance that a Voice of America representative was sent to Johns Hopkins University's Homewood Field, ensuring that the visitors' 4–0 victory was tape-recorded in Icelandic.[24]

The team's final stop in New York City, for an encounter with Israeli club Maccabi Tel Aviv at Downing Stadium, continued in much the same vein. A prematch ceremony saw the Icelandic consul in New York address the crowd, singer Guðmunda Elíasdóttir perform the Icelandic national anthem, and New York State attorney general Jacob Javits take the honorary kickoff. Additionally, the F. & M. Schaefer Brewing Company donated a trophy to be awarded to the winning side. The only issue, it seemed, was the heat wave

(*From left*) Olympic skaters Ronnie Robertson and Catherine Machado meet with Ríkharður Jónsson at the opening of the Ice Capades in Philadelphia. The City of Brotherly Love proved more memorable for its activities off the field than on. Courtesy of the *Philadelphia Inquirer,*

enveloping New York. Following a goalless first half, Iceland wilted in unseasonably high temperatures and Maccabi ran out comfortable winners. Yet the weather was hardly something for which the tour's organizers were at fault and, in any event, it did not prevent the delegation from enjoying visits to Broadway, the United Nations Headquarters, and the Empire State Building.[25]

The Icelandic delegation poses for a photo at the Latin Quarter on Broadway. New York was the group's final stop on its tour of the United States in 1956. Courtesy of Sigmundur Ó. Steinarsson/KSÍ.

By tour's end, the initial sense of foreboding had given way to cheery accord. "We have gotten an opportunity to look around this amazing wonderland," averred KSÍ secretary Ingvar Pálsson, "and everywhere we have gone we have received an equally warm welcome." Ólafur Gíslason, a player, extolled the United States as a land of opportunity and prosperity and praised the fine reception of the tourists. "This trip will undoubtedly be unforgettable for us," he noted, "not least for the opportunity to become acquainted with American football players in their homeland." His teammate, Jón Leósson, was more succinct. "This," he offered, "is the best trip we have ever taken." As he had following the previous year's tour, the State Department's Harold E. Howland wrote the USSFA to compliment it on a job well done. "Our Embassy also reported to us that the Icelandic people were most appreciative of the splendid hospitality the team received," he began. "Needless to say, the Department of State is highly pleased that through the efforts of the United States Soccer [Football] Association so much was done to win goodwill and enhance respect for America in Iceland." The goodwill and respect, of course, came at a cost. At final billing, the national body incurred a loss of $3,396.[26]

More worrying for Washington were some of the impressions left upon the tourists. Following the team's return home, *Tíminn* printed an interview with Gíslason, who recounted his experience over the previous fortnight. The insights he provided spoke not only to the limits of cultural diplomacy, but also the specific challenges associated with bringing athlete-ambassadors into the country. Given the wide array of experiences at their disposal, delegates could—and did—come to their own conclusions about the United States. Gíslason, for his part, drew attention to a pair of narratives that would have troubled policymakers. First, he detailed the squad's visit to the Naval Academy, which would have done little to dispel any perceptions of American militarism. Although Gíslason admired the athletic outlets available to soldiers, he was taken by both the magnitude of the facility and the "harsh" treatment of new recruits. Second, he spoke in detail on civil rights, noting that the country had much progress to make. To wit, he recounted an adventure in a predominantly black neighborhood, where one of the delegates began speaking with children and offering sweets. "When he had stood there for a while, an old man came up to him and told him to scram as quickly as possible if he wanted to keep his life," he noted. "The situation was apparently that white miscreants and child molesters have a practice of luring black children away with them with gifts of candy and such."[27] The dramatic tale conflicted markedly with Washington's efforts to tout the country's progress in race relations.

Football, Diplomacy, and the Reluctant Ally

The Icelandic national team returned home on October 17, 1956. Seven weeks later, on December 6, the American and Icelandic governments reached an agreement to prolong the stay of the defense force. The USSFA did not hesitate to pat itself on the back for its role in the matter. "From my observations," wrote president Edward Sullivan, "the USSFA has completed one of the greatest jobs they ever have on behalf of our country." While one should not diminish the national body's contribution to developments in the North Atlantic, one would be equally wise to not overstate the case. As scholarship on public diplomacy has chronicled, it is notoriously difficult to draw a causal link between cultural means and policy ends. Cultural means, like the elements of soft power more broadly, tend to work subtly and over the long term, creating what Joseph Nye calls an "enabling environment." What is more, they do not exist in a vacuum, but rather within a political, social, and economic context.[28]

Such complexities were at play in Cold War–era Iceland, where a combination of domestic and international circumstances shaped public opinion on the base question. Emily Abrams Ansari has taken these factors into account in her assessment of music diplomacy in the region. According to Ansari, it was not the instruments of soft power, but rather two hard power developments that won the day for Washington. First, the United States helped Iceland stave off financial collapse through a program of grants and loans. Second, the Soviet invasion of Hungary in autumn 1956 dashed hopes that Europe was heading toward peace and undercut support for communism.[29]

None of this is to neglect the importance of cultural cold warriors or the lessons that can be derived from their experiences. American–Icelandic football exchange is informative in several respects. First, it fits into a historiography that has often emphasized the "lack of reciprocity" in Washington's cultural initiatives. Although the tours were ostensibly reciprocal—that is, an American team visited Iceland and an Icelandic team visited the United States—they did not appear to go beyond what Nicholas Cull calls "the drive to project national culture." Once the base issue was resolved, policymakers showed little desire to extend the sporting relationship between the countries. Thus, when the KSÍ invited its counterpart back to the North Atlantic on two separate occasions, Washington appeared less inclined to provide support. Instead, officials set their sights on the Near East, the Far East, and Latin America—a shift that reflected the Cold War's drift to the developing world.[30]

Furthermore, the experience in the North Atlantic shines a light on football's capacity to cultivate goodwill. Although the lofty rhetoric about football as lingua franca should be viewed through a critical lens, on this occasion the global game seemed to transcend the political divide. While the conservative *Morgunblaðið* was perhaps the media outlet most willing to heap praise on the American athlete-ambassadors, Icelandic newspapers across the ideological spectrum were, for the most part, sympathetic to the tours. It is telling that, following the match between the two national teams in Reykjavík, both *Morgunblaðið* and the social democratic *Alþýðublaðið* ran a photograph of the captains exchanging gifts. The pleasant reporting that accompanied the football exchange was a striking contrast to coverage of the American hockey team's tour of Sweden in 1957. Rough play on the ice was the source of much negative comment, prompting ambassador John M. Cabot to declare the venture "a dismal failure in producing better international relations."[31]

Finally, the direct, one-for-one nature of the tours allows for a comparison of sending and receiving cultural ambassadors. While Washington could carefully construct the image that it projected abroad, it exerted far less control when it brought foreigners into the United States. Indeed, visitors could use firsthand experiences to draw their own conclusions about the country. What resulted was a curious dynamic in which football helped cultivate goodwill—delegates shook hands, engaged in pleasantries, and by all accounts behaved affably—at the same time that it failed to fully sell "the American way." Perhaps for this reason, if not for the simple fact that goodwill tours had greater reach without the country than within, the State Department soured on the prospects of hosting football teams in the future.[32] To what extent this affected the American position vis-à-vis the Cold War has yet to be determined.

Notes

Many people have been generous with their time and insight throughout the research process. Special thanks are due to Heather Dichter, J. Simon Rofe, and the anonymous reviewers for their suggestions and guidance as this chapter came to fruition, and to Kendra Willson for her assistance with the translations. The author would also like to express his gratitude to those who tracked down and shared material: in the United States, Valoise Armstrong, Brenda Galloway-Wright, Cara Setsu Bertram, Anne Moore, and Jessica Stremmel; and in Iceland, Óskar Örn Guðbrandsson, Unnar Ingvarsson, Jóhann Gunnar Kristinsson, Sigmundur Steinarsson, and Örn Hrafnkelsson.

1. "Ameríska Landsliðið Komið," *Morgunblaðið*, August 24, 1955, 16.

2. For a brief account of the goodwill tour of Iran by the Pennsylvania State University team in 1951, see David Wangerin, *Distant Corners: American Soccer's History of Missed Opportunities and Lost Causes* (Philadelphia: Temple University Press, 2011), 132–133. Rimet cited in Paul Dietschy, "Making Football Global? FIFA, Europe, and the Non-European Football World, 1912–74," *Journal of Global History* 8, no. 2 (2013): 281.

3. Dwight D. Eisenhower, "Inaugural Address," January 20, 1953, in *Public Papers of the Presidents of the United States: Dwight D. Eisenhower, 1953* (Washington, DC: US Government Printing Office, 1960), 1; Dwight D. Eisenhower, "Annual Message to the Congress on the State of the Union," February 2, 1953, in *Public Papers of the Presidents of the United States: Dwight D. Eisenhower, 1953*, 13;

Kenneth Osgood, *Total Cold War: Eisenhower's Secret Propaganda Battle at Home and Abroad* (Lawrence: University Press of Kansas, 2006), 11.

4. Mission of the United States Information Agency, 1954, Dwight D. Eisenhower: Records as President, White House Central Files, 1953–61, Official File, box 748, OF 247 United States Information Agency, 1954 (2), Dwight D. Eisenhower Presidential Library, Abilene, Kansas (hereafter DDEL); Shawn J. Parry-Giles, "The Eisenhower Administration's Conceptualization of the USIA: The Development of Overt and Covert Propaganda Strategies," *Presidential Studies Quarterly* 24, no. 2 (1994): 263–276; Wilson P. Dizard, *Inventing Public Diplomacy: The Story of the U.S. Information Agency* (Boulder, CO: Lynne Rienner, 2004); Nicholas J. Cull, *The Cold War and the United States Information Agency: American Propaganda and Public Diplomacy, 1945–1989* (New York: Cambridge University Press, 2008); Naima Prevots, *Dance for Export: Cultural Diplomacy and the Cold War* (Middletown, CT: Wesleyan University Press, 1998); Frances Stonor Saunders, *The Cultural Cold War: The CIA and the World of Arts and Letters* (New York: New Press, 2000); Penny Von Eschen, *Satchmo Blows Up the World: Jazz Ambassadors Play the Cold War* (Cambridge: Harvard University Press, 2004); Laura A. Belmonte, *Selling the American Way: U.S. Propaganda and the Cold War* (Philadelphia: University of Pennsylvania Press, 2008); Hugh Wilford, *The Mighty Wurlitzer: How the CIA Played America* (Cambridge: Harvard University Press, 2008); Greg Barnhisel, *Cold War Modernists: Art, Literature, and American Cultural Diplomacy* (New York: Columbia University Press, 2015).

5. Ruth Eckstein, "Ping Pong Diplomacy: A View from Behind the Scenes," *Journal of American-East Asian Relations* 2, no. 3 (1993): 327–342; Zhaohui Hong and Yi Sun, "The Butterfly Effect and the Making of 'Ping-Pong Diplomacy,'" *Journal of Contemporary China* 9, no. 25 (2000): 429–448; Thomas M. Hunt, "American Sport Policy and the Cultural Cold War: The Lyndon B. Johnson Presidential Years," *Journal of Sport History* 33, no. 3 (2006): 273–297; Damion L. Thomas, *Globetrotting: African American Athletes and Cold War Politics* (Urbana: University of Illinois Press, 2012); Kevin B. Witherspoon, "Going 'To the Fountainhead': Black American Athletes as Cultural Ambassadors in Africa, 1970–1971," *International Journal of the History of Sport* 30, no. 13 (2013): 1508–1522; John Soares, "'Our Way of Life against Theirs': Ice Hockey and the Cold War," in *Diplomatic Games: Sport, Statecraft, and International Relations since 1945*, ed. Heather L. Dichter and Andrew L. Johns (Lexington: University Press of Kentucky, 2014), 251–296; Kevin B. Witherspoon, "'Fuzz Kids' and 'Musclemen': The US-Soviet Basketball Rivalry, 1958–1975," in *Diplomatic Games: Sport, Statecraft, and International Relations since 1945*, ed. Heather L. Dichter and Andrew L. Johns (Lexington: University Press of Kentucky, 2014), 297–326; Ashley Brown, "Swinging for the State Department: American Women Tennis Players in Diplomatic Goodwill Tours, 1941–59," *Journal of Sport History* 42, no. 3 (2015): 289–309; Anne M. Blaschke, "Running the Cold War: Gender, Race, and Track in Cultural Diplomacy, 1955–1975," *Diplomatic History* 40, no. 5 (2016): 826–844; Toby C. Rider, *Cold War*

Games: Propaganda, the Olympics, and U.S. Foreign Policy (Urbana: University of Illinois Press, 2016).

6. Valur Ingimundarson, “The Struggle for Western Integration: Iceland, the United States, and NATO during the First Cold War,” *Forsvarsstudier* 3 (1999): 12–15; Sólrun B. Jensdóttir Hardarson, “The ‘Republic of Iceland’ 1940–44: Anglo-American Attitudes and Influences,” *Journal of Contemporary History* 9, no. 4 (1974): 29–34.

7. Donald E. Nuechterlein, *Iceland: Reluctant Ally* (Ithaca: Cornell University Press, 1961); Elfar Loftsson, “The Disguised Threat: Iceland during the Cold War,” *Scandinavian Journal of History* 10, no. 3 (1985): 228–229; Thor Whitehead, *The Ally Who Came in from the Cold: A Survey of Icelandic Foreign Policy 1946–1956* (Reykjavík: University of Iceland Press, 1998); Ingimundarson, “The Struggle for Western Integration.”

8. Whitehead, *The Ally Who Came in from the Cold*, 49–54; Ingimundarson, “The Struggle for Western Integration,” 32–37, quote on 38; Nuechterlein, *Iceland: Reluctant Ally*, 109–111; Valur Ingimundarson, “Immunizing against the American Other: Racism, Nationalism, and Gender in U.S.-Icelandic Military Relations during the Cold War,” *Journal of Cold War Studies* 6, no. 4 (2004): 65–88. Concern about a growing American influence was shared across the spectrum of Icelandic politics. As one briefing note put it, “All political parties very sensitive about impact of American troops on Iceland’s inbred culture and society; no Icelandic politician can afford to adopt ‘unpatriotic’ view.” NSC Briefing Notes: Impasse with Iceland over 1951 Defense Agreement, April 12, 1954, General CIA Records, CIA-RDP79R00890A000300010016–6, Freedom of Information Act Electronic Reading Room (hereafter FOIA).

9. Nuechterlein, *Iceland: Reluctant Ally*, 115–119, 146–148; Ingimundarson, “The Struggle for Western Integration,” 40–41; Current Situation in Iceland: ORE 83-49, October 18, 1949, National Intelligence Council Collection, 0000258578, FOIA; Howland H. Sargeant, “How Can We Defend Free Culture?” *Department of State Bulletin* 26, no. 667 (1952): 535–540. With regard to the first point, the Soviets had broken off trade in 1948 on account of Iceland’s growing ties with the West. The countries reconciled following a fisheries dispute between Iceland and Great Britain, which left the former in search of a new export market for its fish. On the “proto cod war” in greater depth, see Guðni Jóhannesson, “Troubled Waters: Cod War, Fishing Disputes, and Britain’s Fight for the Freedom of the High Seas, 1948–1964” (PhD diss., Queen Mary University of London, 2004), 62–131; Sverrir Steinsson, “The Cod Wars: A Re-Analysis,” *European Security* 25, no. 2 (2016): 256–275. On Soviet cultural diplomacy in greater depth, see Frederick C. Barghoorn, *The Soviet Cultural Offensive: The Role of Cultural Diplomacy in Soviet Foreign Policy* (Princeton: Princeton University Press, 1960); Nigel Gould-Davies, “The Logic of Soviet Cultural Diplomacy,” *Diplomatic History* 27, no. 2 (2003): 193–214; Rósa Magnúsdóttir, “Mission Impossible? Selling Soviet Socialism to Americans, 1955–1958,” in *Searching for a Cultural Diplomacy*, ed. Jessica C. E. Gienow-Hecht and Mark C. Donfried (New York: Berghahn, 2010), 50–72.

10. Memorandum by the Director of the Office of British Commonwealth and Northern European Affairs (Raynor) to the Assistant Secretary of State for European Affairs (Merchant), November 25, 1953, in *Foreign Relations of the United States, 1952–1954*, vol. 6, part 2, *Western Europe and Canada*, ed. David M. Baehler et al. (Washington, DC: US Government Printing Office, 1986), 1522–1525; Porter McKeever, "How to Throw Away an Air Base," *Harper's Magazine*, October 1956, 41.

11. Walter B. Smith to Theodore C. Streibert, December 10, 1953, General CIA Records, CIA-RDP80R01731R003000050008-0, FOIA; Operations Coordinating Board, Interim Report—Iceland, December 21, 1953, General CIA Records, CIA-RDP80R01731R003000050001-7, FOIA; Annex B: Increase in Exchange Program with Iceland, December 21, 1953, General CIA Records, CIA-RDP80R01731R003000050001-7, FOIA; Memorandum by the Executive Secretary of the National Security Council (Lay) to the National Security Council, July 12, 1954, in *Foreign Relations of the United States, 1952–1954*, vol. 6, part 2, *Western Europe and Canada*, 1540; Deborah Cohn, "'In Between Propaganda and Escapism': William Faulkner as Cold War Cultural Ambassador," *Diplomatic History* 40, no. 3 (2016): 409–410; Emily Abrams Ansari, "Music Diplomacy in an Emergency: Eisenhower's 'Secret Weapon,' Iceland, 1954–59," in *Music and International History in the Twentieth Century*, ed. Jessica C. E. Gienow-Hecht (New York: Berghahn, 2015), 166–188.

12. Bill Graham, "Soccer," *Brooklyn Eagle*, September 23, 1954, 20; Report of the International Games Committee, Reports of the Officers and Committees of the United States Soccer Football Association (hereafter USSFA Reports), 1955–56, 35, United States Soccer Federation, Chicago, IL (hereafter USSF); Report of the International Games Committee, USSFA Reports, 1954–55, 43, USSF.

13. Report of the Executive Secretary, USSFA Reports, 1954–55, 4, USSF; Mary Stewart French to Daniel J. Ferris, March 29, 1955, Record Group (RG) 59, General Records of the Department of State, Central Decimal File (CDF) 1955–59, box 4177, 811.453/3-2955, National Archives and Records Administration, College Park, Maryland (hereafter NA); Report of the President, USSFA Reports, 1955–56, 5, USSF; Report of the International Games Committee, USSFA Reports, 1954–55, 43, USSF; Report of the International Players Selection Committee, USSFA Reports, 1955–56, 40, USSF; Milt Miller, "Pinezich Will Make Soccer Trip to Iceland," *Long Island Star-Journal*, July 23, 1955, 7; Report of the International Games Committee, USSFA Reports, 1955–56, 35, USSF. With regard to the question of noncitizen participation, the aforementioned visit to Iran by the Penn State team may be suggestive. Policymakers settled upon the collegians because, in David Wangerin's estimation, the "clean-cut, genial" image of student-athletes posed "less of a diplomatic risk than hyphenated Americans from the semiprofessional netherworld." Wangerin, *Distant Corners*, 132–133.

14. "Soccer Group to Leave," *New York Times*, August 22, 1955, 24; "Ameríska Landsliðið Komið," 16; "Bandaríska Landsliðið í Knattspyrnu Kom til Rvíkur í Gær," *Alþýðublaðið*, August 24, 1955, 1, 7; "Þúsundir Miða Seldir á Landsleikinn," *Vísir*,

August 25, 1955, 1; "Landsliðið Vann Pressuliðið 4–2," *Alþýðublaðið*, August 25, 1955, 5; "Landsleikurinn Er í Kvöld," *Alþýðublaðið*, August 25, 1955, 1; "Ísland–Bandaríkin," *Morgunblaðið*, August 25, 1955, 2; "Landsliðin í Kvöld," *Þjóðviljinn*, August 25, 1955, 12; "Fyrsti Landsleikur Íslands og Bandaríkjanna í Knattspyrnu Verður í Kvöld," *Tíminn*, August 25, 1955, 2; "Landsliðin, Sem Mætast í Kvöld," *Tíminn*, August 25, 1955, 8; "Ísland–Bandaríkin," *Morgunblaðið*, August 25, 1955, 11.

15. "Aukaleyfi til Varnarliðsmanna," *Tíminn*, August 24, 1955, 8; "Ísland–Bandaríkin," *Alþýðublaðið*, August 25, 1955, 7; "Landsleikurinn í Fyrrakvöld: Ísland og Bandaríkin," *Alþýðublaðið*, August 27, 1955, 4, 6; United Nations, *Demographic Yearbook: 1956* (New York: United Nations, 1956), 161. The estimated population of Iceland in 1955 was 158,000. For this match, as with others, the press gave varying attendance figures. The numbers provided, therefore, offer a general rather than a specific picture of what crowds were like.

16. "U.S. Soccer Team Loses," *New York Times*, August 26, 1955, 14; "Íslendingarnir Höfðu Yfirburði í Landsleiknum, Sígruðu Bandaríkjamenn 3–2," *Þjóðviljinn*, August 26, 1955, 1, 3; "Landsleikurinn í Fyrrakvöld: Ísland og Bandaríkin"; "9,500 Sáu Íslenzka Landsliðið Sigra 3–2," *Vísir*, August 26, 1955, 8.

17. "Íslendingar Unnu Bandaríkjamenn 3–2," *Verkamaðurinn*, August 26, 1955, 4; "Landsleikurinn í Gærkvöldi: Ísland Vann Bandaríkin 3–2," *Alþýðublaðið*, August 26, 1955, 1; "Frá Landsleiknum við Bandaríkin," *Þjóðviljinn*, August 28, 1955, 4; "Unir Sér Betur Heima," *Morgunblaðið*, August 28, 1955, 8.

18. "Kappleikurinn á Sunnudaginn: Akurnesingar gegn Bandaríska Liðinu," *Alþýðublaðið*, August 30, 1955, 5, 7; "Akurnesingar Unnu Bandaríkjamenn með 3–2," *Morgunblaðið*, August 30, 1955, 7; "Kappleikurinn í Fyrrakvöld: Urvaslið Reykjavíkurfélaga Vann Bandaríkjalandsliðið," *Alþýðublaðið*, September 1, 1955, 4, 7; "Reykjavíkurúrvalið Vann Bandaríkjamenn 1–0," *Morgunblaðið*, September 1, 1955, 6–7; "Reykjavíkurúrvalið Vann Bandaríkjamennina 1–0," *Þjóðviljinn*, September 2, 1955, 9–10; "Akurnesingar Sigruðu Bandaríska Landsliðið með 3–2," *Tíminn*, August 30, 1955, 7–8; Report of the International Games Committee, USSFA Reports, 1955–56, 35, USSF.

19. "Akurnesingar Sigruðu Bandaríska Landsliðið með 3–2"; "Reykjavíkurúrvalið Vann Bandaríkjamenn 1–0"; "Reykjavíkurúrvalið Vann Bandaríkjamennina 1–0." A translation of the *Morgunblaðið* clipping was entered into the national body's annual reports. See Report of the International Games Committee, USSFA Reports, 1955–56, 35–36, USSF.

20. Report of the International Games Committee, USSFA Reports, 1955–56, 35–36, USSF; Eugene Held, "Who Governs Soccer in America?" Correspondence with National Associations: USA (hereafter USA Correspondence), box 1932–64, folder 1951–58, Fédération Internationale de Football Association, Zurich, Switzerland (hereafter FIFA); Memorandum of Meeting—OCB Working Group on Iceland (NSC 5426), October 26, 1955, White House Office, National Security Council Staff: Papers, 1948–61, Operations Coordinating Board Central File Series, box 35, OCB 091 Iceland 2(10), DDEL.

21. "Landsleikur í Bandaríkjunum Næsta Sumar?" *Morgunblaðið*, August 28, 1955, 16; "A Letter from the Football Association of Iceland to United States Soccer Football Association, Inc.," *Soccer News*, February 1956, USA Correspondence, box 1932–64, folder 1951–58, FIFA.

22. Report of the President, USSFA Reports, 1955–56, 5, USSF; "Fréttabréf frá Ríkisútvarpi Islands," *Lögberg*, October 4, 1956, 2; "Bandaríkjaferðin Verður Landsliðinu Ógleymanleg: Vaxandi Áhugi á Knattspyrnu Þar," *Morgunblaðið*, October 19, 1956, 10, 23; "Olympic Stars Start Arriving Today," *Los Angeles Times*, October 17, 1956, C5; Report of the President, USSFA Reports, 1956–57, 2A–3A, USSF; Report of the Olympic Committee, USSFA Reports, 1956–57, 23, USSF.

23. Although the *Philadelphia Inquirer* included the match in a list of upcoming events, the paper not only placed it after an entry for the Montgomery County Kennel Club all-terrier show, but also misspelled "Iceland." The typographical error read "Icland." "Uhriks Earn Tie with Iceland," *Philadelphia Inquirer*, October 8, 1956, 25; "'Landskeppni' í Knattspyrnu við Bandaríkin," *Tíminn*, October 13, 1956, 5; "Local Sports This Week," *Philadelphia Inquirer*, October 7, 1956, 10; "Iceland Booters Feted at Luncheon," *Philadelphia Inquirer*, October 9, 1956, 33; Mayer Brandschain, "Ice Capades Opener Thrills 3,000 at Arena," *Philadelphia Inquirer*, October 9, 1956, 34.

24. "Bandaríkjaferðin Verður Landsliðinu Ógleymanleg: Vaxandi Áhugi á Knattspyrnu Þar"; "Iceland Booters Boast Good Mark," *Baltimore Sun*, October 8, 1956, 18; "Iceland Team Coming Here," *Baltimore Sun*, October 9, 1956, 24; "Iceland Team Here Tonight," *Baltimore Sun*, October 10, 1956, 23; Edward Sullivan to Dwight D. Eisenhower, October 3, 1956, Dwight D. Eisenhower: Records as President, White House Central Files, 1953–61, President's Personal File, box 469, PPF 1-EE Invitations, Maryland, 1956, DDEL; Bernard M. Shanley to Edward Sullivan, October 6, 1956, Dwight D. Eisenhower: Records as President, White House Central Files, 1953–61, President's Personal File, box 469, PPF 1-EE Invitations, Maryland, 1956, DDEL; The President's Appointments, October 1956, Dwight D. Eisenhower: Records as President, Daily Appointments, 1953–61, DDEL; Edward C. Atwater, "Iceland Trips Local Team," *Baltimore Sun*, October 11, 1956, 19.

25. William J. Briordy, "Maccabi Defeats Iceland by 2 to 0," *New York Times*, October 15, 1956, 33; "Ísraelsmenn Sigruðu Íslendinga í New York Eftir Skemmtilegan Leik," *Tíminn*, October 21, 1956, 4, 8; "Consul Generals [*sic*]," *Soccer News*, November 1956, Colin Jose Soccer Collection, 1910–2010, MS 811, Special Collections and University Archives, UMass Amherst Libraries.

26. "Bandaríkjaferðin Verður Landsliðinu Ógleymanleg: Vaxandi Áhugi á Knattspyrnu Þar"; "Það Varð Aldrei Neinn Landsleikur við USA," *Tíminn*, October 20, 1956, 7, 9; "Ísraelsmenn Sigruðu Íslendinga í New York Eftir Skemmtilegan Leik"; Report of the President, USSFA Reports, 1956–57, 2A, USSF; Minutes of the Annual Meeting of the United States Soccer Football Association, July 26–27, 1958, 7, USSF.

27. "Það Varð Aldrei Neinn Landsleikur við USA."

28. Ibid.; Nuechterlein, *Iceland: Reluctant Ally*, 184–187; Report of the President, USSFA Reports, 1956–57, 2A, USSF; Joseph S. Nye Jr., *Soft Power: The Means to Success in World Politics* (New York: PublicAffairs, 2004).

29. Ansari, "Music Diplomacy in an Emergency," 180–181.

30. Giles Scott-Smith, "Mapping the Undefinable: Some Thoughts on the Relevance of Exchange Programs within International Relations Theory," *Annals of the American Academy of Political and Social Science* 616 (2008): 176; Nicholas J. Cull, "Public Diplomacy: Taxonomies and Histories," *Annals of the American Academy of Political and Social Science* 616 (2008): 33; Circular 917, April 1, 1958, RG 59, CDF 1955–59, box 127, 032—US Olympic Soccer Team/4–158, NA; Report of the President, USSFA Reports, 1957–58, 2, USSF; Report of the National Commission, USSFA Reports, 1957–58, 12, USSF; Report of the National Commission, USSFA Reports, 1958–59, 5, 11, USSF; Report of the National Commission, USSFA Reports, 1960–61, 14, USSF. On the Cold War in the developing world, see Odd Arne Westad, *The Global Cold War: Third World Interventions and the Making of Our Times* (New York: Cambridge University Press, 2005); Hal Brands, *Latin America's Cold War* (Cambridge: Harvard University Press, 2010); Robert J. McMahon, ed., *The Cold War in the Third World* (New York: Oxford University Press, 2013).

31. *Alþýðublaðið*, August 27, 1955, 1; "Akurnesingar Leika við Bandaríkjamenn í Dag," *Morgunblaðið*, August 28, 1955, 16; John M. Cabot to the Department of State, Foreign Service Despatch 1091: Visit of American Ice Hockey Team to Sweden, March 29, 1957, RG 59, CDF 1955–59, box 127, 032—US Ice Hockey Team/3–2957, NA. For a critical appraisal of the peace-promoting potential of sport, see John Hoberman, "The Myth of Sport as a Peace-Promoting Political Force," *SAIS Review of International Affairs* 31, no. 1 (2011): 17–29.

32. Report of the President, USSFA Reports, 1957–58, 2, USSF. This is not to suggest that exporting cultural ambassadors always went according to plan. See, for instance, Witherspoon, "Going 'To the Fountainhead.'"

"Because We Have Nothing"

The 1962 World Cup and Cold War Politics in Chile

Brenda Elsey

The 1962 World Cup has been remembered as one of the least exciting iterations of the world's largest sporting event. The goal average dipped below three for the first time, an injury sidelined superstar Pelé, and violence marred many of the matches. Despite these sporting qualities, the 1962 tournament provides a unique lens on the ways in which non-state actors negotiated Cold War politics, how the national landscape shaped the diplomatic possibilities of sport, and the role of international sport in local political culture. During the years of preparation for the World Cup, Chileans frequently described themselves as living at the "end" or in a "corner" of the world. The attention during the World Cup generated public debate across media. One writer reflected, "We have been, in these moments, the heart of the world, and thousands have come from all nations on Earth to decipher that heart."[1] The World Cup of 1962 was not directed by a political figure or a party; instead, its organization brought together bureaucrats, professional football leaders, amateur football club directors, and media producers.

The six years of preparation for the tournament coincided with a crucial period of the Cold War in Latin America; the years 1956–1962 included the Cuban Revolution, an increase in covert US intervention, and ideological polarization. For many Chileans, 1962 was a moment of social harmony and political cooperation. Chile's political culture fit uncomfortably in the polarized camps of the global Cold War in the early 1960s. Leftist political parties competed in electoral contests with an entrenched oligarchy and a center-right Christian Democratic party. Chile was one of the few countries in the world where socialists and communists could realistically hope to take power through electoral means. The events that transpired after 1962 defined the World Cup's importance in Chilean history as much as the tournament itself. Public memory-making has emphasized the tournament's freedom from the political turmoil that later defined Chile's international image, first during the presidency of socialist Salvador Allende (1970–1973) and then during the dictatorship of Augusto Pinochet (1973–1989). Since the transition to democracy, football "experts," journalists, and politicians have reiterated the interpretation of the World Cup as a force for unparalleled national unity. During the thirtieth anniversary of the Cup, journalists worried that 65 percent of Chileans were less than thirty-five years of age and thus did not have first-hand knowledge of the event. Retrospective pieces have attributed the advent of women's fandom, television, and rock music to the World Cup in Chile.[2]

The case of the 1962 World Cup sheds light on the relationship between the global Cold War and local popular culture in Latin America. Matches between teams from different sides of the Iron Curtain provoked commentaries on life in the Soviet Union and the possible advantages of state-controlled economies. It spoke volumes about the political scenario in Chile rather than in the United States or the Soviet Union. At the same time, football directors navigated Cold War divisions within FIFA to procure their support for Chile's bid to host the Cup. In an effort to sway the Eastern bloc countries, directors emphasized the vibrant Chilean labor movement and respect for Socialist and Communist parties. In their presentation to Western European and North American delegations, Chilean directors highlighted the country's democratic tradition and its "free market" economy. This strategy paid off, garnering the votes of both the Soviet Union and the United States. The 1962 World Cup was the last to exclusively feature European and American (as in Americas) teams. Although African and Asian confederations wielded little power within FIFA, the Chilean federation gained important votes from China and Vietnam.

The informal debates around the Cold War in sports media, clubs, and organizations occurred with little state direction. The reluctance of the conservative government of Jorge Alessandri to invest in the event made it clear that Alessandri had little interest in using the World Cup to promote a political agenda. Club directors, association officials, and members of the organizing committee, however, saw the tournament as a major opportunity for

Chile to raise its international profile, which they believed would attract corporate investment, better trade deals, and, of course, better positions within international sporting organizations. However, Alessandri did not attempt to parlay the Cup into popularity; in fact in the speech he gave to the congress the month prior to kickoff, he simply emphasized the efficiency of the government in procuring funds during a difficult year. In part, this attitude stems from Alessandri's public image as a patriarchal family man whose dignity rose above ideology. The Cup remained only tangentially related to Alessandri, and when he ran again for president in 1970 his campaign hardly mentioned it. However, the World Cup of 1962 demonstrates how informal actors understood themselves as ambassadors, debated the Cold War, and rendered sport a site of political performance.[3]

Chilean Football and the World Cup Bid

The presentation of the Chilean Football Federation to the international community, from making the bid in 1956 to hold the Cup through the tournament's aftermath, masked deep political divisions within national sports communities. Cold War politics aggravated tensions between amateur and professional football associations. Historical studies on Chile, and Latin America more broadly, have paid too little attention to the role of civic associations in practicing everyday diplomacy, as well as how international politics shaped non-state actors in the region. To understand these tensions, a bit of background on the structure of football in Chile is useful. Football clubs in Chile, as in most of South America, were created as cooperatively owned organizations. Clubs retained this structure even after the professional league began in 1933. Clubs elected directors and belonged to football's national governing body, the Chilean Football Federation, in which, putatively, the professionals and amateurs shared equal power. Amateur football clubs were among the largest and most politicized of civic associations. Amateur clubs pushed labor unions and political parties to broaden their goals for workers in the realm of recreation.[4] In response to amateurs' activities in working-class neighborhood politics, professional directors accused them of infusing Marxism into football. Amateurs countered that their clubs were truly democratic because of their participatory culture, inclusiveness, and base among the working class. In the Federation, amateurs and professionals profoundly disagreed on the role of the state, market, politics, and women in football.

The professional league's animosity toward amateur football created obstacles for the participation of working-class and women's clubs, which were de facto amateurs, in the organization of the World Cup.

Debates between amateur and professional football clubs demonstrated how local actors employed and understood the language of the Cold War. Professional club directors, with close ties to major media outlets, viewed international sporting competition as testing grounds to prove the superiority of market capitalism. When barrio clubs began to vie for power in the Football Federation, professionals attacked their leadership abilities and criticized their youth programs for producing undisciplined players. The wealthy businessmen and lawyers who ran professional clubs felt threatened by amateur football's effervescence in the 1950s. Whereas professionals railed against neighborhood clubs' "politicization" of football, they characterized their own involvement with high-ranking members of the government as merely "social." The Conservative tactic of defining right-wing politics as moral and left-wing politics as "ideological" was a staple of Cold War Chile that has persisted up to the present.

The World Cup empowered professional clubs over amateurs, which had far-reaching consequences, such as restricting access to public sports facilities and directing state resources toward a small group of sportsmen. Although, theoretically, amateurs and professionals shared power equally in the Football Federation, in practice, professional clubs dominated the organization.[5] When the Federation decided to bid for the World Cup, professional directors claimed that they alone had the resources necessary to organize the event. Their participation in international sporting bodies, particularly in the organizing committee of the World Cup 1962, afforded them social capital. They awarded lucrative contracts to construction companies, provided business to the hotels, and allotted advertisement spaces.

Chilean football officials masterfully navigated Cold War politics to persuade FIFA delegates to accept their bid. In 1956, they presented their case at the FIFA congress held in Lisbon, Portugal. Prospects for Chile seemed bleak: the national squad had not achieved success abroad, its Federation was nearly bankrupt, and many European delegates admitted that they could not locate the country on a map. The "Three Musketeers," as the press nicknamed the delegates, Carlos Dittborn, Ernesto Alvear, and Manuel Bianchi, focused on the state of political tolerance in Chile. The delegates pointed out the strength of leftist parties and labor unions to sway Eastern bloc countries in their favor. At the same time, they wooed Western European delegates with promises of modernity and a controlled exoticism. In other words, the delegates presented Chile as different, but not too different. Ernesto Alvear recalled years later that the committee decided to first send a diplomat, Manuel Bianchi, who served as Chile's ambassador to Great Britain, as a symbol of the Chilean spirit and "governability."[6] The narrative of Chilean democracy, firmly rooted in popular culture, created a unifying message that shaped the sense of responsibility for and involvement in the political process. At the same time, the romantic picture presented by the football delegates masked the social conflicts that shaped the late 1950s and early 1960s.

Argentina mounted the greatest challenge to the Chilean bid for the Cup. Unforeseen events hurt their case, particularly the turmoil and repression that followed the fall of Juan Perón's government. Chilean delegates warned Eastern Europeans of the anticommunism of the Peronists and the military in Argentina. The antagonistic relationship between Perón and the United States may also have helped to sway the US delegation and their allies in Chile's favor. Despite these developments, sports journalists predicted that Argentina would win the bid. Some Chilean journalists went so far as to ask the Federation to give up, in order to avoid public disappointment. Argentina's presentation, which lasted over an hour, stressed the country's modern infrastructure and contributions to the game. The Argentinean representative ended by stating, "We can have the World [Cup] tomorrow. We have it all."[7]

The Chilean Federation selected Carlos Dittborn, the charismatic director of Catholic University's club, to deliver the speech to FIFA's assembly. Dittborn's rebuttal lasted only fifteen minutes. He highlighted three points: Chile's institutional stability, its openness to diverse ideologies, and its unique style of sportsmanship. According to Dittborn, Chilean football organizations reflected general characteristics of the country, especially a "considerable tolerance for creeds, races, and other ideologies," which would insure that every member country would feel welcome. Carlos Dittborn singled out the modesty, work ethic, and dedication of working-class footballers and concluded by praising the underdog spirit of Chilean football, which he connected with what he felt was a universal belief in football as a meritocracy. In a dramatic finish that became the motto of the World Cup, Dittborn declared, "Because we have nothing, we want to do it all." Despite Chile's lack of tourist and sports infrastructure, the emotive current, which emphasized the country's humility, touched a chord with delegates. FIFA delegates voted in favor of

Chile, 32 to 10 (with 14 abstentions). Crowds gathered in the National Stadium, around newspaper offices, and near radios to hear the decision. Euphoric celebrations followed the announcement of the vote. Carlos Dittborn became an instant star, and his famous phrase, "Because we have nothing," headlined newspapers. During the tournament this phrase became ubiquitous, appearing on the scoreboard of the National Stadium and in most propaganda for the Cup. Dittborn's death from a sudden heart attack at the age of thirty-eight, just a month before the tournament began, gave the slogan even greater meaning for Chilean fans. The national team wore black bands on their uniform throughout the Cup in honor of Dittborn.[8]

The Chilean delegation's speech reflected the sportsmen's conception of their role as cultural ambassadors. Career diplomat Manuel Bianchi, who had served as minister of foreign relations in the early 1940s, offered the group his extensive contacts in Europe and knowledge of the political climate of countries participating in the congress. The delegation also built upon a long history of administrative involvement by Chilean sports directors in international sports, which reached back to the foundation of the South American Football Confederation (CONMEBOL) in 1916 and the Chilean Olympic Committee. Before the phrase "soft diplomacy" was coined, it was practiced in sports' circles. Ambassadors and workers in the Ministry of Foreign Relations played an important role in creating these institutions. Luis Subercaseaux, the first Latin American competitor in the modern Olympics, is an excellent example.[9] After participating in the 1896 Olympics in track and field, Subercaseaux went on to serve as ambassador to Spain, Peru, and the Vatican. Subercaseaux was also a founding member of the football club Santiago Morning and the Federation of Chilean Football. He belonged to a generation of the political elite that viewed sport as part of their life of public service. By the 1960s, however, Dittborn and his colleagues incorporated the working class as central to their construction of Chilean national identity.

Immediately following Chile's successful campaign to host the Cup, organizers began to rally sports organizations, government agencies, and financial resources. The anticipation of a World Cup in Chile also prompted a search for football's origins. Fans, sports directors, and journalists produced historical narratives in the early 1960s and found eager publishers and readers. Many of these accounts expressed nostalgia for football in the era before professionalism. *Estadio* and other sports publications blamed the players' union for changing attitudes. That football histories frequently stressed class reconciliation carried an important message during an era of intense labor agitation. For example, the Braden Copper Company, which volunteered its stadium in Rancagua for the tournament, commissioned a book that highlighted the company's support for workers' football. Pieces published in outlets of the conservative Editorial Zig Zag, which included the national newspaper *El Mercurio* and the sports magazine *Estadio*, downplayed the contributions of working-class clubs. Although there is no denying the existence of violence in football, this characterization of working-class fans as criminals served the broader purpose of undermining their rights to lead cultural institutions, such as the Football Federation and World Cup Organizing Committee.[10]

The Chilean bid for the 1962 World Cup drew upon accepted ideas about what made Chile unique in the region, namely, its democracy and stability. The bid showcased an appealing caricature of a humble country that deserved a chance to organize the tournament, regardless of its historically poor showing on the pitch. Unforeseen political developments in Argentina, including the military coup against Juan Perón and the subsequent persecution of Peronists, helped the Chilean case. The submission of the bid and the subsequent excitement masked the long-standing tensions between amateur and professional clubs in Chile. These tensions pitted professional club directors, largely from the business community, against working-class amateurs. These two camps disagreed profoundly on the role of the state in sport, the value of free market capitalism, and the image of Chile to project abroad.

Organizing the Cup

The official World Cup Committee in Chile included state officials, business leaders, and professional club directors. The committee handled the budget and relations with FIFA, and it oversaw "official publications." The process of appointing members to the committee was far from transparent and seemed to be guided by personal connections among state ministries and professional directors. Once formed, the committee was particularly anxious to establish Chile's reputation internationally. In their monthly magazine, geared toward a foreign audience, the committee stressed the success of Chile's government, informing readers (in several languages) that "[Chile's] political institutions . . . reflect a democracy constantly striving for perfection. Political, social, and racial prejudices are nonexistent. Since 1891 there have been no explosive revolutions in Chile. Chiefs of state walk about the streets and cities as any citizen would."[11] The Chilean committee hoped to attract large numbers of European visitors and felt that to do so they needed to counter international perceptions of volatility in the region.

For the committee, this political stability reflected the country's enviable level of economic development, racial makeup, and modernity. Sportswriters echoed concerns about foreign impressions. One journalist warned that FIFA officials and international visitors would scrutinize the country to see "if people are White or Black, whether Spanish or Portuguese is spoken, if life is easy or difficult, whether the climate is tropical or temperate." Writers worried that Chile would be confused with Brazil or Colombia, supposedly less temperate, less white, and supposedly less stable. Official publications avoided any references to the country's non-European population. The committee reported that Chile was "White, of European heritage; without a population of color or mixes, the population most homogenous of the Americas." Indigenous communities struggled for recognition of their claims for land and autonomy. Thus, this type of rhetorical erasure had far-reaching political consequences.[12]

At times, mainstream media complicated the committee's portrayal of Chile, particularly its picture of an exclusively white nation. For example, in one interview, Waldo Sanhueza explained that he was nicknamed the "Indian" because of his heritage. Moreover, he mentioned that players called one teammate the "Jap . . . because that face of his was *so* Chilean, with that something Asian that our race has in the eyes and cheekbones." These memories contrasted with narratives that emphasized the role of European immigrants in developing Chilean football. Retrospective pieces in *Estadio,* published throughout the 1950s, provided material for the football history written in the midst of the Cup. According to these articles, football's "golden age" began with competition between elite Creoles and British visitors. When state officials commented on indigenous culture they usually "Europeanized" it and also relegated it to the past. For example, the director of the state's Department of Sports, Fernando Renard, claimed, in regard to the indigenous communities, that "we take pride in their Spartan habits, their patriotic feeling and the tenacity that over centuries developed the physical strength of a race that loved the air and sun in the valleys and mountains." When officials included the indigenous in the nation, they stressed the exceptional nature of the Mapuche, the communities in Central and Southern Chile.[13]

Traditional ideals of gender figured prominently in the organizing committee's presentation of Chile. The committee promised tourists a tranquil paradise where they could enjoy traditional South American culture with the comforts of modern infrastructure. Chilean women's beauty and subservience constituted one of the pillars of "traditional" culture that visitors could enjoy. One government publication explained, "The woman of this country is generally beautiful, possesses a well formed body, is exquisitely feminine and knows how to dress with a Parisian simplicity and elegance." Women's relationship to football was frequently a subject for ridicule. In reference to a "mixed-sex" charity match that took place in 1905, one journalist wrote, "And to think 55 years later a match of women's football was prohibited for being considered a circus act!" This claim was hyperbolic and perhaps completely fictitious. In fact, women's football clubs began in the early twentieth century and developed considerably in the years surrounding the tournament, both in universities and within neighborhood clubs. The suggestion of the sports magazine, *Gol y Gol*, that women might one day win the World Cup prompted a lively debate among readers, including women footballers. Tournament organizers recruited young women as "hostesses" for visiting delegations and ticket-holders. Female fans received cursory attention during the 1962 World Cup. In film footage, a significant number of women are visible in the stadiums, yet they were rarely interviewed during or after the tournament. Advertisements that featured the World Cup, for example, ads for televisions, emphasized women's role in facilitating men's enjoyment of the event. Although there were precedents for sportswomen as ambassadors in international competition, including the Pan American Games of the 1950s, FIFA and the Chilean Football Federation excluded women athletes entirely.[14]

As the tournament approached, amateur sports directors realized they had been excluded from the organizing committee. They hoped that the increased attention to football would translate into support for their organizations. However, the state allocated most funds for construction, which was FIFA's primary concern. Cities with stadiums to host matches, including Arica, Ñuñoa (Santiago), and Valparaíso/Viña del Mar, received increased funds from the national government for structural improvements to stadiums and transportation infrastructure. Several well-known amateur clubs criticized government plans to relocate shantytown residents away from the major hotel areas and the National Stadium. In addition, amateurs were disappointed that the committee had not implemented measures to prevent inflation of the price of goods and services during the tournament. Despite these public comments and a barrage of petitions, amateur club directors were neither included in the organizational structure nor given affordable tickets.[15]

An incident between the Italian and Chilean press demonstrated that the World Cup could generate as much ill feeling as goodwill. A group of Italian journalists wrote scathing reports about the state of preparations for the tournament in the newspaper *La Nazione*. Local papers in Chile reprinted the articles, perhaps exaggerating some of the Italians' observations. The accusations of the Italian writers prompted a nationalist response that left little room for domestic criticisms of the tournament's organization. Representatives of various Italian newspapers visited in late 1961 and again in 1962, criticizing everything from the unattractiveness of Chilean women to the living conditions in shantytowns. One journalist remarked, "The atmosphere is so depressing that some federations have sent psychiatrists to prevent their players from becoming depressed." Another described Santiago as "a sad symbol of one of the least developed countries in the world and affected by all maladies: undernourishment, prostitution, illiteracy, alcoholism, and poverty." They described the squatter settlements on Santiago's peripheries as deplorable and barbaric. These reports so offended readers and the World Cup Committee that the Italian ambassador held a formal press conference to apologize. Even the Communist Party newspaper *El Siglo*, which had been most receptive to criticisms of the Cup, felt the Italian journalists had been unfair. They complained that the journalists had not seen the promise of Chileans, who were "healthy in spirit, polite, conscious of their problems, and ready to change the current state of things."[16]

The nationalist fervor in response to the Italians silenced complaints about the tournament's organization; however, it did not entirely appease domestic critics. In particular, the World Cup opened new avenues for discussion of Conservative Jorge Alessandri's presidency. A cautious politician with a sober demeanor, Alessandri inherited the World Cup when he took office in 1958. The son of populist president Arturo Alessandri, who had overseen the construction of the National Stadium twenty years earlier, Jorge Alessandri lacked his father's charisma and anti-oligarchic rhetoric. Moreover, he had little connection to popular civic associations and seemed hardly interested in football. Football club directors, both professional and amateur, criticized Alessandri's reluctance to commit adequate funds to the event's organization. In fairness, Alessandri's administration had been preoccupied with rebuilding southern Chile after the largest recorded earthquake in history, which occurred in May 1960. In 1961, after three years of petitions from amateurs and professionals, Alessandri passed Executive Order 244, which brought the organization of the Cup under the control of the Ministry of Interior. The decree ordered state agencies and their personnel to cooperate in every way with the organizing committee. Alessandri delegated most of the responsibility for the Cup to the minister of interior, Dr. Sótero del Río, who became Alessandri's chief defender. Sótero del Río explained in *Estadio* that Alessandri's apparent lack of enthusiasm was in fact a sign of humility. Sportswriters for *Estadio* praised Alessandri's habit of walking to work each morning, without security detail, as well as his modest dress.[17]

President Alessandri's disinterest during the tournament further alienated football enthusiasts. His official welcome speech maintained the "underdog" rhetoric of the FIFA Lisbon conference; however, his speech awkwardly shifted the tone from humility to humiliation. After welcoming the delegations to "this distant corner of the world," Alessandri stated that "Chile is not a notable power in world sports, but its people are enthusiastic participants in diverse types of physical education and its public admires the skill and ability of those that succeed," continuing, "Our country does not have all of the comforts and advancements that others could have offered." Notwithstanding the support of his conservative base, public criticism of Alessandri continued unabated. At the close of the tournament, coach Fernando Riera recalled that when Alessandri met with the team to congratulate them he admitted to having little understanding of football. Alessandri's supporters, instead, emphasized his strong relationship with the United States and his support for President John F. Kennedy's Alliance for Progress. However, they could not capitalize on this alliance in a direct way since the United States did not participate in the 1962 World Cup.[18]

The meetings of the organizing committee of the 1962 World Cup and FIFA archival documents show that Chile pressured FIFA to expand the number of teams; UEFA, the European Confederation, pressured FIFA to plan preliminary matches earlier to build gate receipts and press; and UEFA pressured Chile to insure that venues would concentrate attendance and could be organized in advance. Essentially all parties pressured one another in the interest of increasing profits from the World Cup of 1962. The meeting notes indicate that the organizing committee viewed the media as *the* biggest determinant to build excitement. That was an obstacle given the landscape in Chile because the club system of amateurs offered a much more extensive network for organizing ticket distribution and travel to venues.[19] The reliance, instead, on radio and print media, with advertisement geared toward consumers, framed the World Cup as a middle-class event. However, in 1960s Chile, the majority of football fans did not belong to the middle class. The growth of an international football market, lucrative European leagues, and corporate sponsorship heightened expectations of the sport's profitability.

A month before the tournament, Chileans were shocked by the announcement that only a small number of tickets had been sold. Amateurs, fans, and some members of the press accused government representatives and professional directors of inflating ticket prices to offset the money they had squandered in contracts to architectural and construction firms. The press criticized Arab Chilean directors of the professional club Palestino, especially Nicolás Abhumor, among the organizing committee members. Racist caricatures portrayed representatives of Club Palestino as greedy and self-serving. Originally, organizers projected that the tournament would bring forty to fifty thousand tourists to Chile. In the end, only a fraction of that number arrived. High prices and poor distribution methods hindered Chileans and neighboring Latin Americans from purchasing tickets. Many of the professional clubs authorized to sell tickets were located in elite neighborhoods far from the city center. Writers for the leftist newspaper *El Siglo* complained that hotel and transportation rate speculation prevented provincial Chileans from traveling to see the events. Some journalists felt the government had conducted the organization so poorly that it would have been better if Argentina had won the bid for the Cup.[20]

Doubts cast upon Chile's level of development, prompted by the Italian journalists, continued to inflame nationalist rhetoric throughout the tournament. Although the controversial remarks could have prompted a discussion of inequality, this was complicated because the critics were foreigners. Popular writer Joaquin Edwards Bello responded to the injurious remarks of Italian journalists, whom he characterized as "country bumpkins" from the provinces who were simply not well traveled. In refutation of the Italian journalists' description of Chilean women as unattractive, Edwards Bello insisted that on the contrary, they were so enchanting they established a virtual matriarchy. Writers objectified women in order to defend national honor. In response to the implication that Chile's poor living conditions caused widespread biological damage, the editorialists of the state newspaper, *La Nación*, used state rhetoric to defend Chile's racial heritage, claiming that Chileans descended from a mixture of the most heroic Spanish conquistadores with the noblest Indians.[21]

The committee's rhetorical presentation of Chile as business friendly, modern, and white had consequences on local popular culture, as well as Chile's international image. The European and Latin American media abroad reproduced the committee's rhetoric, and, when the Italian journalists challenged this view, Chilean media and state officials reacted angrily. The incident exposed how quickly international sporting events could promote as much animosity as goodwill among nations. Although the country rallied around Chilean nationalism, the glossy materials produced to entice visitors to Chile and the committee's presentations to FIFA masked conflict over infrastructural changes and the organization of football.

Experiences of the Cup

Whatever nationalist aims each team brought to the World Cup, a surprising turn of events on the pitch could overturn even the best-planned diplomatic agenda. That occurred even more dramatically for the tournament hosts. As host nation, the Chilean national team automatically qualified to play in the World Cup. Historically, Chile's international performances were disappointing, particularly in comparison to the feats of Argentina, Brazil, and Uruguay. The poor showings sparked soul-searching, with fans asking why Chile could not field comparably talented teams. Chile had played in two World Cup tournaments before 1962. The inaugural tournament in 1930 saw Chile play well but lose to Argentina. They also appeared in the 1950 World Cup but were eliminated in the first round. In 1962 the national team performed beyond expectations. The surprising victories sparked commentaries from all corners of the media, as they tried to frame the significance of this newfound success.

Chile defeated Switzerland in their first match, buoying their confidence for their second match against Italy. Resentful over the Italian media's criticism, the Chilean fans and players were seething when their team confronted the Italians on June 2. The match between Chile and Italy, which ended in a 2–0 victory for Chile, has become known as the "Battle of Santiago." Some claimed it was the most violent game in World Cup history. When British television replayed the match, the commentator introduced it as "the most stupid, appalling, disgusting and disgraceful exhibition of football, possibly in the history of the game." Before the match began, spectators shouted insults and threw rocks, food, and other objects onto the field. On the field, players scuffled and spit at one another. The first Italian player expelled, Giorgio Ferrini, refused to leave the field. Later in the match, a fight broke out between Chilean player Leonel Sánchez and Mario David of Italy. Sánchez punched David in the face, but only the Italian player was ejected, to the surprise of even the Chilean crowd. The police entered the field several times during the match and escorted the Italians out of the stadium. The British referee of the game, Kenneth Aston, was overwhelmed by the level of violence. After further disciplinary problems during the 1966 World Cup, Aston introduced yellow and red cards into FIFA.[22]

The animosity between the Italian and Chilean squads had repercussions off the pitch. A student who attended Scuola Italiana, begun by Italian immigrants, recalled that fights broke out over the controversy. Some professional directors, including the former president of Colo Colo, proposed a ban on immigrant clubs in the professional league. They suggested that the Football Federation force Audax Italiano and Unión Española change their names to those of Chilean historical figures, Caupolicán and Pedro de Valdivia, respectively. Certain immigrant communities in Chile expressed their nationalist allegiances during the tournament. Peter Dragicevic, former coach and leader of Colo Colo, recalled that he rooted for Chile against Yugoslavia, despite pressure from his older relatives. For other immigrants, the appearance of their native country's team was a unifying experience that also served to integrate them into Chilean social life. For example, a Czech couple explained that they had never been to a football match in Chile until the Czech team made an appearance at the World Cup. They continued to follow Czech appearances until they were detained in 1965 for bringing posters reading "Free Czechoslovakia" into the National Stadium.[23]

Coverage of the World Cup reflected the political polarization of media outlets. The Communist newspaper *El Siglo* had developed a substantial sports section by the 1940s and featured more amateurs than other publications. During the Cup, *El Siglo* provided an alternative perspective to mainstream sports journalism. First, they allotted more space to interviews with delegations from the Soviet Union and allied countries. The newspaper covered the Soviet delegation's visits to local schools and tourism, in contrast with the sparse coverage in *El Mercurio* and *La Tercera Hora*. *El Siglo* countered competing newspapers' characterizations of the Soviet delegation as unfriendly and shrouded in mystery. *La Nación* and *La Tercera* spread rumors that the Soviets criticized Chile's organization of the Cup, but the Soviets vehemently denied this, stating emphatically that they were happy with the facilities and treatment in Arica. *El Siglo* also presented a different view of football's history in Chile. They blamed the country's poor international performances on environmental factors that stemmed from class inequalities. Their editorials cited malnourishment, inadequate housing conditions, and abusive working conditions as harmful to Chileans' physical state. Moreover, they paid attention to the sacrifices of working-class neighborhoods during the tournament, such as power rationing and transportation disruptions. Writers for *El Siglo* tried to convince politicians to regulate prices in the face of rampant speculation, but met with little success. Finally, they highlighted the economic hardships that working-class players faced. For example, *El Siglo* described the financial difficulties of player Raúl Toro's childhood. One of ten children, "El Chino" had to leave elementary school after just one year to help his father, who worked as a train mechanic. This biography presented a stark contrast to the entirely upbeat profiles that ran in *El Mercurio*. The concerns of *El Siglo* fell on deaf ears, as neither FIFA nor the Chilean Football Federation considered any policy recommendations that would reduce speculation burdens on the local population.[24]

On June 10, 1962, in the northern city of Arica, the Chilean team defeated the Soviet Union by a score of 2 to 1 to reach the semifinals. One sportswriter described the scene in Santiago's National Stadium. When news of the victory came over the radio, "people jumped from their seats, threw their hats in the air, and whipped their white handkerchiefs in the wind. Strangers hugged, men and women, howling a joyful cry amid laughter and tears. The shout climbed into the sky, above the Andes Mountains and scattered the happiness and fervor of a modest and small people throughout the world." Conservative publications like *El Mercurio* interpreted Chile's win over the Soviet Union as proof of the superiority of free market capitalism and democracy. For others, the event was more akin to David and Goliath than a Cold War parable. The editorial in the centrist *Topaze* stated, "In defeating the USSR, we have not defeated a country, or a regime, as some want to believe." Linking the victory to the state of modernity and progress within Chile, the editorial continued, "We have defeated our own defeatism and we have made a demonstration, not to the world, but to ourselves, of what we are capable of. . . . We have a working and middle-class, to which many of these young men belong that has all the conditions to go forward, not only in the football field, but also in the broadest demonstrations of citizenship." Among the public, the success of the team validated Dittborn's vision of a small country's chance at greatness. Chile went on to finish third, after losing to the eventual champion, Brazil.[25]

The 1962 World Cup marked a new moment in the commercialization of the tournament, furthered by the advance of television and the growing power of FIFA. FIFA president Stanley Rous complained about the challenges that commercial interests and Cold War tensions had posed to planning the 1962 World Cup. Postcolonial nations demanded greater inclusion in FIFA and confronted the organization's paternalism. In regional terms, the World Cup of 1962 came at an important juncture for Latin American sports. The revolutionary government of Fidel Castro made a surprising decision to deprofessionalize Cuban sports. Sympathetic sports directors in Chile paid keen attention to the Cuban model, especially given the financial troubles of the professional league. The 1962 Chilean squad was the last to include players with jobs outside of football. The presence of several Soviet bloc delegations in a country with strong Socialist and Communist parties generated discussions of Cold War politics. *El Mercurio* targeted Soviet players for their violent behavior against Yugoslavia, even though most observers judged the latter to be at fault. When the Soviets lost to Colombia, the newspaper blamed the rigidity of socialism for rendering the players unable to adapt to new circumstances.[26]

As members of the organizing committee predicted, the tournament shone a spotlight on Chile and shaped impressions of the country abroad. Foreign television stations broadcast footage from the Chilean tournament as quickly as they could. The official film of the World Cup, distributed in English, reflected some of what the Chilean committee hoped to project. During aerial shots of the capital, the narrator began, "Santiago . . . is a modern metropolis brimming with life, its broad eight lane streets and spacious squares equal anything that could be found in Europe." While the film highlighted the modernity of the country's infrastructure, it portrayed Chilean people as traditional. For example, the narrator praised automatic traffic lights, but pointed out that no one paid attention to them. The film juxtaposed images of newly constructed airports and stadiums with rural folk troupes. The narrator stressed that the public in this "far off" country received all delegations with Latin warmth. Thus, the official film reiterated the Chilean committee's depiction of the country as exotic, but unthreatening. Criticisms of the last-minute construction of the National Stadium and the level of violence in the matches surfaced throughout the film. As much as political interests sought to harness the enthusiasm for the World Cup, it proved impossible for the government or the organizing committee to completely orchestrate the event. The official film explained that in the "smuggler's paradise" of Arica, "attendance was far below what the Chileans had hoped for." The Brazilian media and fans complained about the paltry attendance numbers, categorizing two hundred thousand spectators over the course of six matches as a failure. Following the Cup, the newspaper *Folha* of São Paulo decided the tournament was in decline.[27]

Despite negative international assessments, the tournament changed expectations of what Chilean football could achieve. The World Cup stimulated the globalization of Chilean football in that sense. For example, because of the World Cup, Chilean clubs received many invitations to play overseas. After their stellar performance, Chilean clubs traveled more extensively and their players received attention from South American and European scouts. Chilean football gained new respect from international football fans for their 1962 performance. A Brazilian journalist remarked, "In one month, Chilean football, considered a 'poor relation' has become an international export." In cafes, clubs, and the press, fans debated how Chilean football could continue to improve. Analysts focused on the team's speed and teamwork. Outside experts echoed what Chilean football fans had claimed since the national team consolidated in the 1910s—that they were the British of South America. This meant they were methodical and drew strength from teamwork, rather than the individual talent that characterized Brazilian and Argentinean football. Players who participated in delegations abroad joined the conversation. Clubs that toured Europe after the World Cup, however, returned with disappointing results throughout the 1960s. Coaches and players pointed out that they were not accustomed to the rigors of travel, which affected their play. Star players, including Leonel Sánchez, stressed that Chileans needed fundamental physical training if they were to perform well in the 1966 World Cup. Despite intense recruiting of Chilean players soon after the tournament ended, few ended up having successful careers abroad. Most notably, Eladio Rojas and Jorge Toro accepted lucrative contracts, only to see little playing time.[28]

Political parties hoped to capitalize on the prestige of football during the World Cup. Centrist parties, the Radicals and Christian Democrats, recruited former players to run for political office. These efforts failed to achieve the desired results. In part, Chileans' party identification was too strong for celebrities to sway voters. Also, these professionals lacked the relationship with civic associations that had enabled leftist parties to mobilize supporters through working-class clubs. For example, legendary footballer for University of Chile Eduardo Simián announced his congressional run as a Christian Democrat in 1958. Simián's friends, such as popular player Sergio Livingstone, organized benefits to support his bid. The campaign advertisements drew upon Simián's reputation among sportsmen and referred to him as the "Octopus," a nickname from his football days. Despite Simián's successful career in engineering, it was his "virile and fair play of sports" that the advertisements promoted. Simián promised that, if elected, he would provide opportunities for youth to participate in sport. In addition, Simián pledged that amateur sports would receive "technical assistance, sports fields, equipment, and physical education teachers." Despite hopes that "footballmania" would buoy sportsmen into office, the Liberal Party defeated Simián in his district. Voters proved resistant to populist overtures that drew upon excitement over the World Cup.[29]

As the tournament drew to a close, the government's actions ignited criticism. *El Siglo*, amateur directors, and sportswriters led the charge. First, despite heavy propaganda, critics pointed out that the Alessandri administration failed to complete the "World Cup Museum of 1962." In addition, state officials showed little concern about the three hundred football fields that amateur associations lost during the five years of preparation for the tournament. Furthermore, barrio clubs protested the government's displacement of residents near the National Stadium. After a year of negotiations back and forth, hundreds of families that CORVI (the Public Housing Corporation) ordered to move still refused to do so. Some residents had lived in the area nearly fifteen years without water, plumbing, sidewalks, and other services that *El Siglo* described as "elemental to life in a civilized country." Despite its challenges, community members who had made improvements to the neighborhood were reluctant to leave without a promise of alternate housing. Amateur football associations across the city demonstrated in support of the shantytown residents, but in the end could not prevent their removal. The creation of a national football lottery also generated controversy. Professional clubs and their political allies hoped the lottery would infuse the league with enough capital to improve its financial situation and build more stadiums. Amateurs objected to the moral and financial burden of such a lottery. They succeeded in thwarting the lottery until 1975, when the administration of dictator Augusto Pinochet instituted it.[30]

While the Chilean organizing committee succeeded in navigating Cold War politics to convince FIFA delegates that they should host the 1962 World Cup, tensions resulting from political divisions erupted throughout the tournament. The animosity of professionals toward amateurs, which was supported by CONMEBOL and FIFA, hurt the attendance and success of the Cup. A focus on the repercussions of an international mega-event on the national political scene and national identity provides us a window for understanding how non-state actors viewed cultural politics during the Cold War.

The World Cup of 1962 intensified the connection Chileans felt with a global community of football fans. Chileans described the mood during the World Cup of 1962 as festive and carnivalesque, and they frequently remember it as a perfectly executed event.[31] The third-place finish of the Chilean team came as a joyful surprise. In interviews, some fans recalled the match between Chile and Brazil as the final of the tournament, rather than the semifinal. Despite their marginalization from the event's organization, amateur clubs worked hard to raise enthusiasm for the Cup in their communities. Club leaders across Santiago organized fundraisers to buy tickets to matches and raffled them off. Many directors dipped into club reserves to buy a television, inviting the neighborhood to watch the matches. When they could not afford a television set, clubs tuned in by radio and opened their doors for neighbors to listen. Vivacious gossip, analysis, and prognosis surrounded matches. Many neighborhood clubs organized social events, such as "happy hours" in honor of visiting delegations. In addition, amateur directors shaped public perception of the Cup through their appearances on radio shows.

The organizers of the World Cup lost an opportunity to harness the passion of football's most ardent fans because of their animosity toward amateur clubs. Meanwhile, professional directors used their role in organizing the Cup to consolidate their power over amateurs. FIFA, accustomed to European models, naturally sought out professional directors to ensure the organization of such a large tournament. Cold War politics charged conflicts between amateurs and professionals. Sportswriters, directors, and fans would likely have denied they were engaging in politics when they discussed the World Cup. Yet, the tournament generated widespread debates and became a site where local politics mediated the Cold War. The case of the World Cup of 1962 in Chile demonstrates an interesting case where non-state actors, namely professional club leaders, orchestrated the spectacle and diplomatic aims. Through these cases, sport offers us a unique window into how global politics shaped everyday cultural life and how local actors interpreted, negotiated, and took part in international relations. Whether in their organization, the public reaction to them, or the performances in the competitions, international sporting events were always cloaked in politics.

Notes

Portions of this chapter have appeared in Brenda Elsey, "Football at the 'End of the World:' The 1962 World Cup." And *Citizens and Sportsmen: Fútbol and Politics in Twentieth-Century Chile* (Austin, TX: University of Texas Press) 2011.

1. Nathanael Yañez Silva, "El fútbol es un arte del mundo actual," *La Nación*, June 5, 1962, 40–42.

2. José Gai, "1962: El Mundial que Recordamos," *Las Ultimas Noticias*, May 31, 1992, 10; *El Mercurio* special edition, 50th anniversary of the World Cup, with Federación de Fútbol de Chile, *Nuestro Mundial* (Santiago, 2012).

3. Jorge Alessandri Rodríguez, *Mensaje de S. E. el Presidente de la República don Jorge Alessandri Rodríguez al Congreso Nacional al inaugurar el período ordinario de sesiones, 21 de Mayo de 1962* (Santiago: Impr. del Servicio de Prisiones, 1962); Margaret Power, *Right-Wing Women in Chile: Feminine Power and the Struggle against Allende, 1964–1973* (College Park, PA: Pennsylvania State University Press, 2002); Jorge Alessandri Rodríguez, *Alessandri Volverá: por que volverá* (Santiago: Impr. Marinetti, 1970).

4. *Boletín de Resoluciones de la Agrupación de Pobladores de Chile,* December 1957, 1.

5. For detailed information on the changes in football's structure, see Elsey, *Citizens and Sportsmen.* See also, Asociación Nacional de Fútbol Amateur, *Congreso Nacional de Fútbol Amateur* (Santiago: San Diego, 1953). It is difficult to assess how many amateurs belonged to clubs. Amateurs claimed around 150,000, but the number is likely much higher since only a fraction of football clubs could afford dues required by an association.

6. "Ernesto Alvear," *Estadio*, May 30, 1972, 24.

7. *Estadio*, June 22, 1956, 5; Chamanto, "Es difícil," *Estadio*, June 8, 1956, 3.

8. *Estadio*, June 22, 1956, 5; Chamanto, "Es difícil," *Estadio*, June 8, 1956, 3; *Estadio,* June 15, 1956, inside cover page.

9. This is contested by the IOC but the Chilean Olympic Committee maintains its veracity.

10. See for example Josafat Martínez, *Historia del fútbol chileno* (Santiago: Impr. Chile, 1961); Hugo Sainz Torres, *Breve Historia del Deportes* (Santiago: Braden Copper

Co., 1961); "El Fútbol Profesional Requiere una Vasta Reforma," *El Mercurio*, February 21, 1960 (no page no., Archivo J. Edwards Bello, Biblioteca Nacional, Santiago, Chile [hereafter BN]); *Sport i Actualidades*, June 28, 1912, 1. See "Los Domingos," *Los Sports*, November 23, 1928, 8; Intendencia Santiago, Archivo Nacional, *Comunicaciones Recibidas*, November–December 1928, ARNIT, isan, v. 627, no. 1681.

11. *Campeonato Mundial de Fútbol*, March 1961, 11.

12. A.V.R., "El Contacto Humano," *Estadio*, June 29, 1956, 1; *Campeonato Mundial de Fútbol, 2*, December–January 1962, 72.

13. Pancho Alsina, "Nacido Para el Fútbol," *Estadio*, May 31, 1957, 20; Don Pampa, "Frente a la Realidad," *Estadio*, October 15, 1959, 3.

There is no further information provided on this "prohibited match," and I have not found it referenced in any other sources. G.L., "La Mujer Chilena," *El Viaje*, May 1962, 55; Martínez, *Historia del fútbol chileno*, 12; *Gol y Gol*, May 15, 1963, 4. The hostesses, as well as female fans, can be seen clearly in film footage of the event. See Plan Publicidad Buenos Aires and Sport Film Munich, *Football World Championship 1962: The Official Film*,

14. http://www.youtube.com/watch?v=eyRUHKW1tbk (accessed February 2, 2013); Brenda Elsey, "Cultural Ambassadorship and the Pan-American Games of the 1950s," *International Journal of the History of Sport* 33, no. 1–2 (2016): 105–126, doi:10.1080/09523367.2015.1117451.

15. See the coverage of the Cup in *El Siglo* throughout June 1962. This happened early on in planning and stayed rather constant. See *Estadio*, January 27, 1956.

16. See John Foot, *Winning at All Costs: A Scandalous History of Italian Soccer* (New York: Nation Books, 2007), for the repercussions of the match in Italy. *El Siglo*, May 29, 1962, no page no.

17. *Estadio*, February 2, 1961, 3; "El Campeonato Mundial de Futbol," *El Viaje*, May 1962, 4. To underscore the Alessandri administration's support for the Cup, Sótero del Río purchased 250 televisions to air the tournament around the country. *Campeonato Mundial de Fútbol*, July 4, 1961, 10; *Estadio*, June 28, 1962, 64.

18. "'Que el triunfo premie a aquellos que lo merezcan' dijo Presidente Alessandri al inaugurar el VII Campeonato Mundial de Fútbol," *La Nación*, May 31, 1962, 13; Jorge Alessandri, "Discurso del Presidente de la República en la inauguración del Mundial de Fútbol," 1, Departamento de Prensa, Archivo Medina, BN; "Recuerdos de un patriarca," *El Mercurio* special edition, 50th anniversary of the World Cup, with Federación de Fútbol de Chile, *Nuestro Mundial* (Santiago, 2012); "'Es una lástima que el Mundial haya . . .'" *La Nación*, June 10, 1962, 18.

19. At a March 1960 meeting of the organizing committee, they stressed the importance of setting the qualifying rounds in advance to spark more press interest and to increase gate receipts (they hoped by 20 to 30 percent); they were mentored by UEFA in this regard. Meeting minutes, World Cup Chile 1962, Organizing Committee, Fédération Internationale de Football Association, Zurich, Switzerland.

20. *El Siglo*, June 11, 1962, 2; *El Siglo*, June 3, 1962, 13; Juan De Porte, "Cómo cubrimos el Mundial," *El Siglo*, June 24, 1962, 12.

21. Joaquin Edwards Bello, "Injurias a Chile?" *La Nación*, May 31, 1962, 15; M. Garfias, "Un puntapie fuera de la cancha," *La Nación*, May 31, 1962, 15.

Elsey, *Citizens and Sportsmen*; Scott Murray, Georgina Turner, and Sean Ingle, "The Knowledge," *Guardian*, November 6, 2003, http://www.guardian.co.uk/football/2003/nov/06/theknowledge.sport (accessed March 15, 2013); *El Siglo*, June 4, 1962, 5; Pedro Gajardo, "Chile, en la hora de su consagración," *La Nación*, June 3, 1962, 6; "Ken Aston—the inventor of yellow and red cards," *FIFA*, January 15, 2002,

22. http://web.archive.org/web/20080606022246/http://www.fifa.com/aboutfifa/developing/refereeing/news/newsid=80623.html (accessed December 15, 2012).

23. José Gai, "1962: El Mundial que Recordamos," *Las Últimas Noticias*, May 31, 1992, 10–12; "'Es una lástima que el Mundial haya . . .'" *La Nación*, June 10, 1962, 18.

24. *La Tercera Hora* reproduced very negative stereotypes. For an in-depth discussion of this, see Diego Vilches, "La representación de la Unión Soviética en el Mundial de Chile 1962," Santiago, inédito, 2012. *El Siglo*, June 13, 1960, 2; "Toro, ídolo de sus padres y de los cabros del barrio," *El Siglo*, May 30, 1962, 5.

25. Raul Leppé, "Más allá de la Crónica," *La Nación*, June 11, 1962, 2; Profesor Topaze, "Abramos los ojos," *Topaze*, June 15, 1962, 5; *Estadio*, May 30, 1972, 24.

26. Alan Tomlinson, "FIFA and the Men Who Made It," *Soccer and Society* 1, no. 1 (2000): 55–71; "Escuti y Ortiz representan la experiencia," *La Nación*, May 30, 1962, 1; Diego Vilches, "La representación de la Unión Soviética."

Plan Publicidad Buenos Aires and Sport Film Munich, *Football World Championship 1962: The Official film*,

27. http://www.youtube.com/watch?v=eyRUHKW1tbk (accessed February 2, 2013); "O Brasil teve pouco public no Mundial," *Folha* (Sao Paulo), June 22, 1962, 13; "Copa de 62: declinio," *Folha*, June 19, 1962, 39.

28. "Gentileza é a marca do futebol do Chile," *Folha*, June 13, 1962, 11; "Echoes of Chile Linger On," *Times* (London), September 8, 1962, 3; "Brazil Fancied to Beat Chile," *Times* (London), June 13, 1962, 4; "Triunfal Regreso de la 'U,'" *Gol y Gol*, May 29, 1963, 3; "¿Nuestros Cracks no son Productos de Exportación?" *Gol y Gol*, May 29, 1963, 29.

29. *Estadio*, March 16, 1961, 32; *El Mercurio*, March 5, 1958, 15; *El Mercurio*, March 21, 1958, 21.

30. *El Siglo*, July 2, 1962, 5; *El Siglo*, June 18, 1962, 2; *El Siglo*, March 22, 1962, 1; *El Siglo*, May 25, 1962, 2; "'Es una lástima que el Mundial haya . . .'" *La Nación*, June 10, 1962, 18.

31. Interview with Guillermo Lamilla, conducted by author, Santiago, 2004.

"Football More Important Than Berlin"

East German Football versus NATO, 1960–1964

Heather L. Dichter

FIFA's World Cup became the flagship international football event shortly after its establishment in the 1930s, and its resumption in 1950 solidified that position. The popularity of the sport around the world, and especially in Europe, led to the creation of other tournaments such as the European Championships organized by the continental body, as well as a comparable tournament for younger players. For the states that did not have the resources to host the larger mega-events, hosting a less prominent world championship or European championship provided a great source of pride and media coverage. Yet while the global public may have viewed these events as less prominent, they were not immune from international politics. Even these "third-order" events became entangled in Cold War politics in the early 1960s as a result of a divided Germany.[1]

When the Federal Republic of Germany (FRG, or West Germany) joined the North Atlantic Treaty Organization (NATO) in 1955, the military organization adopted a policy that refused to grant entry visas to athletes and teams that represented the German Democratic Republic (GDR, or East Germany), particularly because of their use of a state symbol, flag, and anthem, the staples of international sport, at events and particularly on the victory podium. When the political problems of an East German entry in a sporting event arose in member states, the host country often raised concerns at a NATO meeting.

Publicly, they blamed travel problems on NATO or the Allied Travel Office (ATO); this remnant of the occupation of Germany, run by the Americans, British, and French, granted special travel permits, Temporary Travel Documents (TTDs), to East Germans who sought to visit or transit through countries that fell outside of the Soviet bloc or were considered nonaligned. The efforts to maintain NATO's policy of not recognizing the GDR often damaged a country's international prestige and caused a public outcry when these political decisions diminished the level of athletic competition. For example, the Football Association tried to ensure that two East German teams could play in Manchester and Northern Ireland in September 1960, but the lack of TTDs led to the cancellation of these matches, which the East German state-run newspaper claimed had "provoked outrage among the British football fans." Spectators want to see the best athletes from across the globe, and when top competitors are barred from participating, the public can be less inclined to purchase tickets. International sport federations, attempting to prevent politics from interfering with the successful organization of their events, thus became intimately involved in world affairs.[2]

Whereas the International Olympic Committee (IOC) recognized only one German state, FIFA had granted separate recognition to East Germany in 1952. Similarly, the continental football federation, Union of European Football Associations (UEFA), also recognized East Germany separately from West Germany, with both German football federations having UEFA membership since the organization's 1954 founding. As Alan McDougall has shown, football remained an incredibly popular sport in East Germany, even if the national team never achieved much international success, only qualifying for the World Cup once (in 1974). In the early 1960s Portugal and the Netherlands confronted the problem of East German participation in the UEFA junior tournament (for players eighteen and under) and Olympic qualification. Even though these tournaments were not the biggest or most important football matches, their domestic governments feared that not allowing the East Germans to participate could prompt a public backlash against themselves and NATO. The changing politics on the Continent and in the Cold War, as well as within the sporting world, led NATO and its member states to factor these nuances into their decisions regarding these three football cases.[3]

Football became the vehicle through which many Europeans learned about NATO policy—or, at least a specific policy regarding East Germany.

Because enforcing East German nonrecognition resulted in football matches being canceled or changed, NATO and its member states had to counter these unpopular actions by communicating a specific message to their publics. The popularity of sport—and football in particular—forced NATO to confront the issue frequently. NATO discussions about athletes and sports teams often became entwined with broader debates surrounding visits by East German scientists and cultural groups. However, the mass appeal of football, along with the nationalism that it stirred and the use of state symbols, meant that international sporting events could cause a greater threat to national policy and NATO unity than could academics and actors. The ATO and NATO had imposed travel restrictions in response to East German actions that restricted free movement, particularly within Berlin. Ironically, NATO promoted free movement of people, but its policy prevented East Germany from having the freedom of travel abroad because of a flag, symbol, or song.

NATO diplomats, foreign ministries, and the leaders of national and international football federations therefore spent months in protracted negotiations over whether minor football matches involving the German Democratic Republic would even take place during the height of the Cold War, as each group attempted to appear blameless in the court of public opinion. NATO had established an information service in its second year to counter communist propaganda against the organization, and by the end of the 1950s NATO was actively developing campaigns to promote its collaborative and positive efforts. This need to improve its image among its own populations meant that being portrayed as meddling in affairs in which the general public felt it did not belong—such as sport—would further damage NATO's reputation. The diplomats at NATO and back home in the various foreign ministries recognized that if the public perceived that NATO was preventing international football matches or was causing a diminished field in a tournament, they would face a greater backlash. Jens Boyessen, the Norwegian permanent representative to NATO, raised these concerns at NATO, noting that some visa refusals for sport might draw negative attention. Indeed, the American delegate responded to Boyessen's comments by noting the travel regulations should be kept confidential—although that plan quickly went out the window when Norwegian press publicized the travel policy that same day because an East German ice hockey team could not receive travel documents for a tournament in Norway.[4]

These football games thus became tied up with debates over NATO policies, national interest, and public opinion. Though not the only sporting events that NATO discussed, football's popularity prompted some states to attempt to use the national interest exception to the East German travel ban—even for matches that did not grip the nation at the time and have since been largely forgotten. Nonetheless, these football matches brought the Cold War directly into the smaller NATO member states' national boundaries. In contrast to the sense, at least in the Low Countries, that the Cold War "happened 'somewhere else,'" a look at the hosting of sporting events illustrates that the Netherlands and Portugal engaged directly with their NATO allies over Cold War policies with which they did not fully agree or which they believed would cause public opinion problems at home and abroad. Historian Lawrence Kaplan wrote that transforming NATO "meant giving voice to the smaller nations." Sport, especially football, gave some of the less powerful states in NATO the space to assert their positions within the multilateral organization. The Americans, British, and French continued to play a dominant role in NATO, particularly on issues concerning Germany. States that excelled in specific sports—the Netherlands in football, Norway in skiing, Denmark in rowing, for example—could use the opportunities of hosting international sporting events to advocate for their own positions on NATO issues, especially when those sentiments were at odds with those of the United States and Germany.[5]

Football incidents surrounding Olympic qualification and the UEFA junior tournament in the early 1960s reveal the importance of the sport in international relations. The diplomatic discussions on football and sport held at NATO, embassies, and foreign ministries demonstrate how states large and small could contribute to the evolution and implementation of multilateral policy. Even minor sporting events could impact international relations, and Portuguese and Dutch diplomats advocated for the East German football teams to be able to play matches in their countries because these games served their own national interests at home.

Portuguese National Interest

The subject of East German football first arose at a NATO meeting on November 15, 1960, in the Political Advisers Committee (PAC) meeting. As host of the UEFA junior tournament around Easter 1961, Portugal informed

NATO that various countries would be invited to the event, including the Soviet Union, Romania, Poland, and the Soviet-occupied Zone of Germany (as NATO and West Germany called the GDR). Delegations had the opportunity to comment on or object to East German participation.[6] While football ostensibly seemed completely irrelevant to NATO affairs, recent actions by East Germany had prompted responses in NATO that ultimately had an impact on sporting events. The travel ban on East German national teams prompted Portugal to contest NATO's nonrecognition policy because it considered it a matter of national interest to invite East Germany to the UEFA junior tournament. The Portuguese government felt that NATO largely ignored its diplomatic interests, particularly with respect to its African colonies; therefore, it sought to assert its position in NATO when the football tournament arose.

As part of the 1959 celebration of the ten-year anniversary of the founding of the GDR, the country introduced a new flag with the emblem of the worker and peasant state in its center. In response to restrictions on travel to East Berlin in September 1960, the tripartite powers implemented more stringent travel restrictions that same month and informed their NATO allies of these measures, which included a travel ban on athletes purporting to represent the GDR. The ATO banned nine categories of travel (trade, agriculture, medical and scientists, professional [professors, teachers, students, lawyers], political, cultural, sport, press, and tourism) but permitted travel for health, emigration, contractual labor, family visits, and on compassionate grounds. The ATO could grant TTDs "in exceptional cases where an allied or friendly Government certifies that the travel would be in its 'national interest'"—although the ATO never clearly defined what constituted "national interest." The destination country asserted the national interest designation, but the ATO still made the final decision regarding the granting of TTDs (at times to the chagrin of the country seeking to receive East German visitors).[7]

Recognizing the problems related to the travel ban, UEFA, which sanctioned the tournament, sent a letter to NATO urging them to issue visas to the East Germans so that they could participate in the tournament in Portugal. UEFA noted that this tournament contributed to reconciliation and friendship between East and West in Europe and warned that if the East Germans did not receive visas then all Eastern European states would withdraw. At the next PAC meeting the chairman noted that UEFA's letter was the first time such a message had been sent to NATO and asked how it should be treated, which prompted an extensive discussion. As the American delegate reported back to the State Department, most NATO members contributed to the debate: "Dutch favored being lenient with such multilateral sports activities; view shared generally by UK, Norway, Denmark, and Italy. Canadians thought unwise to confirm any of telegram's hypotheses about NATO Committee's activities and suggested deadpan reply that NATO not visa-granting organization. France inclined to favor no answer. Belgian suggested answer that NATO not competent in such matters so apply to Portuguese and ATO. Consensus agreed reply should go promptly." Ultimately PAC agreed to send a simple telegram, stating: "This organization is not competent in matter raised in your telegram. Signed/NATO." Officially, NATO did not grant visas, but the organization agreed to policies that all member states upheld. The Portuguese delegate therefore stated that his government did not object to authorizing the visas but first wanted the views of the other NATO governments.[8]

Discussions within NATO and between PAC representatives and their respective foreign ministries continued over the ensuing weeks as the question of East German participation in the UEFA tournament in Portugal became subsumed by a larger debate regarding a change to the East German travel policy more generally. Immediately upon receiving the NATO response, UEFA sent an identically worded telegram to the Allied Travel Office in Berlin. Because "TTDs cannot be issued unless 'national interest' category is invoked by Portuguese," the ATO planned to respond after March 1 that travel documents would not be granted unless the ATO received instructions otherwise. The State Department informed the ATO to delay a firm response, suggesting instead to recommend that the East German applications be started as early as possible while still remaining noncommittal in tone.[9]

In the meantime, American diplomats met with their counterparts in Bonn, Paris, and Lisbon to prepare for the continued discussion about the UEFA tournament at the next PAC meeting. Another legacy of the occupation of Germany was that the representatives of the American, British, and French embassies in Bonn regularly met with the staff of the Federal Republic's foreign ministry. At the quadripartite meeting on February 27, the German Foreign Ministry expressed its concern about the East German football team participating in the UEFA tournament in Portugal. They recognized that the ATO and NATO were soon likely to lift the travel restrictions imposed in September 1960 and revert to the March 1960 rules, which still prevented teams purporting to represent the East German government, including sport teams. The French representative wondered whether they could "oppose the coming of this team without causing a stir for NATO? Perhaps Portugal could demand that East German athletes do not deploy their flag and do not play their anthem?" The diplomats left the meeting without setting a firm course of action, which the Americans reported the following day at the NATO PAC meeting after the British stated that the East German travel restrictions were in the process of revision and would be reported at the next NATO Council meeting.[10]

While the four powers met in Bonn, an American embassy representative in Lisbon met with the Portuguese Foreign Office secretary general, who "took occasion [to] vent certain amount spleen over fact Portugal called upon from time to time to act in conformity views NATO partners while at same time most of those partners do not support Portugal on matter of prime national interest." In particular, Portugal "did not believe Washington [was] aware of 'realities' in Africa." Portugal was a founding member of NATO, but António de Oliveira Salazar's state (the Estado Novo), in addition to being authoritarian and anticommunist, was also militarily and ideologically unprepared for the challenges of decolonization. Confronted with the growing decolonization movement in Angola and its ensuing problems, Portugal saw the UEFA junior tournament as a source of positive news at home. The possibility that NATO policies could hinder the smooth running of the event and cause problems with the communist bloc—which supported decolonization movements in Africa—was an additional headache that the Portuguese government did not want.[11]

Separate from the issue of whether the East German team would receive travel documents to participate in the UEFA tournament in Portugal was the more general tripartite discussion regarding East German travel. At the beginning of March 1961, the three powers agreed to lift the additional restrictions imposed in September 1960 and return to the guidelines from a year earlier. However, the ATO and NATO would still "exclude all East Germans whose visits have a predominantly political character," which included "persons or groups purporting to represent the D.D.R. Government or State at international meetings, including sports." Yet, as they reverted to this policy, the tripartite powers did not object to the East German team receiving TTDs for the tournament in Portugal. The State Department informed its ATO delegation of the new travel guidelines and in the same telegram then stated: "Application of East German football team desiring travel Portugal obviously no longer a problem." The quadripartite powers determined that athletes under the age of eighteen at a minor tournament would not constitute much in the way of political agitation.[12]

The discussion at NATO followed a similar trajectory when the political advisers next met on March 7. The three powers shared with their NATO allies the new travel guidelines, which prompted a request by Portugal regarding the "special case of E. German football team which desired to come to Portugal." Some NATO members "were inclined to favor allowing team to come so long as it was carefully controlled and no national flags or anthems permitted." In response the United States suggested that the "Portuguese case be handled as special one and, since question of judgement involved, [and] suggested that Portuguese authorities discuss case with ATO before making decision." While the final judgment was up to the Portuguese, the chairman noted that they "should take into account considerations expressed in meeting, especially the advantages and disadvantages which flow from granting visas albeit with stringent limitations as opposed to refusing visas and facing repercussions from an uninformed public." In that discussion the British had argued that refusing visas for sport teams "would have a disproportionately harmful effect on public opinion and, thus, would not be in the best interests of the Alliance." The UEFA junior tournament in Portugal, although it was international and included teams from across the entire European continent, was nonetheless a small event that, on its own, would not garner much media coverage. In England, for example, the *Times* wrote one sentence about England's 4–0 loss to Portugal in its first game and then only included the matches at the bottom of the columns listing football results. However, the communist press played up instances when East German athletes and teams were not allowed to travel to international sporting events, which caused NATO and its member states problems. A military organization barely more than a decade old did not need or want the negative publicity that would prompt its domestic populations to question its value.[13]

Portugal went forward with the approval of the visa request, and the ATO authorized TTDs for the East German team. Instead of a backlash in Portugal and the communist bloc for a possible interference of politics in sport, the East German press lauded the success of numerous protests that had led to the team's ability to participate in the UEFA junior tournament. They even praised the efforts of Peco Bauwens, the president of the (West) German Football Federation (Deutscher Fussball-Bund) and vice president of

UEFA, for his support of East Germany's participation in the tournament. In a letter Bauwens had sent to the ATO in Berlin, he expressed many of the same ideas as the official UEFA telegram, but he also wrote that West Germany desired East Germany's participation to quash accusations that the Federal Republic was responsible for the refusal of the East German visas, accusations that frequently appeared in the Eastern European press. He noted that UEFA anticipated the withdrawal of Yugoslavia, Romania, Poland, and Hungary from the tournament if East Germany did not receive visas. NATO and the ATO were dismissive in their reply to Bauwens, particularly as the German delegation at NATO said that he had acted alone and had not spoken with any government officials prior to contacting the ATO.[14]

At the last minute the East German team withdrew from the tournament in solidarity with the Hungarian and Yugoslavian teams, who did not receive visas. With this action the communist states hoped to cause problems for the Portuguese and the West in general. Even *A Bola*, the Portuguese paper with the most extensive coverage of the tournament, provided no reason why the teams withdrew. Portugal went ahead with the tournament but had to reconfigure the groups, leaving three groups with three teams while the fourth had four teams. Poland and Romania remained in the event, preventing a united front of communist withdrawal—the tactic the bloc used frequently in the following years. The deliberations among NATO member states regarding the participation of a youth football team from East Germany had nonetheless demonstrated their concerns as they sought to balance domestic policy with NATO agreements. Countries such as Norway, which was not even competing at the tournament in Portugal, still considered how these actions could impact them at home during comparable events, which factored into their contributions to the NATO discussions. Particularly when taking action could result in sharp criticism of the Atlantic alliance over an otherwise innocuous sporting event, the less prominent states within NATO struggled to justify maintaining a hard-line NATO position, as evidenced by Portugal's intent to use the national interest argument for allowing the East German junior team to receive travel documents for the tournament in Portugal.[15]

"Gracious Hosts in the Land of the Tulips"

Dutch diplomats, similar to the Portuguese, emphasized national interest in the following few years for multiple football matches scheduled with East

Germany. Football's prominence in the Netherlands is so great that Frank Lechner, in his monograph on the country, globalization, and national identity, spends the entire first chapter on the Orange Nation, football's role in Dutch national identity.[16] Over a period of two and a half years, the Netherlands' strength on the pitch ultimately led to three occasions when they encountered the problem of an East German team: hosting the 1964 UEFA junior tournament and qualifying for the 1962 World Cup and 1964 Olympic football tournament. While on the surface these three cases are similar—the GDR wanted to send a football team to the Netherlands—these situations in fact reveal the multilayered challenges that confronted both diplomats and international sport leaders as they sought to comply with NATO regulations. With the construction of the Berlin Wall in August 1961 and a reimposition of travel restrictions on East Germans, their participation in football tournaments once again became a NATO concern from a diplomatic standpoint as well as for its public perception implications.

In the lead-up to the 1962 FIFA World Cup in Chile, East and West Germany played in different qualification groups. West Germany won all four games played against Greece and Northern Ireland to earn its berth. East Germany, on the other hand, struggled in its group against Hungary and the Netherlands. Hungary won three games and earned a draw against the Netherlands. The second Dutch–East German match was scheduled for October 1961; but, with the construction of the Berlin Wall six weeks earlier in August, NATO supported the Federal Republic and tightened the travel restrictions imposed on East Germans. Because the Berlin Wall completely halted movement between the two parts of the divided city, the ATO immediately suspended all TTDs for East Germans "except for most urgent compassionate cases." The ATO informed NATO of these changes, and NATO's reimposition of the travel ban on East German athletes and sport officials immediately impacted the final East German qualification game, scheduled for October 1 in the Netherlands. Within two weeks of the NATO decision, the Dutch Foreign Ministry had informed its national football federation that East Germany would not receive TTDs, and the Dutch federation immediately wrote to the East Germans about this decision. *Neues Deutschland*, the East German state-run newspaper, reported this refusal of travel visas, citing a Dutch journalist's admission that the refusal fell directly on NATO. Because Hungary had already won the group stage with three victories (their draw against the Dutch came at the end of October), there was no need to reschedule the cancelled Dutch–GDR match. Nonetheless, this event marked one of the first sport casualties of the Berlin Wall.[17]

The beginning of 1962 saw two world championships marred by the denial of travel documents to East German teams, reigniting this debate at NATO. With an East German team unable to participate in the alpine skiing and ice hockey world championships in France and the United States, respectively, the Soviet Union and its allies withdrew their athletes from these events, leaving a depleted field. The political situation had not changed since the erection of the Berlin Wall, and, therefore, the travel restrictions on East Germans should not change, argued the quadripartite powers. Other states, particularly Belgium and the self-styled "cold countries" of Norway, Canada, Denmark, and Iceland, noted the negative public perception of NATO when athletes could not participate in sporting events. The Norwegian delegate in PAC argued that "NATO should avoid a situation where public opinion did not understand its policy. It was important to grasp the 'psychological opportunity' for making some relaxation" of the travel restrictions. The Canadian representative agreed with his Norwegian colleague, arguing that "the difficulty was to rectify a situation where public opinion was not sympathetic to certain aspects of NATO policy." In response, the German delegate said that "any relaxation would convince FRG and Berlin public opinion that 'football [was] more important than Berlin.'" The Norwegian permanent representative to NATO repeated the same arguments the following day in the North Atlantic Council meeting, even calling these restrictions on East German athletes "psychological warfare action at expense only of NATO countries." While NATO recognized these "strong arguments for relaxation travel ban on German athletes in terms of public opinion which would be strongly adverse to NATO if ban maintained," the quadripartite powers, in particular the Americans and Germans, held firm in continuing the travel restrictions imposed in response to the construction of the Berlin Wall.[18]

NATO travel restrictions remained in place two years later, and the issue of the travel of East German football teams to the Netherlands arose again over qualification for the 1964 Olympic Games. Unlike qualification for the FIFA World Cup, for which East Germany and West Germany had separate recognition and teams, the IOC recognized only one Germany. Beginning with the 1956 Olympic Games, the IOC insisted that the two German states compete on a unified Olympic team under one flag, the black-red-gold with the Olympic rings in the middle. Requiring increasingly more negotiations to arrange the details to select the all-German team every Olympiad, this process continued through the 1968 Games. To determine who would represent Germany at the Olympic Games, the best athletes from each state competed against each other. For team sports, instead of selecting the best athletes from both states to build the strongest possible squad, the East German and West German teams played against each other, and the winning team earned the right to compete. Before trying to qualify for the 1964 Olympic football tournament in Tokyo, the East German side first defeated the West German team 3–0 and 2–1 in September 1963. With the side representing Germany selected, the team then needed to defeat both the Netherlands and the Soviet Union to earn the Olympic berth. Obviously, the team of East German athletes would have no trouble entering the Soviet Union to play that home-and-away series, but scheduling two games with the Netherlands, a NATO member, was more complicated.[19]

The Dutch, football crazed but with limited influence or power in NATO, did not want to lose this chance to qualify for the Olympic competition. In contrast to the World Cup qualifications, this time the Dutch argued that East Germany's football team should be permitted to visit the Netherlands because these athletes represented the all-German Olympic team. Working quickly to ensure that the matches could proceed, the Dutch representative to PAC reported just three weeks after the East German defeat of the West German team that this squad, composed entirely of East German athletes, would soon schedule a match in the Netherlands. In contrast with events in 1961, the Dutch reported to their NATO colleagues that this current team "was considered by the West German authorities to be an all-German team" and that the East German "team had undertaken to refrain from political" actions while in the Netherlands. Because of these two stipulations, the Dutch were "prepared to issue visas to the members of the team, provided they were in possession of TTDs." While other NATO member states reported this turn of events to their own foreign ministries, the fact that this squad of East Germans represented the all-German Olympic team, which the Federal Republic government sanctioned, resulted in little discussion at NATO. Embassy representatives at the quadripartite meeting supported the ATO authorization of TTDs specifically for the "German pre-Olympic team," whom the Dutch would instruct to refrain from political activity.[20]

The competitions went ahead as scheduled, and the East German press provided extensive coverage of the first match on March 14 in Amsterdam.

Neues Deutschland journalist Joachim Pitzner detailed the visit, beginning with the team's travel to the Netherlands. He noted that the team received a kind welcome upon their arrival at the Amsterdam airport as well as excellent hospitality from the Dutch in their travels and at their hotel. Pitzner also highlighted the visa situation, writing: "You have to give the meeting a symbolic meaning. You can't read it in the newspapers, but even in small discussions the Dutch football fans easily remember the refusal of entry before the last World Cup, which prevented a qualification match on Dutch soil." To the East Germans, then, the fact that their team was even in the Netherlands to play was "a sign that the ice wall of Berlin's visa blockade is beginning to melt." After the 1–0 victory over the Dutch, Pitzner's postgame recap story, while not mentioning the visa problems, nonetheless described the opponents as the "brave Dutch boys and the great hosts." This game was indeed a victory for East Germany both on and off the pitch.[21]

The UEFA youth football tournament scheduled to begin less than two weeks later presented a different scenario as East Germany sought to send a team separately from West Germany. At the February 11 PAC meeting, the Dutch had addressed football in two consecutive meeting points: the UEFA junior tournament and the Olympic qualification matches. One month before the UEFA junior tournament began, the Dutch representative reported that "the Royal Netherlands Football Association is bound to invite the East German Youth Team for the coming European Youth Football Tournament" because UEFA "competitions shall be open to the representative or club-teams of all the national associations in membership with UEFA." However, as he noted, the Dutch government, pursuant to NATO travel restrictions, concluded "that no sufficient grounds exist for issuing entrance visa to an East German Youth Football Team for participation" in the tournament scheduled to begin at the end of March.[22]

Between this discussion at NATO and the tournament itself, football executives sought to ensure that the East Germans could participate in the tournament. Knowing that the East German–Dutch Olympic qualification match in the Netherlands was proceeding, the FIFA secretary corresponded with International Olympic Committee chancellor Otto Mayer regarding the difficulties the Dutch football federation was having. Mayer responded that the IOC president and two vice presidents (an Englishman, American, and Frenchman) were planning a coordinated appeal to their foreign ministers, but with the outcome unknown he recommended the football federations appeal to the ATO directly. Meanwhile FIFA president Sir Stanley Rous called on the Foreign Office in London regarding the status of travel restrictions on East Germans, particularly whether the East German team would be permitted to travel to the Netherlands for the youth tournament. The Foreign Office representative noted that Rous "accepted all this in very odd spirit, indicating that he quite understood the political background and was personally sickened by the political and propagandist element which the East Germans tried to introduce into what should be simply sporting functions." Rous also scathingly compared the East Germans to the Indonesians, who had recently organized the Games of the Newly Emerging Forces in opposition to the Olympic movement. As an Englishman Rous acknowledged "the special difficulties presented by East German teams"; however, as president of the most powerful international federation, he also remarked that "as time went on exclusion of such teams from NATO countries would tend to cause Western organisations and Governments increasing embarrassment." Rous needed to make a personal appeal to his government on his sport's behalf, but he also knew not to issue any outright ultimatums that would have no real impact on the Foreign Office's policies.[23]

While this decision had clearly been made at the end of February and the FIFA executive knew what would transpire, the Dutch football federation did not publicly announce this lack of travel permits for the East German team until one week before the tournament kicked off. The Dutch and all of its allies in NATO knew the backlash that every visa refusal for East German athletes garnered in the press, both behind the Iron Curtain and within NATO countries, and they sought to minimize protests and efforts to obtain the TTDs for the East German team by leaving little time for protests to be mounted. When *Neues Deutschland* raised the visa refusal on its pages, they did so in typical fashion. On March 24, two days before the tournament began, the headline proclaimed "Visa Was Granted," but the second headline noted "'Travel Office' Prevents GDR Participation in the UEFA Tournament." The paper noted that while the Dutch Foreign Ministry had granted visas, it was the "dishonest" ATO that refused to authorize the travel documents. Many NATO states used this technicality in the 1960s to deflect blame when it came to East German athletes being unable to participate in sporting events.[24]

The East German football federation, not surprisingly, protested this action to UEFA and hoped that the continental organization could force a last-minute change. UEFA's lobbying on behalf of the Dutch football federation and themselves was to no avail. *Neues Deutschland* quoted both the Greek team captain and the Polish team leader; the latter stated: "We are dismayed by this decision. Sports should not be a political football. The youth, the future of the people—one should not separate, but unite." With the East German team unable to travel, UEFA's Youth Committee met the day before the tournament began and modified the group schedule so that Scotland played Switzerland twice (as compared to the typical three-team group stage with each team playing the other two teams once). The tournament then proceeded as planned, with a young Franz Beckenbauer playing well for the West German team. Nonetheless, criticism of the Dutch appeared not only in the East German press but also in the Dutch press and UEFA. The Dutch representative reported at the next NATO PAC meeting, on April 2 in the middle of the tournament, about "the strong public pressure to which his Government had been subjected as a result of the refusal to permit the 'East German Football Association' to compete in this tournament; the Netherlands Government had not given way to this pressure and it was their hope that, in similar future cases, other member governments would react in the same way." Similarly, when the UEFA general assembly met in June 1964 and the Soviet delegate raised this problem, the Dutch repeated what their compatriots had told NATO. The Swiss president of UEFA noted that FIFA, UEFA, and the Dutch federation "had made every possible endeavour—by means of innumerable interventions put forward in personal discussions, at conferences, by cable and in writing—to enable the East German Youth Team to participate."[25]

UEFA reported that the East German team's travel visas were ultimately granted, but too late, not until after the tournament began (although neither the East German press nor NATO member state diplomats reported that the East German team received travel documents). Following this discussion at their general assembly, UEFA used the problems from the youth tournament to push the ATO to confirm that their policies had been changed and that the next UEFA event, the European Club competition, would not be hit by similar problems. The ATO, under the guidance of the British Foreign Office, responded with an explanation of the TTD policy, emphasizing that "it is impossible to foresee precisely what will be the situation when these events are due to take place," and clarifying that the policy is in place for "national" teams. Although the international football community might have been a bit confused about this policy, NATO and the ATO had no plans to change it for a single sporting event, as they had repeatedly maintained that position since the appearance of the Berlin Wall.[26]

These two instances in March 1964 when East Germany sought to send a football team to the Netherlands presented a mixed signal about the travel restrictions on East Germans. As questions regarding travel for East German athletes continued to arise, the Federal Republic's PAC representative made a lengthy statement on the matter. While the statement was about travel restrictions and permissions in general, he also commented on "the problem of sports exchanges, where the restrictive regulations are applied by the Federal Government more stringently than by the other NATO countries." NATO's policy required East German athletes to be part of an all-German team in order to receive travel documents, and the Federal Republic encouraged the creation of these combined teams. They even admitted that, for sports such as football, "what is politically relevant for us in view of the circumstances is that an all-German team can be set up at all—even if it has to be the one coming from the Soviet zone." Other NATO states that wanted to invite East Germans to their events, such as Norway, which wanted one of the world's best ski jumpers to participate in its annual ski jump festival, were becoming increasingly frustrated with what appeared to be an unevenly applied regulation. In fact, quite the opposite was the case: athletes who competed as representatives of the German Democratic Republic were consistently denied travel visas to compete at events held in NATO member states after the construction of the Berlin Wall in August 1961. When East German athletes represented an all-German team, such as during the Olympic football qualification match in the Netherlands, the ATO granted their travel documents so that they could participate in sporting events.[27]

While the sport organizations in most NATO member states confronted this problem of East German teams during the 1960s, the Netherlands and Portugal had problems with football events in quick succession. Although the matches affected in the early 1960s were not major tournaments, they nonetheless were important to NATO's internal diplomatic relationships. Football led smaller states to take a stronger stance within NATO, to show that they were not simply "loyal allies" following the United States.[28] Although neither Portugal nor the Netherlands actually went against NATO, they pushed back a bit on the travel ban on East Germans at first before they ultimately fell in line. The desire of the Portuguese and Dutch to organize successful football events that included East German teams reveals the complicated nature of NATO and the extent to which the less powerful states sought to exert themselves. The tripartite decisions regarding travel ultimately guided the final NATO actions, which ostensibly reinforced the strength of the larger and most powerful states within the organization. However, the Netherlands, Portugal, and several other states repeatedly supported an exception to the travel ban for sport and led numerous debates within the alliance that the quadripartite powers could not easily quash.

Because football matches (or the lack thereof) could impact the perception of the alliance among member states' domestic populations, NATO recognized it could not ignore the public backlash against the impact East German travel restrictions had on sporting events. In fact, NATO had promoted the concept of the Atlantic community and responded to communist criticism by creating its Committee on Information and Cultural Relations in the early 1950s.[29] These actions became more difficult in the 1960s with the growth of peace movements and NATO actions that resulted in tremendous communist criticism—such as the political interference by NATO in sport. Media coverage of the refusal of visas to the East German youth team forced the Dutch government to respond to a strong negative reaction from the Dutch football federation as well as within the media. If the Dutch had to face a backlash for upholding NATO policies, they were adamant that their NATO allies should also hold firm to the alliance's policies. Although, in the view of the media and the general public, the East German–Dutch football matches had been treated differently for no apparent reason, there was in fact a clear distinction between these two events that led to their different treatment.

NATO had a vested interest in the scheduling of football matches during the Cold War, particularly when their cancellation because of their own travel policies resulted in negative publicity for the alliance on both sides of the Iron Curtain. The Western states called the erection of the Berlin Wall a restriction on the freedom of movement, but NATO's retaliatory response further limited travel for East Germans. The GDR claimed the wall served security purposes, but the physical division prevented Berlin residents from moving freely between both parts of the city. The sanctions imposed by the quadripartite states on East Germany and maintained by all NATO states actually further limited opportunities that some East Germans might have had for contact with people from outside the communist bloc. Even when diplomats accepted the premise that the meeting of younger athletes on the football pitch could have positive results, the overriding concern was the political and propaganda implications of recognizing East German state symbols at a football match. Thus, the argument against the GDR's restriction of movement relied on an even greater limitation of travel—which impacted the athletes and spectators, as well as an entire country that wanted to follow the action of its national team, by depriving them of the ability to play football in NATO member states if the team represented the GDR itself. Because of the broad interest in international football matches at all levels, football conveyed NATO policies to the general public. Whereas in 1956 the Portuguese had suggested that NATO "sponsor sports meetings as a means of increasing interest in NATO among youth,"[30] the organization's involvement in football in the early 1960s—and in minor matches at that—instead created a negative backlash against the alliance by communicating a policy that appeared, to the average citizen, to simply prevent football matches from taking place.

Notes

The author would like to thank Francisco Pinheiro and Candace Sobers for their assistance on the Portuguese section, Thomas Junod and Nicholas Bouchet at UEFA, Max Rottenecker for his research assistance, and Andrew Johnstone and the anonymous reviewers for their feedback.

1. David Black, "Dreaming Big: The Pursuit of 'Second Order' Games as a Strategic Response to Globalization," *Sport in Society* 11, no. 4 (2008): 467–480.

2. Telegram 1585, Foreign Office to Bonn, September 14, 1960, Foreign Office (FO) 371/154260, National Archives, London, United Kingdom (hereafter TNA); telegram 891, Bonn to Foreign Office, September 15, 1960, FO 371/154260, TNA; telegram 1279, Guenyveau to Diplomatie Paris, September 19, 1960, 179QO/14, Centre des Archives diplomatiques de La Courneuve, Paris, France (hereafter CADC); "Hockey og politikk," *Aftenposten*, November 3, 1960, 18.1/74 Öst-tyske innreisebestemmelser. Bind IV, Utenriksdepartement, Oslo, Norway (hereafter UD); "Vest-Berlin telte mer enn en ishockey-kamp," *Verdens Gang*, November 4, 1960, 18.1/74 Öst-tyske innreisebestemmelser. Bind IV, UD; Heather L. Dichter, "'We Have Allowed Our Decisions to Be Determined by Political Considerations': The Early Cold War in the International Ski Federation," *Sport in History* 37, no. 3 (2017): 290–308.

3. FIFA Minutes of the XXVIIth Congress, Helsinki, July 24–26, 1952, 25th to 27th Ordinary Congress, 1946–1952 Activity Report Minutes, FIFA Archives,

Zurich, Switzerland; Uta A. Balbier, *Kalter Krieg auf der Aschenbahn: der deutsch-deutsche Sport, 1950–1972; eine politische Geschichte* (Paderborn: F. Schöning, 2007); Alan McDougall, *Youth Politics in East Germany: The Free German Youth Movement, 1946–1968* (New York: Oxford University Press, 2004), 78–98.

4. Linda Risso, *Propoaganda and Intelligence in the Cold War: The NATO Information Service* (London: Routledge, 2014); telegram 548, Leusse, REPAN to Diplomatie Paris, November 2, 1960, 105PO/1, box 10, Centre des Archives diplomatiques de Nantes, Nantes, France (hereafter CADN); telegram 333, UK Delegation to NATO Paris to Foreign Office, FO 371/154264, TNA; "Irritasjon over visumnektelse for østtyskere," *Aftenposten*, November 2, 1960, 18.1/74 Öst-tyske innreisebestemmelser. Bind IV, UD.

5. Kim Christiaens, Idesbald Goddeeris, Frank Gerits, and Giles Scott-Smith, "The Benelux and the Cold War: Re-interpreting West-West Relatons," *Dutch Crossings* 40, no. 1 (2016): 3; Lawrence S. Kaplan, preface to *Transforming NATO in the Cold War: Challenges beyond Deterrence in the 1960s*, ed. Andreas Wenger, Christian Nuenlist, and Anna Locher (London: Routledge, 2007), x.

6. AC/119-R(60)41—Committee of Political Advisers Meeting held on Tuesday, 15th November, 1960, Action Sheet, November 17, 1960, NATO Archives, Brussels, Belgium (hereafter NATO).

7. AC/119-WP(59)112—Internal and External Situation of the Soviet Occupied Zone, October 27, 1959, NATO; Margarete Myers Feinstein, *State Symbols: The Quest for Legitimacy in the Federal Republic of Germany and the German Democratic Republic, 1949–1959* (Boston: Brill, 2001), 40–51; AC/119-WP(60)3—New Flag of the Soviet Occupied Zone of Germany, January 13, 1960, NATO; telegram A 10049, Ambassaden i Bonn to Utenriksdepartementet, September 12, 1960, 18.1/74 Öst-tyske innreisebestemmelser. Bind IV, UD; AC/119-R(60)32—Committee of Political Advisers Meeting held on Tuesday, 13th September 1960, Action Sheet, 16 September 1960, NATO; telegram 936, Bonn to Foreign Office, September 23, 1960, FO 371/154260, TNA; Nic. A. Fougner, Notat—Reiserestriksjoner mot Öst-Tyskland. Presse- og kring-kastingsfolk til idrettsstevne i Norge, February 6, 1961, 18.1/74 Öst-tyske innreisebestemmelser. Bind V, UD.

8. Telegram POLTO 1138, Nolting, Paris to Secretary of State, February 21, 1961, Record Group (RG) 59, Central Decimal File (CDF) 1960–63/862.181, box 2644, National Archives, College Park, Maryland (hereafter NA); Telegram POLTO 1159, Nolting, Paris to Secretary of State, February 23, 1961, RG 59, CDF 1960–63/862.181, box 2644, NA.

9. Telegram 465, Lightner, Berlin to Secretary of State, February 24, 1961, RG 59, CDF 1960–63/862.181, box 2644, NA; telegram 309–11, Chalvron, Haussaire Berlin to Ambafrance Bonn, February 27, 105PO/1, box 10, CADN; telegram TOPOL 1168, Rusk to Amembassy Paris, February 24, 1961, RG 59, CDF 1960–63/862.181, box 2644, NA; telegram 342, Bowles, Department of State to USBER Berlin, February 27, 1961, RG 59, CDF 1960–63/862.181, box 2644, NA.

10. Telegram 901–04, François Seydoux, Bonn to Diplomatie Paris, February 27, 1961, 105PO/1, box 10, CADN; telegram, POLTO 1182, Burgess, Paris to Secretary of State, February 28, 1961, RG 59, CDF 1960–63/862.181, box 2644, NA.

11. Telegram 545, Elbrick, Lisbon to Secretary of State, February 28, 1961, RG 59, CDF 1960–63/862.181, box 2644, NA. For a useful overview of facets of Portuguese decolonization see Stewart Lloyd-Jones and Antonio Costa Pinto, eds., *The Last Empire: Thirty Years of Portuguese Decolonization* (Chicago: Intellect, 2003).

12. POLAD(61)11—Restriction on travel of residents of East Germany, March 3, 1961, NATO; AC/119-WP(60)26—Policy towards Visitors from East Germany, March 9, 1960, NATO; telegram 354, Rusk to USBER Berlin, March 4, 1961, RG 59, CDF 1960–63/862.181, box 2644, NA; Compte rendu de la réunion quadripartite, March 22, 1961, 178QO/1719, CADC.

13. Airgram, POLTO G-1399, Wolf, USRO/Paris to SecState, March 10, 1961, RG 59, CDF 1960–63/862.181, box 2644, NA; AC/119-R(61)9—Committee of Political Advisers Meeting held on 7th March, 1961, Action Sheet, 10 March 1961, NATO; "England Youths Lose in Lisbon," *Times*, April 3, 1961, 2; "Yesterday's Football Results," *Times*, April 5, 1961, 14; "Yesterday's Results," *Times*, April 7, 1961, 20.

14. "Einreise erzwungen," *Neues Deutschland*, March 10, 1961, 10; telegram 393–94, Chalvron, Haussaire Berlin to Ambafrance Bonn, March 13, 1961, 105PO/1, box 10, CADN; P. J. Bauwens to Combined Board Travel Office, February 28, 1961, 105PO/1, box 10, CADN; telegram 331–33, Chalvron, Haussaire Berlin to Ambafrance Bonn, March 2, 1961, 105PO/1, box 10, CADN; letter 619, E. Ulstein, Paris (NATO) to Utenriksdepartement, March 2, 1961, 18.1/74: Öst-tyske innereisebestemmelser. Bind VI, UD.

15. Portuguese newspapers also suffered from censorship under Salazar. *A Bola*'s coverage previewing the tournament, including the three teams that later withdrew, began in March. Compte rendu de la réunion quadripartite, April 13, 1961, 178QO/1719, CADC; "Under 21 Tournament," *O Século*, March 30, 1961, 8; "Wave of Anti-American Feeling Sweeps Portugal," *Times*, April 8, 1961, 7; Heather L. Dichter, "'A Game of Political Ice Hockey': NATO Restrictions on East German Sport Travel in the Aftermath of the Berlin Wall," in *Diplomatic Games: Sport, Statecraft and International Relations since 1945*, ed. Heather L. Dichter and Andrew L. Johns (Lexington: University Press of Kentucky, 2014), 32–36; letter, Knut Hedemann to Norges Delegasjon (NATO), Paris, March 1961, 18.1/74: Öst-tyske innereisebestemmelser. Bind VI, UD; airgram, POLTO G-1399, Wolf, USRO/Paris to SecState, March 10, 1961, RG 59, CDF 1960–63/862.181, box 2644, NA.

16. Frank J. Lechner, *The Netherlands: Globalization and National Identity* (New York: Routledge, 2008).

17. C-R(61)40—Summary Record of a Restricted meeting of the Council held at the Permanent Headquarters, Paris, XVIe., on Thursday, 31st August, 1961, 13 September 1961, NATO; Michalski to Koniklijke Nederlandsche Voetbalbond,

September 15, 1961, Stiftung Archiv der Parteien und Massenorganisationen der DDR im Bundesarchiv, DY 12/2081, Bundesarchiv, Berlin, Germany; "Neue Niederlage," *Neues Deutschland*, September 18, 1961, 6; H. Käser to Otto Mayer, December 27, 1963, included in International Olympic Committee, Request for visas for participation in sport events in NATO countries, January 1964, Republique Democratique Allemagne, Correspondance 1963–1971, Olympic Studies Centre, Lausanne, Switzerland (hereafter OSC).

18. Dichter, "'A Game of Political Ice Hockey"; A. E. Donald to J. S. Whitehead, March 6, 1962, FO 371/163681, TNA; telegram POLTO CIRC 89, Finletter, Paris to Secretary of State, March 7, 1962, RG 59, CDF 1960–63/862B.181, box 2673, NA; POLTO A CIRC 175, USRO/Paris to SecState, March 8, 1962, RG 59, CDF 1960–63/862.181, box 2645, NA; A. E. Donald to J. S. Whitehead, March 6, 1962, FO 371/163681, TNA; telegram POLTO CIRC 89, Finletter, Paris to Secretary of State, March 7, 1962, RG 59, CDF 1960–63/862B.181, box 2673, NA.

19. Balbier, *Kalter Krieg auf der Aschenbahn*; Ergänzungen zum Kommuniqué und Beschlußprotokoll, East-West NOK, November 18, 1959, Heft 208, Deutscher Olympischer Sportbund, Frankfurt, Germany; "Überlegen herausgespielter Sieg der Zonen-Fußballelf," *Frankfurter Allgemeine Zeitung*, September 16, 1963, 9; "DFB-Amateure gewinnen zweite Olympiaqualifikation," *Frankfurter Allgemeine Zeitung*, September 22, 1963, 9; H. Käser to Otto Mayer, October 30, 1963, Fédération Internationale de Football Association (Fifa): Correspondance 1959 - août 1964, OSC.

20. Cees Wiebes and Bert Zeeman, "'I Don't Need Your Handkerchiefs': Holland's Experience of Crisis Consultation in NATO," *International Affairs* 60, no. 1 (1990): 91–113; AC/119-R(63)34—Committee of Political Advisers Meeting on 15th October 1963 Action Sheet, 18 October 1963, NATO; letter 2005, Bjørn Kristvik to Utenriksdepartement, October 15, 1963, 33.12/45. Pass- og visumforhold m.h.t. Ost-Tyskland. Bind II, UD; AC/119-R(64)5—Committee of Political Advisers Meeting on 11th February, 1964 Action Sheet, 14 February 1964, NATO; Airgram A-531, R. Glenn Mays, Jr., USBER Berlin to Amembassy Bonn, 17 February 1964, RG 59, CFPF 1964–66, EDU 15 GER E, box 363, NA; Compte rendu de la réunion quadripartite, February 19, 1964, 178QO/1720, CADC; telegram 453–54, Margerie, Bonn to Berlin, February 21, 1964, 105PO/1, box 9, ACDN; telegram 618–619, Winckler, Haussaire Berlin to Ambafrance Bonn, March 6, 1964, 105PO/1, box 9, CADN.

21. Joachim Pitzner, "DDR-Fussballer herzlich begrüßt," *Neues Deutschland*, March 13, 1964, 8; Joachim Pitzner, "Magerer, aber wertvoller 1:0 Sieg," *Neues Deutschland*, March 15, 1964, 8.

22. AC/119-R(64)5—Committee of Political Advisers Meeting on February 11, 1964, Action Sheet, February 14, 1964, NATO; J. L. van der Kun, Netherlands Delegation to NATO to R. W. J. Hooper, Assistant Secretary General for Political Affairs, NATO, February 28, 1964, 18.1/74. Öst-Tyske innreisebestemmelser. Visumforholdet til Öst-Tyskland. Bind XII, UD.

23. H. Käser to Otto Mayer, February 11, 1964, Fédération Internationale de Football Association (Fifa): Correspondance 1959 - août 1964, OSC; letter, Otto Mayer to H. Käser, February 17, 1964, Fédération Internationale de Football Association (Fifa): Correspondance 1959 - août 1964, OSC; HTA Overton, T.T.D.s, February 26, 1964, FO 371/177987, TNA.

24. "Visa waren erteilt," *Neues Deutschland*, March 24, 1964, 6; Dichter, "'A Game of Political Ice Hockey'"; Dichter, "'We Have Allowed Our Decisions."

25. "UEFA protestiert," *Neues Deutschland*, March 25, 1964, 8; Minutes of VIIth UEFA Ordinary General Assembly, June 17, 1964, 259, box RM00005989, UEFA Archives, Nyon, Switzerland (hereafter UEFA); "Empörung in Holland," *Neues Deutschland*, March 26, 1964, 8; *UEFA Official Bulletin* 27 (May 1964): 259, box RM00000676, UEFA; "Die Jugendauswahl siegt," *Frankfuerter Allgemeine Zeitung*, March 28, 1964, 12; AC/119-R(64)12—Committee of Political Advisers Meeting on 2nd April, 1964 Action Sheet, 9 April 1964, NATO; RD Clift, UK Delegation to NATO to DN Beevor, Foreign Office, April 6, 1964, FO 371/177988, TNA.

26. Minutes of VIIth UEFA Ordinary General Assembly, June 17, 1964, 259, box RM00005989, UEFA; Report of the General Secretary—1964 and 1965, March 1966, 9, box RM0000917, UEFA; A. E. Stoddart to J. L. Bullard, Bonn, July 9, 1964, FO 371/177989, TNA; telegram, ATO Berlin to UEFA, July 7, 1964, FO 371/177989, TNA.

27. Remarks made by the German Representative at the Meeting of the Political Advisors Committee on TTDs, April 6, 1965, 18.1/74 Öst-tyske innreisebestemmelser. Visum forholdet til Öst-Tyskland. Bind 13, UD.

28. Kim Christiaens, Idesbald Goddeeris, Frank Gerits, and Giles Scott-Smith, "The Benelux and the Cold War: Re-interpreting West-West Relatons," *Dutch Crossings* 40, no. 1 (2016): 3; David J. Snyder, "The Dutch Encounter with the American Century: Modernization, Clientelism, and the Uses of Sovereignty during the Early Cold War," *Dutch Crossing* 40, no. 1 (2016): 11.

29. Linda Risso, *Propoaganda and Intelligence in the Cold War: The NATO Information Service* (London: Routledge, 2014), 63–66.

30. C-M(56)5—Implementation of Article 2 of the North Atlantic Treaty, January 13, 1956, NATO.

Sheilas, Wogs, and Poofters in a War Zone

The "Socceroos" and the 1967 Friendly Nations Tournament in Vietnam

Erik Nielsen

Until January 31, 2015, the Australian men's national soccer team had won only one major international trophy. That night's extra-time victory against South Korea in the Asian Cup final supplemented another victory against that country under altogether different circumstances. The 1967 National Day Tournament was won in Saigon during a bloody war, amid great hardship for the team. The aftermath of the tour provoked a tension between the (admittedly partial) archival record and team captain Johnny Warren's belief that the Australian Federal government had sent the team as part of a propaganda offensive. An examination of this tension tells much about the perceived role that sport has played in Australia's diplomatic approach and about the extent to which this perception is supported by the historical record. The inconsistencies that such an examination reveals illuminate the cultural forces that mediate the popular understanding of these diplomatic efforts. This chapter will show that the most important cultural forces that mediated the popular understanding of Australia's involvement in Vietnam in general are particularly relevant to how the diplomatic importance of the 1967 Australian soccer tour to Vietnam is perceived.

Engagement with East Asia was a key plank of Australia's diplomatic approach in the years following the Second World War. While the White Australia policy continued to restrict Asian immigration in particular to Australia, the policy of "Forward Defence" saw Australia militarily and politically project into the Asian theater. Australian military personnel played a key role in the occupation of Japan and participated in the Malayan Emergency. Between 1955 and 1988, the Royal Australian Air Force maintained a base at Butterworth on the Malay Peninsula, complete with the Australian families of servicemen being housed in the nearby town of Penang. Australia also contributed to the Colombo Plan, which saw students from across Asia study at Australian universities. Like military action in Southeast Asia, which included participation in the Vietnam War, the Colombo Plan aimed to prevent the spread of communism in the region.[1]

While the Asian region was an increasingly important focus of Australian diplomacy, the role that sport played in the nation's diplomatic efforts remains unclear. Public servants working on the Colombo Plan expressed sporadic interest in using sport to further the program's goals, although it is unclear whether the idea gained purchase with decision makers. The 1967 Australian soccer tour to Vietnam highlights the difficulties in assessing the role of sport in Australia's diplomatic efforts. The job of historians is made difficult by the National Archives of Australia's opaque approach to allowing access to records. As a result, engagement with unusual sources and debates is necessary to understand and assess the impact of Australian sport diplomacy on Australian and international political culture. The way that the shifting American approaches to memorializing Vietnam have shaped Australian responses to the same conflict is key to understanding Warren's belief that decisions made by the Australian government placed the team at significant and unjustified risk. The dynamic post–Second World War American culture has been at once well-received, begrudgingly accepted, and reviled across the world, and Australia is no exception.[2]

The issue of the treatment of Vietnam veterans provides an exemplar of how American ideas have shaped Australian ideas, regardless of their suitability to an Australian context. American Vietnam warriors and their supporters, including President Ronald Reagan, have from the 1980s onward demanded that the wider culture in general, and "the Left" in particular, atone for perceived mistreatment of soldiers upon their return from Vietnam. Their Australian counterparts adopted similar arguments and strategies to heal the dislocation from wider society that many Australian returned servicemen experienced. However, specific characteristics of the Australian experience of the war mean that American experiences of the war and its aftermath are unsuitable proxies. The immense power of the American social, political, and cultural machine has penetrated Australian society and influenced the way that its citizens have perceived this conflict. The society, politics, and culture of America therefore influence the impact that Vietnam has had on Australian individual and national identities.

Historians such as Chris Dixon have demonstrated that Australian participants in the Vietnam conflict have followed the lead of their American counterparts despite significant differences in the Australian context. They have sought to redress perceived slights at the hands of internal enemies by using American tactics, even though the experience of returning soldiers was different in Australia than it was in America. Warren has engaged in a similar process to that of Australian returned servicemen seeking succor in American examples by attributing the danger he experienced to a duplicitous and conniving government. While the government played an important role in facilitating the tour, apportioning all blame to the state neglects the agency that the Australian Soccer Federation (ASF) had in organizing the tour to a known war zone. Grand plans for a world tour by the Australian soccer team in 1967 were unfulfilled, leaving a trip to Vietnam as the only opportunity for vital international experience. This perspective allows another story to be told about the tour, and points to the complexities involved in understanding governmental action in the sporting sphere. The nexus between national and individual identities contributes to the way that the role of the state influences the way that individuals make sense of their experiences.

Australia's Experience of Vietnam

Despite significant differences between the two countries, the American cultural revisionism in regard to Vietnam that occurred during the 1980s heavily influenced the meaning that Australians attributed to Vietnam. Dixon argues that "it was during the 1980s that Vietnam veterans in Australia—like their American counterparts—found their political voice and insisted on political and cultural recognition of their plight." American veterans were aided by synergies between their goals and the New Right challenge to the permissive society that developed during the late 1960s and was fueled by anti–Vietnam War activism. Defeat in Indochina in 1975 and the resulting shock to confidence saw American political culture afflicted with a "Vietnam Syndrome," with American capabilities questioned further by incidents such as the hostage crisis that followed the Islamic Revolution in Iran. President Ronald Reagan's cultural agenda rested on a reformulation of the reasons for America's defeat. Reagan held that America was defeated not on the battlefields of Vietnam by a more committed adversary, but at home by the lack of resolve by liberal politicians and media. Bates argues that, in the course of a speech to the Veterans of Foreign Wars conference in August 1980 as Reagan was campaigning for the presidency, he "shifted any blame for the loss of the Vietnam conflict from the veterans and instead pointed a finger at elements within American society that had been duped by the enemy." Reagan's message rested easily with the laments of some defeated American soldiers that the strategy of a limited war had reduced their effectiveness.[3]

In March 1981 Reagan lamented that when American servicemen returned home "they were greeted by no parades, no bands, no waving of the flag they so nobly deserved." He also called for "a rising America—firm of heart, united in spirit, powerful in pride and patriotism," during his 1986 State of the Union address. In doing so, according to Beattie, he was setting the stage for "the Vietnam veteran [to emerge as] a hero and [take] his place alongside other American heroes." Reagan successfully deployed the anxieties and grievances of American veterans of the Vietnam War, regardless of scholarly doubts about the extent to which returning soldiers were treated poorly.[4]

This political revisionism found voice in a number of cultural representations that were as easily digestible in Australia as they were in America. Earlier representations of dislocation—"the Vietnam vet as a sadistic baby killer or brooding drug abuser"—were replaced by "a more positive picture that included the elements of Reagan's account." This progression is revealed in the production history of the *Rambo* film series. A story first novelized in 1972 in the tradition of earlier negative stereotypes, the films contained a more sympathetic protagonist and story arc that were "more in line with Reagan's consistent message on Vietnam." Beattie argues that, despite his dislocation from American society, John Rambo represents a hero that "performs his duty in the name of his country, whereas he may be abused and betrayed by bureaucratic officials."[5]

A vocal segment of the Australian veteran community felt similarly slighted and framed their political campaigns on American lines. Campaigns around issues such as potential harm from the use of Agent Orange and post-traumatic stress disorder drew heavily on American precedents. The American influence was felt culturally as well, as "welcome home" parades were held in both countries during the 1980s. Such parades were held in America throughout spring 1985, with another "Thankyou Vietnam Veterans" parade held in May 1987. The nature of American deployment in Vietnam, as individual tours of duty made by draftees, meant that parades during the war were an unwieldy way of marking their return. On the other hand, Australian returned servicemen were greeted with parades that marked the return of their unit from the conflict. No less than fifteen parades that welcomed home battalions or contingents occurred between 1966 and 1972 across a number of Australian cities. Nevertheless, Australian politicians copied their American counterparts and held a similar march in Sydney in October 1987—several months after the American "Thankyou Vietnam Veterans" parade. The claim that, despite the marches held between 1966 and 1972, Australian soldiers were not welcomed home until 1987 is expressed in official sources today. Dixon argues that the notion that Australian servicemen were not welcomed home until October 1987 is "wrong, and [reflects] the widespread conflation of Americans' and Australians' Vietnam experiences."[6]

Nevertheless, American myths of mistreatment provide an effective model that frames the anxiety of Australian ex-servicemen about their experiences. Ironically, the "most infamous" example of protestor mistreatment of soldiers in Australia, Nadine Jensen's smearing of paint, kerosene, and turpentine over First Battalion commander Lieutenant-Colonel Alex V. Preece, occurred at a parade explicitly held to welcome these soldiers home in Sydney in 1966. The notoriety attributed to Jensen's action by "veterans and their defenders routinely [ignores] the fact that the First Battalion was being welcomed home. Instead, Jensen's protest is often exaggerated into a commonplace rejection of veterans." The adoption of Jensen's act as representative of the protest movement in general, despite its isolated nature and Jensen's peripheral role within the organized anti-war movement, saw the act "exploited and misconstrued as a means of according blame on anti-war protesters for the alleged mistreatment of [Australian] Vietnam veterans."[7]

The Archival and Contemporary Record

The complexity that surrounds the tour is also reflected in other contemporary sources. Reports from Sydney soccer periodical *Soccer World* reflect the fact that the ASF had been planning a major international tour well before the notion of competing in Vietnam materialized. When leading ASF officials returned from a visit to the 1966 World Cup in England, they claimed to have attracted offers to host the Australian team from the football associations of Scotland, India, Japan, Denmark, Norway, and Italy. At the beginning of January 1967, the ASF announced plans for an ambitious eight-week tour of Asia; and in April *Soccer World* also reported the possibility that the team could be invited to play against leading Brazilian team Flamengo in Hong Kong. It was not until late September that *Soccer World* reported that the tour would take the team to Saigon and complained that "Vietnam is not ideal for talent scouting." By this time, it was clear that most of the Australian planning had come to naught. Previous offers were not consummated, and French-born journalist Lucien "Lou" Gautier affirmed that "it is now evident that without the invitation to Saigon there would be no Asian tour this year." In Gautier's view the ASF deserved "no credit" for the arrangements, "as they received an invitation from the South Vietnamese Government, via Canberra, to participate with all travelling and expenses paid." This offer was "a God-send, a face-saver for the ASF" who had returned from the World Cup with big plans that could not be delivered. Gautier clearly puts the influence on the South Vietnamese government, rather than the Australian government.[8]

The long-standing plans and negotiations undertaken by the ASF shed a different light on Warren's claims of a governmental conspiracy. The wider Australian football community and not just the ASF were keen to involve themselves in Asia through this Vietnam tour. Responding to criticism in an unnamed Sunday newspaper that the team's visit to the war zone was "indecent," Hungarian-born editor of *Soccer World* Andrew Dettre (writing under the pseudonym "Paul Dean") countered that through the tour "we indicate to the people of Vietnam that Australia is keen to participate in their sporting life, not just their war." Engagement with Asia was a long-standing concern of contributors to *Soccer World* throughout the 1960s; and, after the team returned, the paper printed a collection of extracts calling for closer footballing relations between Australia and Asia that dated from throughout the decade. Dettre's contribution is indicative of a sporting community with agency in the process of engaging with Vietnam, not one naively drawn along by the government.[9]

Assessing the extent to which the Australian government was responsible for sending the team from archival records is complicated by several factors.

The Australian government retains tight control over records that it has generated, and the Australian Freedom of Information Act of 1982 applies only to records created after its enactment. The Archives Act of 1983 provides that records can be exempt from public view for a host of reasons, including those that can "reasonably be expected to cause damage to the security, defence or international relations of the Commonwealth." Under this act, a series of cables from the Australian embassy in Saigon has been closed from public view. Included in this closure are cable number 1738 and perhaps an attached memorandum (number 1549) that provides advice about the tour. The closed selection contains some 350 cables on a raft of issues, which means it is unclear which cable was found objectionable by archives staff. Noted historian of Australian soccer Roy Hay also suggests that "the file relating to the tournament was never transferred to the National Archives and has been destroyed." These circumstances present constraints for a historian attempting to assess the role played by the Australian federal government in organizing the tour.[10]

Despite these gaps in knowledge about governmental involvement, much can be gleaned from the archival record. While Warren suggests that the invitation "came via the Australian government," the extant archival record shows that the ASF provided the organizational initiative for the tour from the Australian side. Rather than taking the lead, cables relating to the tour between the Australian embassy and the Department of External Affairs (EA) show that the Australian government played a reactive role in the tour's administration. Given the complexities involved in organizing participation at such short notice, both the Football Federation of Vietnam (FFV) and the ASF appear to have used Australian government agencies to provide advice and act as a conduit with which to expedite the negotiation process. The ASF seems to have opened communication with the Australian government in August after receipt of the South Vietnamese offer. On August 11, EA cabled the Australian embassy in Saigon with the information that the ASF had "received [an] invitation from Vietnamese counterpart to participate in football festival 1st to 14th November" and that the "Vietnamese would meet all costs." While the ASF was keen to accept the offer, they had two queries. First, they sought the advice of External Affairs as to whether it was safe to travel to Vietnam. That they felt compelled to do so speaks to the apprehension that the ASF may have felt about sanctioning the tour. The ASF was also eager to know which other teams had been invited to take part in the competition and would be "grateful [for an] urgent reply." Unfortunately, the embassy's response is among the cables restricted from view.[11]

The ASF's urgency was underscored in early October, when EA relayed to the Australian embassy that the "Federation is anxious to learn result of their letter of acceptance sent to Vietnam Football Federation." Reflecting an urgency that belies team coach Joe Vlasits's claims of inattentiveness, the next day embassy staff were able to inform EA that "Mr. Vo Van Ung, chairman of the Football Federation of Vietnam, yesterday confirmed that he had replied to the Australian Federation's letter of 1st September." To the doubtless relief of soccer officials reeling from earlier organizational failures, the cable contained more good news, as the financial terms stipulated by the ASF were agreed to by the FFV.[12] The archival record thus represents a middle ground between Vlasits's charge of ambassadorial neglect and Warren's allegation of governmental manipulation. EA and Australian embassy staff played key roles as a conduit between the ASF and the FFV, but the football authorities keenly prosecuted the tour's arrangements.

That the ASF did not always take advantage of EA's expertise is reflected in the problematic issue of accommodation. The nature of the conflict meant that quality accommodation in Saigon was limited, and Warren cites the conditions the team stayed in at the Golden Building to highlight the difficulties the team experienced in Vietnam. If Warren's description of the hotel referred to earlier is any indication, the team would have been bemused by the Vietnamese "International Tourist Year" brochure's promises of "excellent accommodation" in Saigon. This brochure does not mention the Golden Building, though, and it was also left off a list of principal hotels in Saigon compiled by the Australian Department of External Affairs as part of its Saigon Post report in December 1966. On August 2, the Australian embassy in Saigon warned the Department of External Affairs back in Canberra that an "accommodation shortage may be acute in September/October during the elections," a period that roughly correlates to the team's visit. John Holland also warned readers of *Soccer World* that the best of the city's hotels were reserved for "visiting military brass or . . . international businessmen" with extra pressure being placed on supply by the policy of American, Korean, and Australian governments to billet their Saigon staff in permanently leased hotel rooms. Original plans had the team staying at the President Hotel, and Australian embassy staff relayed to the ASF via the Department of External Affairs that it was "a recently constructed hotel." In fact, this hotel was not complete prior to the team's departure, and they and the teams were shifted to the Golden Building. Ironically, prior to the tour the ASF requested that the whole party (including officials and accompanying media) be housed together in the Golden Building. The imperatives of housing the team together, rather than in more acceptable conditions, caused the team some discomfort.[13]

Despite the passivity of the Department of External Affairs regarding the organization of this tour, some saw the propaganda advantages of the tour. Warren himself suggested in his newspaper column that the tour could help win the battle for hearts and minds among the South Vietnamese. The tour was also doubtless seen as a potential propaganda coup by the South Vietnamese. Scott Laderman has argued that the South Vietnamese government recognized that tourism "served an important ideological purpose, which the government . . . did not to [*sic*] hesitate to pursue. Just as the United States saw tourists as 'ambassadors of good will' in promoting American foreign policy objectives, so, too, did the Saigon government hope that foreign visitors would champion its cause." Most international governments recognized the public relations potential of sport, meaning that the South Vietnamese government was particularly keen for this tour to take place with Australian participation. Their keenness is reflected in the reputed half-time offer from Vice President Nguyen Cao Ky to the South Vietnamese team of six months' salary in exchange for beating Australia. However, large sections of the Australian government were influenced by a laissez faire approach to sport also evident in Britain, which saw sport as outside the scope for governmental interference.[14]

Other sections of the Australian diplomatic corps were keener on sport, as exemplified by the advocacy in 1956 of Australian consular figures such as A. H. Borthwick in Singapore and Colin Moodie in Burma for Australian athletes to visit the countries and play roles similar to those played by American athletes for the State Department. Sport had some influence on Australian efforts in the mid-1950s, even if athletes were generally kept at home: "From the mid-1950s, diplomatic posts were instructed to distribute Australian sporting magazines and newsletters and Radio Australia was directed to give greater attention to sporting events. Provision . . . was later made for the supply of sporting equipment, the construction of sporting fields and arenas, and physical education scholarships." This approach was also reflected in the Australian government's approach to Vietnam. Sometime in late 1966 or early 1967, Sydney media figure Clif Cary volunteered to tour Vietnam "as an individual or as a member of a team of sporting personalities" in a letter to Prime Minister Harold Holt. Cary felt that such a tour could sate troops who were "homesick for sport." While Holt thought the idea had "some merit," Minister for the Army Malcolm Fraser affirmed that the committee charged with reviewing proposals for troop entertainment had decided that "the proposal would not provide the type of entertainment sought in Viet Nam." Fraser argued that sports fans in Vietnam were served by Radio Australia and United States Armed Forces Radio broadcasts, the "bi-weekly 'Australian News'" and metropolitan newspapers, and films of sporting events supplied by commercial sponsors. Holt had to inform Cary that "the emphasis in the special circumstances of Viet Nam is on sending entertainers—musicians, singers and the like" rather than sportspeople. Cary was offered and accepted a role as a correspondent for Radio Australia, on the suggestion of Holt's assistant secretary A. T. Griffith, however. Holt, in contriving a role for Cary, represents a continuation of the view of Borthwick and Moodie, while Fraser represents the view that simply sending materials off was sufficient.[15]

Just as it is problematically assumed that the American veteran experience applies to Australia, it is problematically assumed that the Australian government used athletes in the same way that the American government used athletes. Throughout the Cold War, the US government developed a sophisticated program of sporting diplomacy that deployed athletes through the State Department as part of their struggle for international preeminence. Heather L. Dichter argues that the State Department "consciously used sport to promote the American way of life during the tense decades of the early Cold War." Toby C. Rider has shown that the State Department and the National Council for Free Europe (NCFE) backed the Union of Free Eastern European Sportsmen (UFEES), which attempted to negate the propaganda boost gained by the Soviet Union through its first appearance at the Summer Olympic Games in Helsinki in 1952. With financial and moral support from the NCFE, the UFEES agitated for a team of exiled Eastern Europeans to compete at Helsinki. While this attempt was unsuccessful, it demonstrated that "some of [the Eastern Bloc's] greatest cultural assets—its athletes—preferred to live in the 'free world.'" The State Department used a host of African American athletes to represent the United States abroad, including tennis players Althea Gibson and Arthur Ashe and basketballers Bill Russell, Kareem Abdul-Jabbar, Oscar Robertson, and the Harlem Globetrotters. Kevin B. Witherspoon argues that the use of African American athletes as cultural ambassadors was aimed at negating "the ultimate trump card [that the Soviets held] in the battle for the hearts and minds" of the nonwhite people "at the periphery of the Cold War"—that American racism "undermined true democracy." This international framework is vital in considering how Warren made sense of his time in Vietnam.[16]

Johnny Warren and the 1967 Tournament

As well as being the Australian captain during the 1967 tour, Johnny Warren is perhaps the most significant figure in Australia's soccer history. He captained the Australian team from 1967 until 1970, when his career was interrupted by a knee injury. He recovered in time to represent Australia at the 1974 World Cup, but his greatest influence was arguably in his post-playing career. He was a long-serving commentator for the Special Broadcasting Service (SBS), and played a key role in introducing Australians to the world game. SBS was established following a federal government inquiry in 1977 to provide programming aimed at Australia's growing migrant communities. Australia engaged in a large-scale migration program after the Second World War, largely from Eastern and Southern Europe, and soccer was a key cultural marker that these migrants brought to Australia. The game became central to SBS's programming, and Warren presented a number of programs and served as SBS's chief football analyst. Warren, along with colleague Les Murray, became the public face of soccer in Australia, keeping so-called New Australians abreast of international developments and introducing the game to the rest of the country. Just before his death in 2004 he was awarded the FIFA Order of Merit. His autobiography, entitled *Sheilas, Wogs, and Poofters*, was published in 2001, and it was in this forum that he brought the story of Australia's visit to Vietnam to light.[17]

The provocative title of Warren's book reflects the tone of advocacy he adopts throughout the book. Association, or "soccer," football has traditionally accepted a marginal place in Australia's variegated sporting landscape. Not content with supporting high-level competitions in the three major codes of football exported by the British to the rest of the world (soccer, rugby union, and rugby league), Australians invented a code of their own—Australian rules football. These sports represent the tip of the iceberg in terms of leisure choices in Australia, where the temperate climate means that sports restricted to summer in other parts of the world, such as tennis, golf, and even ocean swimming, can be enjoyed in Australia throughout the year. Soccer has found it difficult to find a niche in this competitive sporting environment, and other codes, jealous of the "World Game's" international appeal, have contributed to the situation through political and cultural means. Soccer has been denigrated as a game for females (Sheilas), foreigners (Wogs), and homosexual men (Poofters) by supporters of other codes in the Australian mainstream media. Warren appropriated these slurs in a clarion call for soccer's central place in Australian sporting culture. Traditional high participation rates have been matched by improved performances on the world stage by men and women since the book's publication, vital in a country where international success is a key indicator of sporting worthiness. Warren poignantly provided a motto for the appearance of the "Socceroos," Australia's men's national team, at the World Cup in 2006 after a thirty-two-year wait. Prior to his death, he promised that Australia's sole previous appearance in 1974 would not be its last, and that when it reached the competition for the second time he would declare "I told you so." This statement retains significant meaning for Australia's soccer community. From a marginal place and aided by the declining fortunes of challengers like the Australian rugby union team (the Wallabies) and the Australian men's national cricket team, the Socceroos have staked a claim to be Australia's "national team." While Australia had played international football for decades prior to the 1967 tour, Warren argues that the hardships experienced in Vietnam provided the real birth of the team. Warren's account is extremely significant to Australia's sporting culture.[18]

Warren devoted chapter 6 of his autobiography to the tour, contextualizing it in both footballing and political terms before offering a travelogue of the team's time in Vietnam. His description of the situation underscores the danger that the team was placed in while in Vietnam. In doing so, Warren clearly aligns himself with the soldiers in country. Traveling around the city and even training were made difficult by the constant threat of violence. Land mines on an adjacent field made training in a park inadvisable, and the team trained on the hotel roof instead. The team was also informed later that Vietnamese security forces had arrested Viet Cong operatives that had intended to "blow up the floor on which the Korean team was staying." The Korean team was situated a floor below the Australian team, so this act would have had a disastrous impact on the Australian team as well. Warren was also unimpressed by the team's accommodation at the Golden Building hotel: "I can't imagine a more inappropriate name. I remember one of the boys turning on a light switch when we first arrived and literally being thrown across the room by a mini-explosion. It was only some bad wiring but it's not the sort of incident that helps the nerves in a war-torn country. The place was also filthy. There were gecko lizards everywhere and we were immediately banned from eating any food there or consuming any local drinks." The team often ate at the Australian officer's mess in Saigon as a consequence, and there was a minor skirmish outside the compound during one of their visits. The resulting gunfire saw the players head "under the [billiards] table in the blink of an eye."[19]

Warren adopted the apprehension of Western soldiers in Vietnam about the loyalty of the South Vietnamese as well: "We simply didn't know which people in the street belonged to the Viet Cong but we were warned about them and we knew they were always around. The person serving breakfast could well be working for the Viet Cong at night. It was impossible to know." He also represented the Vietnamese crowds as intimidating, particularly when Australia defeated South Vietnam. However, the team's experience in the final against the unpopular South Korean team was markedly different, as the local fans vociferously supported Australia. In a collection of quotes collected by *Soccer World* after the team returned to Sydney, Warren commented, "I'll never forget the knowledgeable and friendly Saigon crowds. In the final against South Korea it was almost like playing at home."[20]

The most incendiary statement that Warren makes in his book is that the Australian federal government saw the team as expendable. Warren suggests that "soccer was considered the perfect public relations vehicle [for the South Vietnamese regime] because it was the most popular sport in Vietnam." Warren also implies connivance between the Australian and South Vietnamese governments, stating that "the behind-the-scenes politics of the trip were never really contemplated by our young and rather naïve minds. . . . It wasn't until years later that I realised how the team had been blindly steered into helping the war effort." Of course, the passage of time that saw Warren come to this conclusion was marked by the cultural revisionism of the Reagan Era. His claims to naïveté are undermined by his admission that, despite being "fascinated by the politics behind the war . . . soccer generally put such considerations, at best, on the backburner. It was difficult to get involved in the politics behind our war effort when I knew I was there to play soccer." Warren's approach is distinct from the American experience; Jabbar and Robertson in 1970–1971 explicitly disavowed the Vietnam War while they were in

Tanzania. Both basketballers exhibited an alert political consciousness, with Jabbar a keen participant in "the revolt of the black athlete" in the late 1960s and Robertson a "vocal and stubborn" militant head of the National Basketball Players Association. Jabbar and Robertson proved hard to handle for their diplomatic minders, missing events and complaining about arrangements. Witherspoon suggests that "increasingly militant black athletes like Jabbar and Robertson . . . reopened the issue of racism that State Department officials hoped was closing." The conduct of Jabbar and Robertson demonstrates that, regardless of governmental oversight, athletes retained some agency over their conduct and were not necessarily mere "dupes" of the government.[21]

Nevertheless, Warren claims that "the Australian government was only too willing to lend their support [to the cause of winning over the South Vietnamese through a major sporting event]. Suddenly, the Australian soccer team, usually of little consequence to the national interest, became a necessary part of the war effort." Warren also expressed amazement that the team was placed in such a dangerous position, and points out that, later on, teams in more popular sports like cricket and rugby league had avoided terror threats. Warren's view from hindsight is contradictory to the contemporary view of team coach Joe Vlasits, who was extremely critical of the lack of attention paid to the team by the Australian embassy in Saigon both prior to the tour and after the team arrived.[22]

Warren's remembrance of the tour has strongly influenced recent retellings of the story. Given that Warren recovered the story of the tour from historical obscurity, it is not surprising that his belief that the Australian government sent the team for propaganda reasons has influenced popular representations of the tour. Warren's story was the basis of an article by Richard Cooke on the Guardian Australia website. Cooke begins his account by describing the difficult context within which the tour took place; he repeats the notion that the tour was a "delusional propaganda exercise" but does not name the government he sees as responsible. Cooke also affirms that "the birthplace of the Socceroos success wasn't Sydney, it was Saigon" as per Warren. Cooke employs his own historiographical flourish by suggesting that "from Botany Bay to Gallipoli Australian history was built on bad ideas" and that the country's football history was no different. He also relays the fact that the team hotel (but not the Koreans) was a target of the Viet Cong, and notes that "a bomb attack might have been an improvement." Cooke adds further detail to the volatility surrounding the South Vietnamese game by alleging that rampant betting added to the tension. Apart from Warren's tale, Cooke's main sources appear to be interviews with players Ray Baartz, Atti Abonyi, and Stan Ackersley. Cooke provides an alternative explanation for the response of the Vietnamese crowd to the South Koreans and the Australians as participants in the final. Warren recounts the shock the team experienced when they realized that the crowd was cheering them, but is unable to provide a reason for this support. Baartz is similarly vexed, but tentatively suggests that the Australian style of play might be a reason for the support. Cooke is more positive about the playing style thesis, and also suggests that the Australians found favor for their habit of "mingl[ing] in the city." This behavior was in distinction to the conduct of the other teams, who were more likely to spend their time in the hotel. This is despite Warren's suggestion that team spirit was built because "the conditions of the tour had the effect of pushing us all together because no one was ever out sightseeing, shopping or on the town by themselves." Cooke also noted that the Korean team were "strong favourites with a sense of superiority about them."[23]

The positive response to the Australian team in the final against Korea can perhaps better be attributed to the low regard in which Korean soldiers were held by the Vietnamese population. Korean troops were sent to Vietnam under Lyndon Johnson's "More Flags" policy, and have been accused by Robert M. Blackburn of constituting a mercenary force. The presence of Koreans in Vietnam allowed the United States to "maintain the image that the United States was not acting unilaterally," even if the government of the Republic of Vietnam was less than enthusiastic about receiving a force of nonnative Asians in the country. Reviews of the Korean forces in Vietnam, both approving and critical, note the vigor with which they acted. The subject of Korean atrocities in Vietnam has also been an important political issue in South Korea itself, not least because of the challenge that such claims provided to a persistent Korean self-image of victimhood following Japanese occupation and the Korean War. In this context, it is probably not surprising that the Viet Cong decided to target the hotel accommodation of the Korean team in particular. The local politics of the war provide an explanation for the response of the Vietnamese crowd toward the Korean team.[24]

On the tenth anniversary of Warren's death, November 8, 2014, Sydney journalist Daniel Lane repeated the story in the *Sun-Herald* newspaper. Lane provides the most militaristic reading of the tour, and clearly aligns the team with Australia's soldiers in Vietnam. The hyperbolic tone of Lane's piece is reflected in its title: "When the Socceroos Won behind Enemy Lines." In fact, the team was in "friendly" territory given that South Vietnam was allied to Australia throughout the war, although the particular nature of this conflict meant that this position was not altogether secure. Lane refers to the tracksuit that the team was allowed to keep for winning the tournament as the one that "Johnny Warren and the 1967 national team went to war for" and says that the team was on "active duty" in Vietnam. Lane repeats the stories about the dangerous and unsanitary conditions in which the team played and stayed, but he is more circumspect about the issue of whether the Australian government sent the team for propagandistic reasons. Like Cooke, he ambiguously states that the team "arrived as part of a government offensive to try and win over the hearts and minds of the locals," a statement that does not identify which government was responsible.[25]

Lane's article was accompanied by a piece by Warren's successor as SBS chief football analyst, former Australian national team player Craig Foster. Foster does not specifically mention the tour in his article and, in fact, provides an alternative reading. Foster followed Warren in being an outspoken critic of soccer's marginal place in Australian sporting culture during the early stages of the twenty-first century. He suggests that Warren's advocacy of the sport marks him as a countercultural figure. Foster thus inverts the trope that had previously been deployed in analyses of this tour, aligning Warren with the leftist betrayers of veterans imagined by Reagan. Foster's former boss at SBS, the late Les Murray, put the story back on track around the hundredth anniversary of Anzac Day in April 2015. Murray repeats the claim that the Australian government sent the team abroad and describes the decision as "a dumb and ill-conceived propaganda exercise to further the cause of the dumb decision to involve Australia in a dumb war." The tenor of Murray's statement makes it clear that he was not a supporter of the Vietnam War, and his argument shows that conservative American reimaginings of Vietnam have influenced even the Australian Left. In fact, all these examples derive from what could loosely be described as liberal sources, even if the word has a different meaning in Australia than it does in America. The *Guardian* is explicitly liberal, and the *Sun-Herald* and its stablemate the *Sydney Morning Herald* pass for the alternative to Rupert Murdoch's avowedly conservative News Limited, as its Australian operations are known. SBS is explicitly progressive, with its focus on giving Australia's migrant communities a voice.[26]

Conclusion: Vietnam, Soccer, and the Development of Identities

Roy Hay correctly argues that "we simply don't know [whether the Australian government took the initiative to send the Australian soccer team to Vietnam in 1967] because the key files are no longer available."[27] The state of limbo that historians face has not prevented meaning and motive being attributed to the tour, by Johnny Warren in particular and those that followed his lead. The process of attributing meaning to this tour has not occurred in a vacuum. More accessible sources of knowledge in the form of American cultural reimaginings have influenced Australian understandings of the Vietnam War and its aftermath, including this example. Warren's "realization" is another example of Australians adopting the American process of dealing with the aftermath of the war, as identified by Chris Dixon. The Vietnam War had a clear influence on the development of individual and national identities, particularly in the 1980s and beyond. Social dislocation experienced by individuals contributed to an American national trauma that found voice in art and entertainment as well as politics. Despite vast differences in the experiences between the two countries, this process influenced Australia as well as the United States. The case of Johnny Warren shows that this process influenced other tourists to Vietnam, as well as soldiers. The story of soldiers betrayed by an uncaring government influenced Warren's attempts to make sense of his own experience. Like soldiers sent to Vietnam (not necessarily willingly), Warren and his team found themselves in extreme danger for reasons that make little sense. The contemporary record suggests that the Australian Soccer Federation played the key role in driving this tour, although the narrative of governmental negligence provides an easily digestible framework with which to make sense of this confusion. The construction of a duplicitous and uncaring government that would risk the welfare of civilians for dubious propaganda reasons explains the sheer absurdity of sending a sports team without any military training to a war zone. Warren's claim can be best understood in terms of the impact that American remembrance of Vietnam had on Australian culture, despite significant differences between the experience of the war in both countries.

The contemporary media and the archival record provide another perspective on the matter, with more hands (particularly those of the Australian Soccer Federation) on the decision to send the soldiers to the country. By this reading, the potential propaganda benefit was not the sole reason for the tour, which also included the ASF's need to find an overseas market for the team. Warren clearly did not have access to the archival account, and more digestible cultural products necessarily informed the tour's role in the formation of his own identity. But historians also have a limited perspective about this tour, due to both archival practices and the partial nature of archival records. Records that could shed light on the motivation of the government have been destroyed and restricted from public view. There is no perfect archival record that can debunk Warren's understanding of the tour and therefore completely undermine the message he took from the tour. Scholars are therefore left with two partial understandings of the tour, an individually resonant understanding based on a personal experience informed by wider culture and a more detached understanding based on restricted documentary evidence.

Notes

1. Graeme Cheeseman, "From Forward Defence to Self-Reliance: Changes and Continuities in Australian Defence Policy 1965–90," *Australian Journal of Political Science* 26, no. 3 (1991): 429–445; Dan Halvorson, "From Cold War Solidarity to Transactional Engagement: Reinterpreting Australia's Relations with East Asia, 1950–1974," *Journal of Cold War Studies* 18, no. 2 (2016): 130–159; Christine de Matos, "Occupation Masculinities: The Residues of Colonial Power in Occupied Japan," in *Gender, Power, and Military Occupations: Asia Pacific and the Middle East since 1945*, ed. Christine de Matos and Rowena Ward (New York: Routledge, 2012), 23–42; Robin Gerster, *Travels in Atomic Sunshine: Australia and the Occupation of Japan* (Carlton North: Scribe, 2008); Peter Dennis and Jeffrey Grey, *Emergency and Confrontation: Australian Military Operations in Malaya & Borneo* (St. Leonards: Allen & Unwin in association with the Australian War Memorial, 1996); Mathew Radcliffe, *Kampong Australia: The RAAF at Butterworth* (Sydney: New South, 2017); Daniel Oakman, "The Politics of Foreign Aid: Counter-Subversion and the Colombo Plan, 1950–1970," *Pacifica Review: Peace, Security & Global Change* 13, no. 3 (2001): 255–272.

2. Oakman, "The Politics of Foreign Aid," 269; "A Note on Archives and Archival Practices in Australia" in bibliography to *Australia's Vietnam War*, ed. Jeff Doyle, Jeffrey Grey, and Peter Pierce (College Station: Texas A&M University Press, 2002), 185; Roger Bell and Philip Bell, eds., *Americanization and Australia* (Sydney: UNSW Press, 1998).

3. Chris Dixon, "Redeeming the Warrior: Myth-Making and Australia's Vietnam Veterans," *Australian Journal of Politics and History* 60, no. 2 (2014): 222; Toby Glenn Bates, *The Reagan Rhetoric: History and Memory in 1980s America* (DeKalb: Northern Illinois University Press, 2011), 47.

4. W. H. Capps, *The Unfinished War: Vietnam and the American Conscience* (Boston: Beacon, 1990), 146; Keith Beattie, *The Scar That Binds: American Culture and the Vietnam War* (New York and London: New York University Press, 1998), 93.

5. Bates, *The Reagan Rhetoric*, 64–68; Beattie, *The Scar That Binds*, 94.

6. Jeff Doyle, "Other Contingents: Australian Veterans beyond Vietnam," in *Australia's Vietnam War*, ed. Jeff Doyle, Jeffrey Grey, and Peter Pierce (College Station: Texas A&M University Press, 2002), 82–85; Beattie, *The Scar That Binds*, 92; Dixon, "Redeeming the Warrior," 225.

7. Dixon, 225–226.

8. "World Tour Likely by Aust. This Year," *Soccer World*, July 15, 1966, 1; "Tour of Asia Certain," *Soccer World*, January 27, 1967, 1; "Crack Brazilians May Meet Us Next Oct.," *Soccer World*, April 21, 1967, 1; "Vietnam is Not Ideal for Talent Scouting," *Soccer World*, September 22, 1967, 3; "Australia's Tour Preparations," *Soccer World*, October 20, 1967, 8.

9. "Sth Vietnam our First opponents," *Soccer World*, October 27, 1967, 1; "We Helped Steer Our Soccer to Asian Waters," *Soccer World*, December 8, 1967, 4.

10. "A Note on Archives," 185; Austlii, Commonwealth Consolidated Acts, "Archives Act 1983—Sect 33: Exempt Records," www.austlii.edu.au/au/legis/cth/consol_act/aa198398/s33.html (accessed September 15, 2016); National Archives of Australia, "Item Details: Saigon cables—Inwards. Cables 1700 to 2050," https://recordsearch.naa.gov.au/SearchNRetrieve/Interface/DetailsReports/ItemDetail.aspx?Barcode=3043705&isAv=N (accessed April 15, 2015); Roy Hay, *Football and War: Australia and Vietnam 1967–1972, A Missing Part of the National Narrative* (Bannockburn: Sports & Editorial Services Australia, 2016), 21.

11. Johnny Warren with Andy Harper and Josh Whittington, *Sheilas, Wogs, and Poofters: An Incomplete Biography of Johnny Warren and Soccer in Australia* (Milsons Point: Random House, 2003), 83; Department of External Affairs, Outward Cablegram 1470: "Accommodation," August 11, 1967, Saigon cables outwards chronological numbers 1400 to 1899, series A6366, item SA1967/08T, National Archives of Australia, Canberra, Australian Capital Territory (hereafter NAA).

12. Department of External Affairs, Outward Cablegram (Australian Embassy, Saigon): 1839—"Australian Soccer Federation," October 3, 1967, South Vietnam Visit of Australia Notables and Officials, series A1838, item 3014/10/11/2 part 3, NAA; Department of External Affairs, Inward Cablegram (Australian Embassy, Saigon): 2019—"Visit by Australian Soccer Team," South Vietnam Visit of Australia Notables and Officials, series A1838, item 3014/10/11/2 part 3, NAA. For Vlasits's claim of inattentiveness, see "This Is How We Lived and Played in Saigon," *Soccer World*, November 24, 1967, 4.

13. Brochure, "Travel Guide—Viet Nam: 1967, International Tourist Year," 1967, item no.: 9860106005, John Proe Collection, Vietnam Virtual Archive, Texas Tech University, www.vietnam.ttu.edu/virtualarchive/items.php?item=9860106005, 7; Australian Embassy, Saigon, Report: Commonwealth of Australia: Department of External Affairs: Foreign Service Conditions—Saigon: December 1966, Decem-

ber 16, 1966, 10–11, Saigon—Post Report, series A1838, item 1362/5 part 2, NAA; Inward Cablegram 1571: "Accommodation," August 2, 1967, Saigon cables—Inwards. Cable nos. 1301 to 1699, series A6364, item SA1967/06, NAA; "Saigon Tough Place by Any Standard," *Soccer World*, October 27, 1967, 5; Department of External Affairs, Inward Cablegram: 2019—Visit by Australian Soccer Team, October 4, 1967, South Vietnam Visit of Australia Notables and Officials, series A1838, item 3014/10/11/2 part 3, NAA; Department of External Affairs, Inward Cablegram: 2128—Visit of Soccer Team, October 18, 1967, South Vietnam Visit of Australia Notables and Officials, series A1838, item 3014/10/11/2 part 3, NAA; Department of External Affairs, Outward Cablegram: 1948—Visit of Soccer Team, October 20, 1967; South Vietnam Visit of Australia Notables and Officials, series A1838, item 3014/10/11/2 part 3, NAA.

14. Hay, *Football and War*, 70; Scott Laderman, *Tours of Vietnam: War, Travel Guides, and Memory* (Durham, NC and London: Duke University Press, 2009), 22; Warren et al., *Sheilas, Wogs, and Poofters*, 93; Martin Polley, "The Amateur Ideal and British Sports Diplomacy, 1900–1945," *Sport in History* 26 no. 3 (2006): 450–67.

15. Oakman, "The Politics of Foreign Aid," 269; Clif Cary, letter to Harold Holt, n.d., broadcast of sporting items by Radio Australia for servicemen in Vietnam, series A463, item 1967/1172, NAA; A. Eggleton, letter to Malcolm Fraser, February 14, 1967, broadcast of sporting items by Radio Australia for servicemen in Vietnam, series A463, item 1967/1172, NAA; Malcolm Fraser, letter to Harold Holt, March 15, 1967, broadcast of sporting items by Radio Australia for servicemen in Vietnam, series A463, item 1967/1172, NAA; A. T. Griffith, Memorandum: "The Prime Minister," n.d., broadcast of sporting items by Radio Australia for servicemen in Vietnam, series A463, item 1967/1172, NAA; Harold Holt, letter to Clif Cary, March 23, 1967, broadcast of sporting items by Radio Australia for servicemen in Vietnam, series A463, item 1967/1172, NAA; J. Hall, letter to the Secretary of the Prime Minister's Department, April 11, 1967, broadcast of sporting items by Radio Australia for servicemen in Vietnam, series A463, item 1967/1172, NAA.

16. Heather L. Dichter, "Sport History and Diplomatic History," *H-Diplo Essay*, no. 122, December 17, 2014, https://networks.h-net.org/node/28443/discussions/55645/h-diplo-essay-122-sport-history-and-diplomatic-history-h-diplo (accessed September 1, 2016); Toby C. Rider, "Political Warfare in Helsinki: American Covert Strategy and the Union of Free Eastern European Sportsmen," *International Journal of the History of Sport* 30, no. 13 (2013): 1502; Kevin B. Witherspoon, "Going 'To the Fountainhead': Black American Athletes as Cultural Ambassadors in Africa, 1970–1971," *International Journal of the History of Sport* 30, no. 13 (2013): 1509.

17. Warren et al., *Sheilas, Wogs, and Poofters.*

18. Warren's influence is underlined in a statement made by Football Federation Australia Chief Executive Officer David Gallop on the tenth anniversary of Warren's death. David Gallop, "Johnny Warren's Legacy Lives in Us All," November 6, 2014, www.footballaustralia.com.au/article/johnny-warrens-legacy-lives-in-us-all/1gk7kfyx385ml1h446sa0ll00o (accessed July 1, 2016). The recent development of

Australian football into a mainstream sport is examined by James Skinner, Dwight Zakus, and Allan Edwards, "Coming in from the Margins: Ethnicity, Community Support and the Rebranding of Australian Soccer," *Soccer & Society* 9, no. 3 (2008): 394–404.

19. Warren et al., *Sheilas, Wogs, and Poofters*, 88–92.

20. Ibid., 91; "Aussie Team Feted in Sydney Fiesta," *Soccer World*, December 1, 1967, 1.

21. Warren et al., *Sheilas, Wogs, and Poofters*, 84–91; Witherspoon, "Going 'To the Fountainhead,'" 1513–1519.

22. Warren et al., *Sheilas, Wogs, and Poofters*, 87, 91; "This Is How We Lived and Played in Saigon," *Soccer World*, November 24, 1967, 4.

23. Warren et al., *Sheilas, Wogs, and Poofters*, 95, 98; Richard Cooke, "The forgotten story of . . . the Socceroos in Vietnam," June 6, 2013, www.theguardian.com/sport/blog/2013/jun/06/australia-friendship-tournament-vietnam-1967 (accessed July 1, 2016); Cooke, "The forgotten story of . . . the Socceroos in Vietnam."

24. Richard M. Blackburn, *Mercenaries and Lyndon Johnson's "More Flags": The Hiring of Korean, Filipino, and Thai Soldiers in the Vietnam War* (Jefferson, NC: McFarland & Company, 1994), 31, 52; Stanley R. Larsen and James L. Collins Jr., *Vietnam Studies: Allied Participation in Vietnam* (Washington, DC: Department of the Army, 1975), 135, 141–145; Bruce Palmer Jr., *The 25-Year War: America's Military Role in Vietnam* (Lexington: University Press of Kentucky, 1984), 52; Guenter Lewy, *America in Vietnam* (New York: Oxford University Press, 1978), 58, 97; Jonathan Colman and J. J. Widén, "The Johnson Administration and the Recruitment of Allies in Vietnam, 1964–1968," *History* 94, no. 316 (2009): 500; Sean Brawley, "Hangkuk, Daihan, Korean: Korean Voices of the Wol-nam-jon/American War/Vietnam War," in *War, Society and Culture: Approaches and Issues: Selected Papers from the November 2001 Symposium Organized by the Research Group for War, Society and Culture*, ed. Chris Dixon and Luke Auton (Callaghan, NSW: Research Group for War, Society and Culture, 2002), 82–85.

25. Daniel Lane, "When the Socceroos Won behind Enemy Lines," *Sun-Herald*, November 8, 2014, www.smh.com.au/sport/soccer/when-the-socceroos-won-behind-enemy-lines-20141108–11j4nk.html (accessed July 1, 2016).

26. Craig Foster, "A Decade On, Johnny Warren's Star Burns as Bright as Ever," *Sun-Herald*, November 8, 2014, www.smh.com.au/sport/soccer/a-decade-on-johnny-warrens-star-burns-as-bright-as-ever-20141108–11j0ia.html (accessed July 1, 2016); Les Murray, "Remembrance for the Socceroos," The World Game, website of Special Broadcasting Service, April 21, 2015, https://theworldgame.sbs.com.au/remembrance-for-the-socceroos (accessed July 1, 2016).

27. Hay, *Football and War*, 70.

Entrenching Apartheid Football and Failed Sports Diplomacy

Recalcitrance, Reform, and Retreat, 1951–1977

Chris Bolsmann

The anti-apartheid movement across a number of countries engaged in a range of activities that highlighted the atrocities of the Pretoria regime and the plight of the majority of the population in South Africa. Despite the ban on and harassment of political organizations and individuals within South Africa from 1950 onward, actors within the country resisted apartheid. The sphere of sport represented an important site of struggle against apartheid. The anti-apartheid movements in Australia, Great Britain, New Zealand, and the United States in particular recorded significant victories against apartheid sport through the boycott of and the ban on participation of South African teams in international tours, tournaments, and events.

A number of scholars and activists highlighted the role of the international anti-apartheid movement and campaigns against apartheid sport. These accounts considered the International Olympic Committee's (IOC) initial reluctance to engage with the issue of apartheid through to the suspension of apartheid sports organizations. Detailed studies address the successful campaigns to halt and disrupt South African sport tours to Britain. The struggle of actors against apartheid sport within South Africa's borders has also received attention. The role of sports organizations that implicitly and explicitly supported apartheid has received less attention. Their engagement with the anti-apartheid sports bodies within South Africa and international bodies abroad is an important component in their attempts to steer debates, control organizations, and preserve the status quo within apartheid South Africa.[1]

In contrast to international organizations working against apartheid, the whites-only South African Football Association (SAFA) and the South African government attempted initially to maintain and thereafter reform apartheid sport in general and football in particular. The failed sports diplomacy played out at the international level of the Fédération Internationale de Football Association (FIFA). Football was an important component of the South African government's attempt to circumvent the sport boycott and to counteract the image of the pariah status of the Pretoria regime. The football authorities and organizations aligned to apartheid and the South African government more generally engaged in a campaign of failed sports diplomacy.

Sport, Segregation, and Apartheid

The United Nations (UN) was formed in the aftermath of the Second World War "to save succeeding generations from the scourge of war" and "to reaffirm faith in fundamental human rights, in the dignity and worth of the human person." The issue of racism and South Africa became an important agenda item for the UN. In 1946, fellow founding member state India placed the issue of the treatment of people with Indian heritage in South Africa on the UN agenda. Afrikaner nationalists under the leadership of Daniel Malan were victorious in the first postwar election held in South Africa in May 1948. A factor in the victory was an electoral system that favored rural constituencies in which Afrikaner farmers were in the majority. The Reunited National Party and the Afrikaner Party formed a government despite winning 41.2 percent of the vote as compared to the United and Labour parties' 50.93 percent. The Nationalist held a five-seat lead over Jan Smuts's United Party. Smuts had played an instrumental part in the formation of the League of Nations in 1921 and of the UN, even helping craft the preamble of the new world body. Smuts had convincingly won the 1943 election with a majority of over twenty-five seats in parliament. By the 1953 election, the National Party further consolidated their hold on power by winning the popular vote and the majority of seats in parliament.[2]

After their 1948 election victory, the Nationalist passed several laws that enforced apartheid. In 1943, the Afrikaans newspaper *Die Burger* first coined the term. In parliament Malan declared in 1944 that "I do not use the term 'segregation,' because it has been interpreted as fencing off but rather 'apartheid,' which will give the various races the opportunity of uplifting themselves on the basis of what is their own." Apartheid further consolidated white power and control in South Africa and enforced segregation and racism. A central tenet of the apartheid project was race classification. The Population Registration Act of 1950 established a national register that classified at birth a person's race. Moreover, the act "introduced the principle of biological ancestry into every aspect of social existence [and] became internalized by the vast majority of South Africans." While the Population Registration Act had no precedent in the pre-1948 era, a range of legislation introduced after 1948 built on existing customs. The Group Areas Act of 1950 enforced racial segregation in residential and business areas while the Reservation of Separate Amenities Act of 1953 enforced segregation in terms of public premises among others.[3]

Apartheid permeated all facets of economic, political, and social life in South Africa. However, and significantly for this analysis, no laws were enacted that prohibited racially mixed sport in South Africa. No need for any legislation on sport existed as the Group Areas and Reservation of Separate Amenities made interaction across racial lines of the sports field virtually impossible. Douglas Booth succinctly remarked there was no need for such legislation as "custom and 'tradition' kept sport segregated." Moreover, the "'vast majority of [white] South Africans' support racial segregation and 'have no desire to part from it.'"[4]

South Africans had played a range of sports since the middle of the nineteenth century, including cricket, football, and rugby among others, and in the overwhelming majority of cases they played along segregated lines. By the latter half of the nineteenth century, several regional and national sporting organizations and associations existed in the Cape and Natal. These clubs and associations were for white men only. South Africans of Indian heritage established cricket and football associations. At the national level, the South African Cricket Association (SACA) and the South African Rugby Board (SARB) were formed in 1889, and SAFA in 1892—all three for white men only. From the outset, these national associations established close ties with similar bodies in Britain and, in certain instances, became honorary members. The primary reason was to garner support for tours to Britain and South Africa that could generate handsome profits. Tours in the three major sports regularly occurred from 1889 onward.[5]

In 1894, one of the finest South African cricketers of his day was the Malay bowler H. "Krom" Hendriks. The South African authorities excluded him from the team to tour Britain. The local newspaper, the *Cape Argus,* reported in March 1895 that "the races are best socially apart, each good in their way, but terribly bad mixture" in relation to sport. Richard Parry writing in the *Cape Times* in 1894 noted that "the idea of a black player representing South Africa was politically dangerous and, for a large proportion of the white population, emotionally intolerable." George Parker, author of *South African Sports* (1897), stated that a "strong line of distinction is drawn between the white and black population in South Africa, consequently the membership of athletic clubs is strictly confined to whites." Black South Africans established a range of sports clubs, organizations, and associations during this period. The South African Coloured Cricket Board, formed in 1902, arranged national tournaments for cricketers. The following year, the South African Indian Football Association (SAIFA) came into existence, followed in 1932 by the South African African Football Association (SAAFA) and, in 1933, the South African Coloured Football Association (SACFA).[6]

Within South Africa during this period, there were very few instances of racially mixed sport.[7] Segregated sport was customary; however, while abroad, white South African tour sides competed against sportsmen considered not white. In 1921 the South African rugby team, the Springboks, played against a Maori XV. A South African journalist wrote, "The most unfortunate match was ever played. . . . It was bad enough having to play a team officially designated 'New Zealand Natives,' but the spectacle of thousands of Europeans frantically cheering on a band of coloured men to defeat members of their own race was too much for the Springboks, who were frankly disgusted." In football, SAFA's constitution and rules stated members had to be "of full European descent"; as a result, they turned down an invitation to play against a racially mixed team in Java in 1931 and refused to compete against an Indian side on tour in South Africa in 1934. Sporting authorities, clubs, and teams segregated sport along racial lines from the 1880s to the early 1950s in South Africa. In 1948, after the Nationalists' electoral victory, the new government enacted further segregation and discrimination through apartheid legislation. However, sport became an important site of resistance and struggle against apartheid, with football, in particular, thrust into the international spotlight during the following decade.[8]

Football in Apartheid South Africa

Within South Africa, a range of competing national associations vied for control of the game at the local and national levels and to control representation at the international level. This manifested in attempts to consolidate representation at the international level and claim authority over South African football. White football authorities used existing networks in Britain and FIFA to consolidate power and exclude nonracial football authorities who challenged their position within the country and abroad. South African football authorities maintained close links to the Football Association (FA). From the late nineteenth century onward, a South African representative was based in London and attended FA meetings. SAFA periodically affiliated to the Football Association. After withdrawing its FA affiliation in 1907, FIFA invited SAFA to join the newly established international body. SAFA joined FIFA in 1910 and became the first non-European member. Despite the international orientation of the local South African officials, their primary concern was to maintain cordial ties with Britain and secure visits by British teams, which generated good financial returns for local coffers.[9]

SAFA's affiliation to FIFA lapsed during the First World War, although the federation temporarily reaffiliated to the world body in 1924. The association withdrew from FIFA and reaffiliated to the Football Association in 1926. At the 1948 Olympic Games in London, several football associations from the British Commonwealth met under the banner of the Empire Football Association. Nothing substantial materialized from these discussions, and members of the Commonwealth increasingly looked to FIFA for membership. In 1951, SAFA reapplied to FIFA for membership; although SAFA represented only 18 percent of South African footballers, it was granted membership at FIFA's Helsinki Congress. SAFA's readmission into the international fold did not go unchallenged. Its membership in FIFA was a rallying point in and outside the country against apartheid sport and football in particular.[10]

Three black soccer federations came together to form the South African Soccer Federation (SASF) in 1951 and spearheaded the challenge against the whites-only SAFA. SASF brought together SAAFA, SACFA, and SAIFA under the leadership of Durban-based lawyer George Singh. SASF represented a "multiracial umbrella body opposed to apartheid" with a membership of forty-six thousand. Soon after the reaffiliation of SAFA to FIFA, the anti-apartheid SASF applied to the world body for affiliation. SASF claimed the "body has no race or colour restrictive rules and is in fact open to all races." As a result, SAFA hastily called a special general meeting in October 1952. It proposed that the constitution be amended but retained the racist rule restricting membership to "Europeans" and added the clause "save such affiliated members who cater for and control Non-European Football Associations, and whose Constitutions have been approved by this Association." Moreover, SAFA informed SASF that they could come under "its wings" and that there was no need to apply to the world body. Nothing came of the proposed amendment, and the racist clause was only removed from SAFA's constitution in 1956. SASF again applied to FIFA for membership at the Bern Congress in 1954. In an attempt to strengthen their case with FIFA, SAFA noted they were "the only governing Body for Europeans [and] there is a clear line of demarcation between Europeans and Non-Europeans (called Apartheid) in this Country." SAFA stated that apartheid was the law in South Africa and that "there is no intermingling between Europeans, and Non-Europeans either Socially or particularly on the field of Sport." SAFA accepted and enforced apartheid laws and respected the norms of separation and segregation in South African society.[11]

In 1955, FIFA declared that SAFA "does not compromise and control all the clubs and players in South Africa and therefore it has not the standing of a real national association." Despite the declaration, FIFA reported that the "fusion" of SAFA and SASF "clashes with the Laws and customs of the country." In effect, FIFA sided with SAFA in their analysis of the sociopolitical situation in South Africa. FIFA established a commission of inquiry that visited South Africa in 1956. The Lotsy Commission insisted on the removal of the racist clause in SAFA's constitution, but it also claimed that "it is absolutely necessary that the present administration of the game be left unchanged" and that to "replace [SAFA] . . . would retrogade [*sic*] football in South Africa." This suggested the whites-only association would be best suited to remain custodians of the game in South Africa. At the 1956 FIFA Congress in Lisbon, Karel Lotsy remarked that SAFA were not responsible for the segregation in South African soccer but rather that "it is the unwritten law of the country!" SAFA renamed itself the Football Association of Southern Africa (FASA) the following year to suggest change within the organization of the game in the region. The change was in name only, as the body continued to follow the Pretoria regime's line on apartheid sport. While FIFA continued to back the apartheid-supporting FASA, the South African government clamped down on dissenting sporting organizations. They denied passports to the SASF delegation that planned to travel to Lisbon and make their case for integrated nonracial soccer in South Africa.[12]

In other sports, the black South African Table Tennis Board, formed in 1948, applied for international affiliation. The International Table Tennis Federation granted this membership at the expense of the white organization. Black bodybuilders, cricketers, and weight lifters similarly applied for affiliation to international organizations. As a response, Theophilus Dönges, the South African Minister of the Interior, issued Pretoria's first sport policy in June 1956. He stated:

> Whites and Non-Whites should organize their sporting activities separately, there should be no inter-racial competitions within the Republic's borders, mixing of races in teams should be avoided and sportsmen from other lands should respect the country's customs, as she respected theirs. Within that framework, Non-White sportsmen from outside would not be debarred from entering South Africa to compete with Non-Whites. The Government would prefer Non-White sports organizations seeking international recognition to do so through the aegis of White associations already enjoying such benefits. It would not support Non-White sporting divisions by any process squeezing White South Africans out of international competitions. No travel facilities would be granted to people guilty of such subversive intentions.

In football, FASA followed this policy and co-opted some black football authorities into the white governing body without voting rights. On the one hand, this action signaled to FIFA that FASA was not exclusively white, while on the other, black footballers could enjoy municipal facilities, coaching opportunities, and the possibility of foreign tours. FASA corresponded with Minister Dönges and highlighted its complacency with apartheid: "Notwithstanding the fact that there is no specific Law prohibiting matches between Europeans and Non-Europeans, does the Department favour matches of this nature or matches between teams composed of Europeans and Non-Europeans? [and] would the Government, if necessary, take all steps to insure the observance of the South African traditional way of life in regards to matches of this Nature?"

The Department of the Interior's response was clear: "Definitely not [and] Yes, that is the policy of the Department."[13]

Discussions to form a continental African football body began in the early 1950s. The Confédération Africaine de Football (CAF) was established in 1957, comprising the founding members Egypt, Ethiopia, Sudan, and South Africa represented by FASA. The South Africans committed to send a team to CAF's inaugural tournament in Khartoum the following year. South Africa's scheduled game against Ethiopia did not take place because the South Africans withdrew from the tournament. They claimed that due to the crisis in the Suez and the lack of communication on the part of the African body they would not fulfill their commitment to compete in the inaugural tournament, which was eventually won by Egypt. It was, however, more likely that white South African footballers were not particularly keen on participating on the African stage against nonwhite players. In 1958, FASA suggested it would consider sending two teams "European and non-European" to the second African tournament to be held in Egypt in 1959. FASA claimed "there was no objection to Europeans, and Non-Europeans playing matches outside the Union of South Africa" and agreed to participate in the event. FASA, however, rescinded this decision allegedly because of the tour by English team Bolton Wanderers to South Africa at the same time. FASA had committed to sending teams to the first two African tournaments in 1957 and 1959, respectively. On both occasions, they withdrew their teams due to the geopolitical situation in the region and the money-generating tours by British teams.[14]

In March 1960, the South African police killed sixty-nine protesters in Sharpeville. International condemnation was swift and resounding. At FIFA's 1960 Rome Congress six months later, CAF expelled FASA from the continental confederation that now comprised nine members. This represented the first major setback for apartheid football. Moreover, FIFA passed the resolution that national associations could not practice racial, religious, or political discrimination. The international federation gave FASA twelve months to abide by the resolution. FASA president Fred Fell was "pleased [with the] reprieve," although FIFA suspended his organization the following year. The Pretoria regime responded that should the white body be expelled from the world body, SASF officials would (again) be denied passports to send or invite teams from abroad. The Ministry of the Interior stated: "There is no legislation in this country prohibiting inter-racial competition. . . . It will not support non-White sporting activities designed to force the country to abandon the South Africa custom that Whites and non-Whites should organize their activities, in whatever field, separately. . . . Competitions between White and non-White teams within the Republic, will . . . not be tolerated. There is no objection, though, that a non-White team from South Africa competes against a White team abroad." The Pretoria regime sided with FASA against SASF. It threatened to withhold passport facilities for anti-apartheid sports officials who lobbied to have white sports organizations barred from international associations. Pretoria again reiterated its stance that no mixed sport should take place within the country.[15]

While the apartheid government remained steadfast in its resolve to keep black and white sides from playing against each other within the borders of South Africa, it slowly adopted a somewhat more flexible and pragmatic approach with teams abroad due to the increased focus on apartheid sport by the anti-apartheid movement. The increasingly powerful semiprofessional National Football League (NFL), under general manager Vivian Granger, suggested to FASA in 1961 that white teams touring overseas should play against black teams in South Africa and "that a multi-racial game should be arranged" between FASA and "the non-European Associations . . . in order to test the Government's sincerity in respect to their attitude towards such games." FASA eventually sanctioned a racially mixed match in 1962 between the white South African team Germiston Callies and Black Pirates in the neighboring country Lesotho. The actual playing of this game suggested a repositioning of FASA in which black and white South Africans could play against one another. In the space of a decade, FASA's position on racially exclusive football changed. In the first half of the 1950s, FASA adamantly claimed no racially mixed football should take place within the country or abroad. Due to the opposition of SASF within the country, suspension by FIFA, and expulsion by CAF, FASA attempted to reform apartheid football by permitting differently defined racial teams to play against each other. It would take a further decade for this to occur on a regular basis.[16]

Anti-Apartheid Football and the Struggle against Pretoria

The 1960s represented the height of white football in South Africa. The fledgling professional league became the most popular sport among all racial groups within the country, attracting record crowds. A host of international teams and foreign players competed in apartheid South Africa during the decade. Foreign tours and visits to South Africa by international players occurred against the backdrop of increased state brutality and the banning of anti-apartheid organizations by the Pretoria regime. Moreover, South Africa withdrew from the Commonwealth and became a republic in 1961 in the context of worldwide condemnation of apartheid, particularly in relation to sport. Resistance to apartheid football remained an important component of this struggle. White football officials continued to tinker with race and football team selections. This attempt at football reform was evident when the NFL's Vivian Granger proposed to FIFA president, Stanley Rous, that a FASA "non-White" side enter the 1966 and a white side the 1970 World Cup qualifying stages. FASA's paternalism and control over the collaborative South African Bantu Football Association (SABFU) was clear. SABFU's president, Bethuel P. Morolo, accompanied a white delegation to the 1962 FIFA Congress in Chile. According to FASA, his "main duty was to mix as much as possible with the Afro-Asian delegates and explain the position of his association with the FASA." FASA and SABFA established the "Top Level" committee in 1962 to address the concerns of FIFA but also to "undermine the activities of the anti-racist South African Soccer League [SASL]." The Top Level committee members were able to deny anti-apartheid football organizations access to municipal sports grounds through their collusion with municipal authorities. Moreover, FASA attempted to project a new multiracial appearance in the hope of having the FIFA suspension lifted.[17]

In 1963 FIFA temporarily lifted FASA's suspension after the visit of Stanley Rous and James McGuire to South Africa. The officials incredulously reported that "there is no wilful discrimination on the apart of the F.A.S.A. in respect to any Organisation . . . and if the suspension is not lifted . . . the progress of the game . . . will be retarded." As a result, FASA entered the draw for the 1966 World Cup qualifying rounds. South Africa was grouped with Australia, North Korea, and South Korea. FASA's apartheid mentality was evident when it informed the Ministry of the Interior that it intended to field a "non-European" team against the "non-white countries" and a white side against Australia. Pretoria agreed to issue passports for the "non-White" side "provided that the team be under white supervision whilst overseas." FASA tested the regime's resolve by asking whether a racially mixed South African side could play abroad. Pretoria rejected this proposal. The efforts to field two different teams for World Cup qualification never materialized after FIFA suspended FASA again in 1964 and cancelled South Africa's participation in the qualifying rounds for the 1966 World Cup. South Korea withdraw from participation and North Korea defeated Australia and went on to play in the finals in 1966.[18]

The South African Games were staged in the run-up to the 1964 Olympic Games in Tokyo. In the selection of a team to represent South Africa in Japan, separate events for black and white events were staged. South African athletes competed against foreign competition with national selectors in attendance. South African Olympic officials announced they would include seven black athletes in the sixty-two-member team. The IOC, however, revoked South Africa's invitation to participate in the games. Moreover, the IOC demanded that discrimination in sport be rejected and competition allowed among races in the country. The IOC upheld the ban, and the South African Olympic team was not invited to participate in the 1968 Mexico City games. Pretoria responded to the exclusion of South Africa from the Olympic Games and the suspension of FASA from FIFA by making reforms about who could represent South Africa in international sport.[19]

Multinationalism and the Failure of Apartheid Sports Reform

By the late 1960s the political mood in South Africa had changed due to the ongoing international focus on apartheid sport. In 1960, New Zealand rugby authorities agreed not to include Maoris in the All Blacks side to tour South Africa. In 1964, protestors demonstrated against South African cricketers on tour in Australia and New Zealand. Prime Minister Verwoerd requested the exclusion of Maoris from the 1967 New Zealand tour of South Africa. The New Zealand rugby authorities rejected the request and cancelled the tour. In 1968, England cricket selected South African–born cricketer Basil d'Oliveira for England's tour of his country of birth. In response to his selection, South African prime minister B. J. Vorster exclaimed, "It's the team of the anti-apartheid movement" and added that the player would not be welcome in South Africa. English cricket authorities cancelled the tour. Large-scale protest organized by the Stop the Seventy Tour met the South African rugby Springboks on their tour of Britain and Ireland in 1969–1970. Similarly, while the Springboks toured Queensland, Australia, in 1971, Australian authorities declared a state of emergency due to large-scale demonstrations. Apartheid sport became a rallying point for the anti-apartheid movement around the world.[20]

Despite the increased international pressure on Pretoria, the regime remained intransigent. In 1969, separate events were staged for black and white athletes during the South African Games. Pretoria reaffirmed its stance and noted: "The government is in no way whatsoever going to be intimidated by the demands made for integrated multi-racial sport in South Africa. . . . The ultimate objective is in fact the political control of the country. The Government also rejects a policy which would allow for White teams to compete with non White teams . . . nor will it consider any form of mixed trials."[21] In 1970, the IOC expelled South Africa as a result of Pretoria's failure to bring about real change in South Africa's sporting landscape.

During the 1960s, Pretoria developed a new policy intended to replicate decolonization in parts of Africa and offset international condemnation of apartheid. Homelands for black South Africans were to be granted political "independence." "Nations" were ethnically determined in line with apartheid thinking more generally. In line with this development, Minister of Sport Piet Koornhof introduced the policy of multinationalism in 1971. Sports teams of racially defined "nations" were permitted to compete against one another and against foreign opposition. Mixed national teams were permitted in the Olympics, Davis and Federation Cups (tennis), and Canada Cups (golf). In football, FASA reported in 1972 that 70 percent of its affiliates agreed in principle to play multiracial football. The overtures toward multiracial football were conditional for white affiliates: mixed football at school and club level must remain segregated. In addition, FASA noted the increased power of SASF in discussion with Koornhof. FASA requested the state limit the use of football fields to FASA affiliates only.[22]

In a break with previous editions of the South African Games, Pretoria permitted racially mixed competition during the 1973 games. In football, FASA arranged for racially mixed amateur international sides to compete against multinational (i.e., racially defined) South African teams. FIFA provided "special dispensation" due to FASA's suspension from the international body and sanctioned the event. The South African state agreed to cover all expenses of foreign teams. The Brazilian and English football authorities provisionally accepted invitations to compete in the Pretoria event. FIFA queried whether the South African teams and stadiums would be racially mixed or segregated. Stadiums would be segregated and teams selected on the basis of race, FASA confirmed. FIFA withdrew its sanction and no foreign teams participated in the event. FIFA noted, "We regret the executive was misled and wrongly interpreted the term 'multi-racial.'" Despite the setback for FASA, matches between racially defined South African teams were played. The South African "Whites" twice beat the "Blacks" in football. In the same year, a British All Stars XI that included players contracted with South African and British clubs played against black and white sides. In 1974, the Embassy Multinational Series was staged. The tournament, sponsored by a tobacco company, pitted racially defined sides against each other. In 1975 the US multinational automobile manufacturer Chevrolet sponsored the "Champion of Champions" event, in which black and white club teams played against one another. The tournament generated profits for the organizers. The NFL's Vivian Granger noted that racial integration in football was a matter of time and asked, "Why delay the inevitable?" During the 1960s, South African and foreign companies sponsored separate black and white sporting events. Increasingly, during the first half of the 1970s, local and foreign companies sponsored events that included black and white participants.[23]

Despite increased levels of state brutality and repression within South Africa, resistance to apartheid continued. In 1973, nonracial anti-apartheid activists established the South African Council of Sport (SACOS). SACOS embraced the principles of nonracialism, rejected multinationalism, and demanded the end of apartheid. In the late 1970s, SACOS adopted a more militant position of noncollaboration. SACOS president Hassan Howa argued that "no normal sport in an abnormal society" was possible and stated that nonracial sports organizations could not participate in or be associated with racial segregation or multinationalism. Internationally, the anti-apartheid movement increasingly isolated Pretoria. FIFA adopted a more critical position in relation to apartheid football with the election of Brazilian João Havelange as president of the world body, succeeding Englishman Stanley Rous. The latter maintained close ties with apartheid football authorities and was sympathetic to Pretoria's position. At its 1974 congress in Frankfurt, FIFA agreed that national associations would be barred from the world body if they upheld discriminatory laws. The new policy made the expulsion of FASA imminent.[24]

In July 1976 FIFA expelled FASA at the Montreal congress. FASA's expulsion from FIFA had grave consequences for the NFL. Local clubs would lose players and lucrative transfer fees. FASA's previously dominant position in South African football was under threat. The body suggested to Koornhof that soccer be used "as the guinea pig for experimenting with multi racial sport." In 1975 FASA had argued they "should gradually be expanded into a multi racial body [to include] a multi racial Executive." A "supreme council" for football in South Africa that included the SACOS-affiliated SASF was proposed. FASA's proposal included a rotating presidency; it was designed to primarily benefit the white association, leave control of football to respective racial groups, and allow for the white body to dictate relations with FIFA. Unsurprisingly, SASF rejected the proposal. FASA remained keen to entice international teams to play in South Africa.[25]

Foreign football teams had toured to South Africa since the 1890s, and the country was a popular tour destination for national and club teams. During the early 1960s, several elite clubs such as Arsenal, Real Madrid, and Tottenham toured apartheid South Africa and generated profits for the teams and local football associations. Tour teams played against whites-only teams in segregated stadiums. In 1975, FASA negotiated with Argentinean football authorities to field a team to play against a racially mixed South African team. Rather than only a financial endeavor, FASA hoped this game would persuade FIFA of the nonracial character of the game in South Africa—albeit only at the elite level. FASA noted that "a mixed S. A. team, selected on merit" would show the visiting FIFA delegation that "blacks and whites can and want to play together."[26]

Koornhof remarked that he "would be very happy to sanction such a game" played by a South African side picked on merit from all racial groups in the country. The visit by the Argentinean team coincided with the FIFA delegation visit to South Africa in March 1976. The FIFA executive sent the delegation to South Africa to report back to the FIFA Congress to be held in Montreal later that year. The "Chev Argentine Stars" team was composed of former international players, with some of the players well into their late thirties and early forties. It was clear the Argentineans did not constitute a representative team. Harry Cavan, FIFA vice president from Northern Ireland, Juan Goni from Chile, and Hiram Sosa from Guatemala made up the FIFA delegation that watched the first match of the Argentinean tour in which a racially mixed South African side defeated the winners by five goals to nil. The remaining matches were played against a White XI, a Coloured XI, a Black XI (twice), and a racially mixed side. The black and white press in South Africa enthusiastically reported on the tour and the South African victories.

The South African press printed numerous photographs of black and white players embracing each other in goal celebrations and bathing together in postmatch locker rooms. SASF, however, noted in a memorandum handed to the FIFA delegation that the tour was merely "window dressing" and was in violation of FIFA statutes.[27]

The FIFA delegation met with Koornhof and a range of South African football authorities. Until a new inclusive body in South Africa formed, FIFA suggested the suspension of FASA remain in effect. In the build-up to the 1976 FIFA Congress in Montreal, FASA engaged in a concerted campaign to canvass support from FIFA members to allow South Africa to remain a member and have the suspension lifted. FASA sent letters in French, German, and Spanish to seventy FIFA members. The mailing included an accompanying promotional pamphlet published in four languages that depicted "White and non-White players enjoying the game together." Any support that these efforts might have gained for FASA was undone by the state brutality inside South Africa: the June 16 massacre of protesting schoolchildren in Soweto on the outskirts of Johannesburg. FIFA met in Montreal the following month and unanimously voted to expel FASA. Of the 100 votes cast, 78 members voted in favor of the expulsion, 13 abstained, and 9 voted against, despite the efforts of the chair of the FA, Sir Harold Thompson, who spoke in support of FASA.[28]

FASA's president Ian Taylor noted in his address at the 1977 annual general meeting: "From the blacks' point of view we must be prepared to admit that we have shown prejudice to them, we have obtained the best facilities and we have organized overseas tours and visits to their exclusion. All this is admitted but we must now show that it is our earnest desire to change all this so that we can normalise our sporting relationships." In 1978 FASA noted that they "accepted the basic principle of non-racial soccer from grass-roots level." FASA retreated into the amateur and junior game in South Africa and within a decade were engaged in secret talks with the exiled African National Congress (ANC) in Lusaka, Zambia. The once all-powerful whites only football body merged with a range of nonracial organizations and became part of the newly established South African Football Association in 1992.[29]

The introduction of apartheid in 1948 thrust the Pretoria regime into the international limelight, due to increased levels of state brutality and violence, particularly after 1960, and the recalcitrance of apartheid sporting authorities to engage in meaningful change. International sporting bodies such as

FIFA and IOC were at the forefront of isolating apartheid South Africa internationally. This isolation manifested itself in sporting boycotts and protest against touring South African teams and suspensions and expulsions from international bodies. As a result, Pretoria introduced superficial reforms to portray change within South Africa to its international critics. The anti-apartheid movement targeted cricket and rugby in particular and recorded significant victories in their struggle against apartheid sport.

CAF in particular spearheaded the struggle against apartheid football abroad, and SASF led from within the country. White football authorities remained recalcitrant and paternalistic in their dealing with local anti-apartheid opposition. Despite this, and after FASA's suspension from FIFA, South African football officials were forced to engage with opposition bodies in the country. FASA suggested superficial reforms in an attempt to create a favorable impression with FIFA and yet remain firmly in control of resources and facilities within the country. With the introduction of multinationalism, Pretoria projected an image of reform within apartheid sports and sought to leverage international opinion through superficial reforms, with football at the center of these efforts. While football was one of the first sports in South Africa to integrate and ultimately challenge apartheid sport, this integration was not the intended outcome of Pretoria and white football authorities. As a consequence of this integration, white football authorities retreated from the professional game and focused their energies on youth and amateur football in white neighborhoods. Within a decade they engaged in discussions with nonracial sports bodies to bring about nonracial football in South Africa. Their efforts before this were, however, attempts at failed sports diplomacy in which they sought to uphold apartheid and maintain privilege and control of the game in South Africa.

Notes

1. Richard Lapchick, *The Politics of Race and International Sport: The Case of South Africa* (Westport: Greenwood, 1975); Peter Hain, *Don't Play with Apartheid: Background to the Stop the Seventy Tour Campaign* (London: George Allen and Unwin, 1971); Robert Archer and Antoine Bouillon, *The South African Game* (London: Zed, 1982); Douglas Booth, *The Race Game: Sport and Politics in South Africa* (London: Frank Cass, 1998); Christopher Merrit, "'In Nothing Else Are the Deprivers so Deprived': South African Sport, Apartheid and Foreign Relations," *International Journal of the History of Sport* 13, no. 2 (1996): 146–165.

2. Preamble of the United Nations, http://www.un.org/en/sections/un-charter/preamble/ (accessed June 10, 2018); Saul Dubow, *Apartheid, 1948–1994* (Oxford: Oxford University Press, 2014), 2–3; Saul Dubow, "Smuts, the United Nations and the Rhetoric of Race and Rights," *Journal of Contemporary History* 43, no. 1 (2008): 43–72.

3. Quoted in Hermann Giliomee, *The Afrikaners: Biography of a People* (Charlottesville: University of Virginia Press, 2003), 475; Dubow, "Smuts, the United Nations," 37–38.

4. Booth, *The Race Game*, 58.

5. Goolam Vahed, "Deconstructing 'Indianness': Cricket and the Articulation of Indian Identities in Durban, 1900–32," *Culture, Sport, Society: Cultures, Commerce, Media, Politics* 6, no. 2–3 (2003): 144–168; Goolam Vahed and Surendra Bhana, *Crossing Space and Time in the Indian Ocean. Early Indian Traders in Natal. A Biographical Study* (Pretoria: University of South Africa Press, 2015), 31–35.

6. *Argus*, March 23, 1895, 2; Quoted in Jonty Winch, "'I Could a Tale Unfold': The Tragic Story of 'Old Caddy,'" in *Empire & Cricket: The South African Experience 1884–1914*, ed. Bruce Murray and Goolam Vahed (Pretoria: University of South Africa Press, 2009), 67; *Football Evening News*, September 2, 1899, 3; Peter Alegi, *Laduma! Soccer, Politics and Society in South Africa* (Scottsville: University of KwaZulu-Natal Press, 2004), 18.

7. Chris Bolsmann, "The 1899 Orange Free State Football Team of Europe: 'Race,' Imperial Loyalty and Sports Spectacle," *International Journal of the History of Sport* 28, no. 1 (2011): 81–97.

8. Quoted in Booth, *The Race Game*, 23; South African Football Association (SAFA), Circular to Divisional Association, February 1930, Football Association of Southern Africa (FASA), 1892–1992, AG3365, Historical Papers Research Archive, William Cullen Library, University of the Witwatersrand, Johannesburg, South Africa (hereafter WCL); Chris Bolsmann, "White Football in South Africa: Empire, Apartheid and Change, 1892–1977," *Soccer and Society* 11, no. 1–2 (2010): 29–45.

9. Minutes of the 7th Annual Congress, May 15–16, 1910, FIFA Archives, Zürich, Switzerland (hereafter FIFA); Mike Huggins, "Sport, Tourism and History: Current Historiography and Future Prospects," *Journal of Tourism History* 5, no. 2 (2013): 107–130.

10. SAFA, Report from Fred Fell, July 30, 1948, FASA, AG3365, WCL; Alegi, *Laduma*, 112.

11. Alegi, *Laduma*, 10; letter, SASF to FIFA, August 19, 1952, FASA, AG3365, WCL; SAFA, Minutes of Special General Meeting, October 11, 1952, FASA, AG3365, WCL; letter, SAFA to SASF, November 4, 1952, FASA, AG3365, WCL; letter, SAFA to FIFA, September 20, 1954, FASA, AG3365, WCL.

12. Alegi, *Laduma*, 112–113; letter, FIFA to SAFA and SASF, June 29, 1955, FASA, AG3365, WCL; FIFA, report, March 2, 1956, FASA, AG3365, WCL; Lotsy, Report about the football-situation in South Africa, FASA, AG3365, WCL; Peter Alegi, *African Soccerscapes: How a Continent Changed the World's Game* (London: Hurst and Company, 2010), 51.

13. Archer and Bouillon, *The South African Game*; Mary Draper, *Sport and Race in South Africa* (Johannesburg: South African Institute of Race Relations, 1963), 6; Alegi, *Laduma*, 114; Peter Alegi, "Katanga v Johannesburg: A History of the First Sub-Saharan African Football Championship, 1949–50," *Kleio* 3 (1999): 55–74; letter, FASA to Minister of the Interior D. T. Donges, May 26, 1958, FASA, AG3365, WCL; letter, Department of the Interior to FASA, n.d., FASA, AG3365, WCL.

14. "'Rangers' European Tour Offered to S.A.F.A.," *Rand Daily Mail*, October 29, 1956, 14; "Pan-African Soccer: On or Off?" *Rand Daily Mail*, November 21, 1956, 20; "S.A. Out of Khartoum Tournament: Now Rangers can Ask for Tour of Europe," *Rand Daily Mail*, December 29, 1956, 12; "S.A. Soccer Teams May go to Egypt," *Rand Daily Mail*, July 18, 1958, 20; SAFA, Minutes of Half Yearly Meeting, November 1, 1958, FASA, AG3365, WCL; FASA Minutes, April 14 and 16, 1959, FASA, AG3365, WCL.

15. "All-Africa Soccer Group Expels F.A.S.A.," *Rand Daily Mail*, August 25, 1960, 17; Alegi, *Laduma*, 117; Paul Darby, *Africa, Football and FIFA: Politics, Colonialism and Resistance* (London: Frank Cass, 2002), 73; "'Indians Won't Play Ball' Says Mr. Fell," *Rand Daily Mail*, August 23, 1960, 18; letter, Ministry of the Interior to FASA, June 20, 1960, FASA, AG3365, WCL.

16. FASA, Minutes of FASA Half-Yearly Meeting, November 18, 1961, FASA, AG3365, WCL; *Star*, February 26, 1962.

17. Bolsmann, "White Football"; letter, Vivian Granger to Stanley Rous, August 27 1962, FASA, AG3365, WCL; Fred Fell, Report to FASA, January 12, 1963, FASA, AG3365, WCL; Quoted in Peter Alegi and Chris Bolsmann, "From Apartheid to Unity: White Capital and Black Power in the Racial Integration of South African Football, 1976–1992," *African Historical Review* 42, no. 2 (2010): 3.

18. Stanley Rous and James McGuire, Report, 1963, FASA, AG3365, WCL; Letter, FASA to the Minster of the Interior, February 27, 1964, FASA, AG3365, WCL; letter, Ministry of the Interior to FASA, March 12, 1964, FASA, AG3365, WCL; letter, FASA to the Ministry of the Interior, April 7, 1964, FASA, AG3365, WCL; letter, Ministry of the Interior to FASA, April 20, 1964, FASA, AG3365, WCL.

19. Christopher Merrett, "From the Outside Lane: Issues of 'Race' in South African Athletics in the Twentieth Century," *Patterns of Prejudice* 38, no. 4 (2004): 233–251; Marc Keech, "The Ties That Bind: South Africa and Sports Diplomacy 1958–1963," *Sports Historian* 21 (2001): 71–93; Malcolm Maclean, "Revisiting (and Revising?) Sports Boycotts: From Rugby against South Africa to Soccer in Israel," *International Journal of the History of Sport* 31, no. 15 (2014), 1832–1851.

20. Trevor Richards, *Dancing on Our Bones: New Zealand, South Africa, Rugby and Racism* (Wellington: Bridget Williams, 1999); Basil D'Oliveira, *D'Oliveira: An Autobiography* (London, Collins, 1968); Basil D'Oliveira, *Time to Declare: An Autobiography* (Johannesburg: Macmillan, 1980); Hain, *Don't Play with Apartheid*; Christopher Merrett, "Aurora: The Challenge of Non-Racial; Cricket to the South African State of the Mid-1970s," *International Journal of the History of Sport* 18, no. 4 (2001): 95–122; Goolam Vahed, "Cultural Confrontation: Race, Politics and Cricket in

South Africa in the 1970s and 1980s," *Culture, Sport, Society* 5, no. 2 (2002): 79–107; Quoted in Andre Odendaal, *The Story of an African Game* (Cape Town: David Philip, 2003), 175; Hain, *Don't Play with Apartheid*; David Black and John Nauright, *Rugby and the South African Nation* (New York: Manchester University Press, 1998).

21. Quoted in Merrett, "Patterns," 243–244.

22. Dubow, *Apartheid*, 106; Dan O'Meara, *Forty Lost Years: The Apartheid State and the Politics of the National Party, 1948–1994* (Athens: Ohio University Press, 1996); Jamie Miller, *An African Volk: The Apartheid Regime and its Search for Survival* (New York: Oxford University Press, 2016); Christopher Merrett, "'If Nothing Else. Are the Deprivers so Deprived': South African Sport, Apartheid and Foreign Relations, 1945–71," *International Journal of the History of Sport* 13, no. 2 (1996): 146–165; Alegi, *Laduma*; Archer and Bouillon, *The South African*; Booth, *The Race Game*; quoted in Gustav Venter, "Slippery Under Foot: The Shifting Political Dynamics with South African Football, 1973–1976," *South African Historical Journal* 69, no. 2 (2016): 265–287.

23. Letter, FIFA to FASA, January 26, 1973, FASA, AG3365, WCL; letter, FIFA to FASA, November 28, 1972, FASA, AG3365, WCL; telegram, FIFA to Dave Marais, n.d., FASA, AG3365, WCL; Alegi, *Laduma*, 141–142; Venter, *Slippery*, 11; Alegi and Bolsmann, "From Apartheid to Unity."

24. Douglas Booth, "The South African Council on Sport and the Political Antinomies of the Sports Boycott," *Journal of Southern African Studies* 23, no. 1 (1997): 51–66; Booth, *The Race Game*; Marc Keech, "Contest, Conflict and Resistance in South Africa's Sport Policies," in *Power Games: A Critical Sociology of Sport*, ed. John Sugden and Alan Tomlinson (London: Routledge, 2013), 161–180; Paul Darby, "Stanley Rous's 'Own Goal': Football Politics, South Africa and the Contest for FIFA presidency in 1974," *Soccer and Society* 9, no. 2 (2008): 259–272; Venter, *Slippery*, 7.

25. Venter, *Slippery*, 8–10; FASA, Minutes of the Executive, August 10, 1974, FASA, AG3365, WCL; FASA, Minutes of the Executive, March 7, 1975, FASA, AG3365, WCL.

26. Venter, *Slippery*, 8–10, 14.

27. Ibid., 12, 17.

28. Letter, FASA, January 5, 1976, FASA, AG3365, WCL; "SA Expelled from FIFA," *Rand Daily Mail*, July 17, 1976, 1.

29. FASA, AGM President's Report, March 12, 1977, FASA, AG3365, WCL; FASA, Minutes of Officers Meeting, April 1, 1978, FASA, AG3365, WCL; Alegi and Bolsmann, "From Apartheid."

High Jack

Soccer and Sport Diplomacy in the Caribbean, 1961–2018

Roy McCree

During England's bid efforts to bring the 2018 FIFA World Cup to its shores, former England captain David Beckham visited Trinidad and Tobago to garner support. While there, he publicly commented that it was great "having the opportunity of talking with Jack [Warner] about the bid and our thoughts going into the final stages of the bid. We have to think positive, we have to believe we're in a good position."[1] Beckham's comments provide a relevant backdrop to examining two major related issues that have not figured prominently in the narrative surrounding sport and international relations: the specialized diplomacy of sport exemplified in the use of sport celebrities like Beckham and the relevance of smaller soccer tournaments and nations to the staging of global sport events whether they are considered mega or meager.

The historical examination of the significance of sport as an aspect of international relations has focused mainly on its utility as an instrument of traditional interstate diplomacy. Admittedly, while this still remains highly relevant, the utility of the specialized diplomacy of sport as a framework for explaining the character and dynamic of international sport competition has received much less attention. This framework distinguishes between the traditional use of sport as an instrument of diplomacy and international-sport-as-diplomacy. While the former is centered on the relationship between (nation) states, the latter focuses on non-state actors like FIFA and the International Olympic Committee, as well as the relationship between them.[2]

This specialized diplomacy of international sport relates to the communication, bargaining, and negotiation that take place between non-state actors such as FIFA, IOC, or the other international sport federations and state actors as well as with other non-state actors such as media companies, firms, and sponsors in the staging of particular sport events. Some of the major issues that require bargaining and negotiating relate to the rights over hosting, media coverage, and advertising as well as arrangements for transportation and security for the particular event. In light of the global reach of these supranational sport organizations, and the mega-events they organize, the specialized diplomacy that they generate is seen to be "arguably even more significant than the effects of international sport upon diplomatic relationships." In this context, in order to demonstrate its analytical utility, the specialized diplomacy of sport framework is critically applied to the staging of the 2001 FIFA Under 17 Boys World Cup in Trinidad and Tobago and the senior men's World Cups of 2006 and 2018. In applying it to the analysis of these events, a particular focus will be former controversial FIFA vice president Jack Warner, due to the influential role he assumed in these tournaments and the organization as a whole. In addition, the examination of the Junior World Cup departs from the dominant trend in the literature, where the principal focus has been on such mega-events as the Olympic Games, the senior men's World Cup and on the bigger nation states and powerhouses in sport on the whole.[3]

The small Caribbean nation-state of Trinidad and Tobago, with a population of just around 1.4 million inhabitants, assumed major visibility in the global organization of soccer due largely to former controversial FIFA vice president Jack Warner's dominant role in soccer on his native island. Although the country has been one of the major soccer-playing countries in the English-speaking Caribbean historically and achieved its first World Cup qualification in 2006, it can hardly be considered a soccer power. For instance, while these rankings have fluctuated over time, at the end of 2019 it was ranked 104th out of 210 countries in FIFA's global soccer rankings, compared to 63 at the time of its qualification for the 2006 World Cup finals in Germany. Nevertheless, in the figure of Jack Warner, Trinidad and Tobago has played an outsized role within soccer politics.[4]

Warner held numerous roles within the world of soccer: domestically, in FIFA, and in one of the regional zones of FIFA's supranational infrastructure, the Confederation of North, Central American, and the Caribbean Federation

(CONCACAF). In addition to his work in soccer, Warner was also an influential figure in the politics of Trinidad and Tobago during the bidding process and staging of these events. The position assumed by Jack Warner within FIFA, and the influence he came to exercise on the organization of the game globally, may seem at odds with the country's global soccer, economic, and political status.

The historical antecedents to soccer and diplomacy in the Caribbean deal largely with the sport of cricket and, to a lesser extent, athletics. The examination of these antecedents briefly explains how these cases correspond more to the traditional diplomatic use of sport than the specialized diplomacy of sport that the staging of international sport competition generates. Although Caribbean states played an active role in international attempts to dismantle apartheid in the 1970s and 1980s through their support of resolutions under the auspices of the UN as well as the British Commonwealth, they had no clear public policy guideline on the use or role of sport in their foreign policy. Such a policy may have articulated their particular development goals, values, and interests, and the possible role of sport as a diplomatic strategy in negotiating or managing relations with other state and non-state actors in accordance with that policy.[5]

During this period, it is important to note that several Caribbean states had only recently gained political independence from Britain in the 1960s and 1970s and were still devising their foreign policy as independent nations, which had previously been the purview of Britain. Caribbean states also acted in unison by boycotting the 1986 Commonwealth Games over the continued refusal of white-dominated countries like Britain, Australia, Canada, and New Zealand to support sanctions against South Africa.[6]

Apart from cricket and, to a lesser extent, athletics, no other sport in the Caribbean has been used to such an extent as an active instrument of foreign policy by state actors or by non-state actors to deal with any political problem or struggle. However, unlike this study, the focus in these two rare cases of Caribbean sport and international relations was more on relations between states and the traditional use of sport as an instrument of foreign policy or diplomacy to (re)shape those relations, as opposed to a focus on the specialized diplomacy of sport. In the latter regard, it is also important to examine the organizational structure of soccer regionally and globally, together with the role assumed by Jack Warner in its operations.

Caribbean Soccer, FIFA, and Jack Warner, 1961–2017

In the global structure of FIFA's soccer empire, CONCACAF is responsible for the organization and development of soccer in this subregion. This body was established in 1961 and consists of forty-one countries, of which the English-speaking Caribbean accounts for nineteen, or almost 50 percent of its membership. These members however are distributed across three subregional organizations, including the North American Football Union (NAFU), with three members; the Central American Football Union, with seven members; and the Caribbean Football Union (CFU), with thirty-one members.[7]

The CFU was founded in 1978, and its members are spread across the English-, French-, Dutch-, and Spanish-speaking Caribbean but not in Central America, Mexico, or the United States. Jack Warner was a founding member of the CFU; he served as its first secretary from 1978 to 1983, and then as its president from 1983 until his resignation from FIFA in 2011. Warner was elected CONCACAF president in 1990 but was first made a member of FIFA's Executive in 1982 and then was elevated to the position of vice president in 1997. The composition of CONCACAF's membership and the voting structure within FIFA enables the senior executives of the former to exercise considerable influence over the decision-making process for hosting events and football development in general, across the world. The peculiar regional organization of soccer in the Caribbean is therefore essential to understanding the relevance of the sport as diplomacy framework in the Caribbean and the critical role assumed by Jack Warner in this process.[8]

Although CONCACAF has only two teams that can be considered to be among the top soccer countries of the world, Mexico and the United States, the structure of the voting within FIFA has enabled it to exercise tremendous influence in the organization. This influence relates particularly to the election of presidents, the selection of host countries to stage competitions like the World Cup, and the running of its various committees; for instance, the election of the FIFA president is based on the principle of "one country, one vote" among its two hundred plus members. This means that regardless of their territorial size or status in world football, nations like Trinidad and Tobago have the same right to one vote as soccer powers Brazil or Germany.

In addition to this democratic principle, the various regional associations of FIFA can also vote as a block in FIFA's presidential elections. This organizational practice gives a region like CONCACAF significant voting power to elect the president since the votes of its more than thirty members can make the difference in securing the two-thirds majority necessary to become FIFA president. And in fact, this is what happened in the election of Joseph "Sepp" Blatter as president in both 1998 and 2002: the votes of CONCACAF enabled him to defeat his presidential rivals.[9]

As president of CONCACAF during these periods, Jack Warner would have played a crucial role in helping Blatter to secure victory. This would not only have endeared him to Blatter but, invariably, would have strengthened his own position and influence in the organization. In the latter regard, Tomlinson notes that following Warner's rise to the CONCACAF presidency in 1990, "within a decade, 72 persons from the confederation were on FIFA's 21 standing committees, boosting Warner's and his confederation colleagues' profile in FIFA's top committee." Additionally, in one of two self-commissioned biographies, it is revealed that, up to 2005, Warner himself was on at least ten of FIFA's subcommittees, serving as chairman or deputy chairman on several of them. In addition, it must also be noted that the selection of World Cup host countries was determined by FIFA's twenty-four-member executive committee, in which CONCACAF had three members and invariably three prized votes.[10]

Jack Warner's involvement in the CFU, CONCACAF, and eventually FIFA stemmed from his involvement in the Trinidad and Tobago Football Association (TTFA). TTFA was established in 1908, just four years after the formation of FIFA in 1904, although it only joined FIFA in 1963 following the granting of political independence from Britain in 1962. Warner served as secretary of TTFA for around sixteen years, from 1974 until his resignation in 1990. He resigned under a cloud of suspicion and public furor over the fraudulent selling of tickets for a home game against the United States, in the final playoffs to qualify for the 1990 World Cup in Italy. However, following his resignation from TTFA in 1990, the new TTFA president, Oliver Camps, appointed Warner to serve as its special advisor in 1992. Although he no longer held any formal position within the organization, he "was still exerting extensive control of the federation's business and activities." After serving these various organizations for well over twenty-five years, Warner simultaneously resigned in 2011 from all positions in FIFA, CONCACAF, CFU, and TTFA, again, over allegations of corruption.[11]

In addition to playing a prominent role in the organization of soccer regionally and globally, as a member of FIFA's inner executive sanctum, Warner also assumed a prominent role in the national politics of Trinidad and Tobago beginning in the mid-1990s. He eventually served as a member of parliament and minister in the Ministries of Works and Transport as well as a minister of national security in the period 2007–2013. Moreover, Warner was not just a minister, but a senior member of both the government and political party, of which he was the chairman, deputy political leader, and also a major financier. However, as happened with TTFA in 1990 and FIFA in 2011, Warner also resigned from the government in April 2013 over allegations of corruption, again, following an internal investigation by CONCACAF's Integrity Committee. Subsequently, in 2015, the US Department of Justice indicted Warner along with thirteen other officials for "racketeering, wire fraud and money laundering conspiracies, among other offenses, in connection with the defendants' participation in a 24-year scheme to enrich themselves through the corruption of international soccer." Following this development, Interpol placed Warner on its most wanted list, but ever since, he has been fighting extradition to the United States to answer these charges. Although Warner lost his appeal questioning the legality of this extradition in 2017, he is still currently challenging these proceedings.[12]

As a parliamentarian, senior government minister, president of CONCACAF and CFU, de facto head of TTFA (in his capacity as its special advisor), and globetrotting senior executive member of FIFA, Warner appeared to be a larger-than-life figure and a major power broker both within FIFA and without. In the latter regard, for instance, the English 2018 bid team openly stated that "they placed emphasis on winning over Jack Warner" because he was seen as having a "disproportion[ate] amount of power in terms of voting" since he controlled "a block of votes." Within this broader organizational and sociopolitical context, the roles of CONCACAF, Trinidad and Tobago, and Warner must be analyzed as they relate not simply to the development of world football but also to the peculiar diplomatic processes generated by the staging of international football competition at both the senior and junior levels.[13]

FIFA 2001 Under 17 World Cup

The study of international sport competition has been dominated by an almost exclusive focus on certain mega-events like the Olympic Games (summer and winter) and the FIFA senior men's World Cup to the neglect of smaller or more junior events across a range of sports. In this regard, international sport events have been stratified into three major categories: first-order events like the two above, second-order events like the Commonwealth Games, cricket, and rugby World Cups, and third-order events like the Asian Games, Pan American Games, and the African Cup of Nations. However, this classificatory schema does not include female or age-based competitions, which might perhaps be relegated to fourth- and fifth-order events. Yet, what all these events have in common is the lack of journalistic and academic analysis compared to their first-order counterparts.[14] In this context, the staging of the 2001 FIFA Boys Under 17 World Cup in Trinidad and Tobago helps with understanding the peculiar diplomacy generated by international sport events, big or small, notwithstanding the size of the event itself or the country where it is held. It does so by highlighting the range of negotiations and transactions that had to be undertaken in relation to facility construction; the provision of information technology (IT) services, security, and travel arrangements for the various foreign teams; the sale of media rights; and even winning the bid.

In order to win the bid to stage this tournament, Trinidad and Tobago had to beat rival bids of countries like Peru, Japan, Finland, and Scotland, who may have fancied their chances more compared to a much smaller island nation. Parliamentary debates in Trinidad and Tobago justified organizing the 2001 FIFA Boys Under 17 World Cup on several grounds. It was argued that the event formed part of national development plans and also promoted the development of the sport in the country. Additionally, hosting the event would contribute to human development through "developing the sporting capabilities of one's people." Furthermore, this type of event gave smaller countries or members of FIFA the opportunity to stage international soccer events, which appealed to Trinidad and Tobago.[15]

It was Warner, however, who played the instrumental role not only in winning the bid but also in the eventual organization of the tournament. In this regard, he was the chairman of the FIFA youth committee that decided on the bids, chairman of the tournament's organizing committee that determined the budget for the event, deputy chairman of the finance committee that approved the budget, and vice president of FIFA's Executive Committee, which rubber-stamped it.[16] This rubber-stamping underlines Warner's location in FIFA's structure of authority and the leeway it provided him to negotiate and influence decisions that served his particular interests.

Having used his position within FIFA and surely the voting strength of CONCAFAF to win the bid, Warner was also able to use his close association with the then government of Trinidad and Tobago to negotiate for the construction of four new stadiums, as well as the renovation of existing facilities, to stage the tournament. This close association stemmed from the fact that he was known to be a major financier of the political party that had formed the government—so much so, that he was even provided with a special diplomatic passport by the government. Because of his political influence, Warner was able not only to negotiate the construction of new sport facilities but also to secure the contracts to construct them through his own construction company. In addition, Warner was even able to persuade the then government to replace the original financiers for the construction of the new stadiums estimated to cost over US$70 million. And that was not all; he was also able to secure several other lucrative contracts that included the media rights for the tournament, although this was legally challenged by a local media company, Caribbean Sport Television Network (CSTN). CSTN claimed to have bought the rights previously, from FIFA's former marketing partner ISL before it went bankrupt in early 2001. In his internal lobbying within FIFA for the broadcast rights, Warner reportedly threatened, in an e-mail to Blatter, "to withdraw from all activities related to the event" if the rights were not granted to him and instead went to CSTN.[17]

Apart from securing construction and media deals, Warner also obtained contracts for his other family-owned businesses. These included the provision of food and drinks at all five stadiums for the competition, accommodation and travel arrangements for the fifteen competing foreign teams through his family-owned travel agency, and the provision of security through a private firm with which he was linked. And if that was not enough, he was also able to secure an IT contract for a Florida-based company (SEMTOR), in which his son was a "project manager," to disseminate news and results for the tournament after his own lobbying within FIFA.[18]

This apparent conflict of interest was questioned within FIFA as well as by the local and international media, led by corruption buster Andrew Jennings. Jennings, for instance, asked Blatter pointedly at a post-tournament news conference: "Jack Warner's family has won a mass of lucrative contracts generated by the tournament here in Trinidad. Might there be a conflict of interest?" Michael Zen-Ruffinen, then general secretary of FIFA, had also submitted a report to Blatter, in which he stated: "The President has constantly taken decisions which are favorable to the economic interests of Jack Warner and some of his family members, and thus are contrary to the financial interests of FIFA." Echoing the same sentiments, the *Trinidad Express*, in its editorial of September 11, 2001, noted in part "that the country is owed an explanation as to why one family appears to have gained from an international tournament being staged with national facilities at the expense of what appears to be just about everybody else."[19]

In spite of these complaints, however, the matter fell on deaf ears. Rather, Walter Gagg, one of Blatter's aides, came to Warner's defense as he made the following comments on the matter at a post-tournament news conference: "Why do people still have to ask the questions about what happened and why this happened? Without Jack Warner, I don't really think we would have been able to host this FIFA Under 17 Championship in Trinidad and Tobago and we have to be very, very happy to have him in the organisation." Jennings suggests that Warner was given this amount of leverage or influence within FIFA because the bloc of votes Warner commanded as president of CONCACAF could have benefited Blatter's reelection as president of FIFA in 2002. Evidence of this comes from the fact that following the end of the 2001 Junior World Cup, Warner wrote to President Blatter, stating: "I am pleased to advise that all member federations of CONCACAF are fully supportive of your re-nomination as President of FIFA for a second term just as they were for your election in 1998."[20]

Given Warner's support for Blatter, it is not surprising that Blatter described him as "a wonderful and loyal friend" as he heaped praises on him at the 2001 Under 17 World Cup. He stated, "Jack Warner has been in FIFA since 1981 and I have to say he is a very hard worker. . . . For me, in FIFA, he is a wonderful and loyal friend. He is very competent and reliable and I just have to say that Jack Warner is one of the top personalities in the world of football."[21] The comments of both Gagg and Blatter serve to further confirm Warner's past standing within FIFA and the leverage that this gave him to act and negotiate in his own interest.

However, apart from the negotiations over the economic spoils for organizing the tournament, security became a much bigger issue following the September 11 attacks in the United States, which happened just two days before the start of the competition. As a result, FIFA held an emergency meeting to consider canceling the tournament. In his capacity as chair of the local organizing committee, Warner approached the Trinidad and Tobago government to provide state security in order to ensure the continuation of the tournament. In this regard, the then prime minister reportedly stated that "special security measures have been put in place to ensure the safety of all visiting delegations, officials, visitors and the general public" taking part in the championship.[22] Warner's efforts led to direct action on the part of the Trinidad and Tobago government to ensure the smooth running of the event in light of the changed global political and security situation that followed the September 11 attacks.

The actions of Jack Warner to stage and organize the 2001 FIFA Under 17 World Cup are significant at four broad levels. First, they offer a concrete illustration within the Caribbean context of the utility or relevance of the specialized diplomacy of sport framework as it pertains to making representation or negotiating for such issues as construction of stadiums, contracts for transportation, IT services, accommodation, media rights, and security in the staging of a Junior FIFA World Cup. In the latter regard, the provision of security by the state is normally a major requirement; but, in the aftermath of the 9/11 attacks, the importance of such extra security was even more critical as a direct response to the threat it posed to relations among states and to world peace. It should also be noted, however, that securing the various contracts rested clearly on the machinations of one individual and not so much on some collective non-state actor, as has been the case elsewhere.[23] Second, it helps to show how the negotiations to host international sport tournaments, such as the Junior FIFA World Cup, are greatly aided by the nature of the link between the state and non-state actors involved. In this case, Warner's close ties with the Trinidad and Tobago government at the time had clearly facilitated the material and logistical support of the latter in the staging and saving of the tournament in the aftermath of the 9/11 attacks. The problem of security became even more critical since the United States was also competing in the tournament. Third, at the same time, this close link serves to problematize, at best, the distinction between state and non-state actors upon which the specialized diplomacy of sport is premised. This stems from the fact that Warner had his feet in both camps or jurisdictions since he was a high-ranking member of FIFA, the non-state actor, and also a high-ranking member of the governing party of Trinidad and Tobago. Fourth, Warner's use of his unique position and influence within FIFA to win the bid for the tournament, as well as to seek his own apparent financial interests, clearly demonstrates that the diplomacy of sport entails negotiations that take place within the sport organization itself and not just between the sport organization and the state or other non-state actors. Thus, the specialized diplomacy of sport should not only be based or structured around the state–non-state actor dyad but should also incorporate the intraorganizational processes of bargaining and negotiation that may take place within non-state actors like FIFA among its officials. However manipulative or underhanded they may seem.

World Cup Bids 2006 and 2018

The examination of the 2001 Under 17 Boys World Cup served to demonstrate the applicability of the unique diplomacy of sport in relation to a range of contractual issues as well as the negotiating power exercised by a single individual, who was a central figure both within FIFA and the government of Trinidad and Tobago. While the examination of the 2006 and 2018 World Cups also serves to demonstrate the relevance of this framework and the negotiating maneuvers of Warner as an agent of FIFA, it focuses more narrowly on the bidding process in relation to their staging. Relatedly, it also focuses on the way Warner made use of his position within CONCACAF to advance his own particular agenda. The bidding process for such events sets in train a process of resource mobilization involving non-state actors: national soccer federations negotiating with their governments, private sponsors, and the machinery of FIFA. The latter machinery would of course include organizations such as CONCACAF and critical actors like Warner. Bidding therefore activates a process of negotiation, bargaining, and communication in the staging of international sport events that underlies its value in demonstrating the peculiar diplomacy that such events generate.

During England's campaign to stage the 2006 World Cup, Warner used the opportunity to negotiate for work permits to allow players from CONCACAF, and from Trinidad and Tobago in particular, to play professional football in Britain. This was in exchange for his vote and that of the CONCACAF region, which, as earlier noted, had three votes on FIFA's ExCo. In this regard, the former secretary of the English FA, Graham Kelly, noted that in negotiations, Warner "would want every consideration being given for work permit applications for players from the region and he wouldn't hesitate to ask," a situation that he described as "a pain" and "very difficult." Warner's negotiation strategy in asking for these work permits was also likened to "a form of emotional diplomatic blackmail" since he tried to gain these concessions by referring to the perception of Britain as "stuck up, imperialistic," with "a very bad attitude towards us downtrodden colonials." However, although Warner succeeded in obtaining permits for several players from Trinidad and Tobago, the English were not as successful, for it was Germany who narrowly won the bid, albeit under very controversial circumstances, by a margin of 1 vote (11–12).[24]

Nevertheless, the failure of the English did not discourage them from attempting to secure the 2018 World Cup, which required that they again lobby Jack Warner due to his voting power. As part of the lobbying and negotiation process to win the bid, concessions had to be made by both Warner and the English FA. The first major concession involved Warner getting the English national team to play a friendly game against Trinidad and Tobago, in his home country of Trinidad and Tobago. The game took place in June 2008 and was also promoted as part of the centennial celebrations of TTFA. For CONCACAF, for the country, and for Jack Warner, it can be considered a major soccer coup to pull off such a match given the contrasting histories and strengths of the two sides, whose only previous encounter was in the group stages of the 2006 World Cup, which England won. Commenting on the historical significance of playing a match against England on home soil, Warner stated: "Here we are on the cusp of our renewed efforts at qualifying for World Cup South Africa 2010 and the near impossible is achieved, that is, a warm-up match between a full strength England football team and Trinidad and Tobago played right here at the Hasely Crawford Stadium." He noted further, "In most parts of the world, pulling that off would have been lauded by all local sports officials and media." The general secretary of TTFF, Richard Groden, also noted, "This game is of extreme national importance as it is unprecedented that England would play in a country the size of Trinidad and Tobago on home ground."[25]

However, after the English agreed to the game, in turn, Warner had to concede the broadcast rights to the English FA for England and Europe. This was a condition precedent or a precondition for them to play in Trinidad among other unstated conditions. The arrangement also involved the accreditation of seventy British journalists as well as eighty from the CONCACAF region. Additionally, in order to stage the match, the local football association, with the involvement of Warner, also had to negotiate access to the national stadium through the Ministry of Sport as it required paying a rental fee. The negotiations that Warner had to undertake with both the English FA and the local state authorities to bring off this game are reflective of the peculiar diplomacy that the bidding for and the staging of international sport events can entail.[26]

However, apart from agreeing to play against Trinidad and Tobago, the other major concession for the English FA involved getting the renowned David Beckham to visit the country in order to hold soccer clinics for both coaches and young footballers as part of the David Beckham Football Academy. This visit took place in 2010, just four months after England had submitted its bid for the 2018 World Cup. Acknowledging that they were courting his vote, the *Guardian* reported Warner stating: "I've said before, if any country can host a World Cup tomorrow, England can. . . . So it is one of the few countries that is prepared. But we have to meet together as a confederation to make a final decision and we will do that soon. He [Beckham] adds a lot of weight and I think that this is a plus for them [England]."[27]

The involvement of Beckham and his soccer academy had formed an integral component of the English bidding strategy. This strategy was structured around not just the development of football both in England and internationally but also, the development of society as a whole by using football as an intervention strategy to help deal with such issues as education, discrimination, and social integration, consistent with FIFA's bidding requirements. In its evaluation of the English bid, FIFA had noted: "The objective of the Bidder's programme is to create positive change in England and worldwide. The proposals include the creation of a global fund for football development and development through football; support for the expansion of the football for Hope movement; the creation of a global network of 'learning zones' to promote education; a widening of the activities of the David Beckham academy to promote life skills; measures to fight discrimination and promote social integration and the influencing of international policy."

This use of the English soccer team, David Beckham, and the wider lobbying of FIFA by the English FA was a clear use of soccer as part of broader public diplomacy efforts in general, and the specialized diplomacy of sport in particular, in order to win the 2018 bid. In the case of Beckham, however, it was not just public diplomacy per se but celebrity-driven public diplomacy involving a major "global icon" in soccer, in order to help win votes as well as "hearts, minds and global wallets."[28]

In addition, consistent with the specialized diplomacy of sport, the bidding processes were not just narrowly between two sport organizations or non-state sport actors, the English FA and FIFA. On the contrary, they also involved the British government and monarchy, which had provided material, legal, and symbolic support for the bid:

> In May 1999 all 24 members of the FIFA ExCo, plus wives and partners were flown to and from London, put up in the best hotels, offered circle seats at *Phantom of the Opera*, entertained at a royal party with Prince Charles at his Highgrove residence, and given VIP tickets for the FA Cup Final. The Foreign and Commonwealth Office helped gain access to key decision-makers; provided assessments of the attitudes of international sporting bodies; offered high-level hospitality within the UK to selected individuals and opinion-formers; facilitated visa applications; helped with dissemination of publicity; briefed journalists on positive image-making; organized special events at overseas missions and residences; and arranged formal and informal approaches to key personnel by heads of mission and senior diplomatic staff.[29]

These actions serve to highlight the enormous extent to which a state can become involved as a partner in the bidding process to host certain major sport events as part and parcel of the specialized diplomacy of sport or the lobbying entailed in their staging. While state support is one of the requirements of FIFA's bidding process in order to provide guarantees for such matters as customs entry, visas, tax exemptions, security, ambush marketing, and intellectual property, it does not limit how far the state can go in their bid campaigns, once they do not violate the integrity of the process. However, it should be noted that the actions of Warner were not particularly new or unusual to the FIFA bidding process and the specialized diplomacy of sport that has come to characterize it. For instance, in the lobbying to host the 2006 World Cup, Dr. Joe Mifsud, the president of the Malta Soccer Federation, was also able to get both the English national team and top German club, Bayern Munich, to visit and play in Malta "in exchange for the prospect of his vote." And for their 2018 bid, the president of the Thailand Soccer Federation, Worawi Makudi, requested a game between England and his national team, although that game never materialized. Whereas for the 2006 World Cup bid Warner had negotiated to get Caribbean players to play in Britain by getting them work permits, for the 2018 bid he further expanded his negotiations by achieving visits from both the English team and megastar David Beckham to the Caribbean.[30]

The visit of the English national team and Beckham, however, were not the only demands made by Warner in the English attempts to secure the CONCACAF vote as part of their 2018 bid. The 2017 FIFA report about the bidding for the 2018 and 2022 World Cups reveals more about the extent to which Warner had tried to use his position to negotiate various benefits from the World Cup bidders. For instance, his wish list for "England 2018" included the following: providing employment for his friends; helping develop his local club team in the areas of coaching, sport management, and playing through sponsoring a trip to England; organizing and funding trips to England for male and female national youth teams of Trinidad and Tobago; the building of new sport facilities in his parliamentary constituency in Trinidad; and even the purchase of media rights so that Haitians could have watched the World Cup. While most of his requests were not met for reasons linked to scheduling or cost, the English bidding team did agree to sponsor, as well as attend, the reception for the 2010 annual conference of the Caribbean Football Union, at Warner's suggestion, in order to promote their World Cup bid.[31]

For making such requests, however, FIFA found Warner guilty of "exerting undue influence over a bidder" and concluded that "accordingly, both Mr. Warner's demand and England 2018's response undermined the integrity of the bidding process," which precipitated his resignation from FIFA in 2011. The 2017 report also showed the important role played by bidding entrepreneurs such as consultants, lawyers, and bidding teams as non-state actors in their collusion or collaboration with FIFA Executive Committee members as part of the specialized diplomacy of sport. The actions of Warner, serving as the agent of a non-state actor (FIFA), as well as the efforts of the English FA in relation to the bidding negotiations for the 2006 and 2018 soccer World Cups, demonstrate the workings and relevance of the specialized diplomacy of sport as an analytical prism to understand the international significance of the staging of such sporting events because they speak to the issues of negotiation, bargaining, and communication, which are fundamental to the diplomatic process within sport and without.[32]

Whether in relation to big states or small states, the use of sport for political purposes to deal with such issues as sovereignty, self-determination, political legitimacy, and international visibility in the world system has been part of the dominant narrative in the study of the sport–diplomacy–foreign policy nexus or conundrum. In this context, the examination of Jack Warner's role in the bidding process for the senior men's World Cups of 2006 and 2018, as well as the staging of the 2001 Under 17 Boys World Cup in the Caribbean, broadens the study of the "diplomatization of sport" or the "sportification of diplomacy" regionally and globally. Moreover, the examination of the Under 17 Boys World Cup challenges the mega- or "first-order" sport event bias, demonstrating that smaller or lower-order events also involve significant planning, resource requirements, and negotiating activities consistent with the specialized diplomacy of sport. In addition, they may also entail significant economic gains that may not always redound to the benefit of the country as a whole.

In small states like those that dominate the makeup of CONCACAF, with no economic, military, or political might, the use of soft power through sport and its specialized diplomacy serve as a major means not only to attract global attention and create positive images of nation but also to influence or affect the fortunes of other (larger) states in the global system. In this regard, in spite of its relatively obscure status as a football power, and dominated by member nations who might be considered political and economic minions in the global realpolitik, the region of CONCACAF in general, and its former president in particular, were still able to command global attention and exercise some measure of influence on a major football power in the world (in this case, England) as well as beat others to host the 2001 Under 17 Boys World Cup. This was due in large measure to their strategic position within FIFA and, in the case of Jack Warner, within the government of Trinidad and Tobago.

However, Warner's multiple positioning and personal machinations point to two major limitations of sport as diplomacy as an analytical framework for examining the sport diplomacy nexus. First, such positioning serves to blur the distinction or simple dualism between state and non-state actor that underpins sport's specialized diplomacy as articulated by Murray and Pigman since Warner was both a member of FIFA and the government, as well as party financier. Second, Warner's personal machinations within FIFA, particularly in the staging of the 2001 Under 17 Boys World Cup, clearly demonstrate how such specialized diplomacy of sport can involve particular forms of negotiation within non-state actors themselves and can provide opportunities for possible unethical conduct, which can lead to the reputational damage of the actors involved. In addition, to associate the use of public diplomacy with the FIFA World Cup bidding process is rather ironic or problematic since the apparent secrecy and closed-door manner in which the organization has conducted its business or governance is hardly consistent with a supposedly more open and transparent approach to diplomacy. Given the bold and seemingly brazen patterns of self-enrichment that have characterized the staging of such international sport events, whether mega or meager, the actions of certain FIFA officials reveal not only the specialized diplomatic power of soccer but also, perhaps, a specialized corruption of diplomacy in sport or the diplomacy of sporting corruption.[33]

Notes

1. "David Beckham Goes World Cup Vote Hunting for England in Trinidad," *Guardian,* September 26, 2010, https://www.theguardian.com/football/2010/sep/26/david-beckham-england-world-cup-bid (accessed August 1, 2017).

2. Stuart Murray and Geoffrey Pigman, "Mapping the Relationship between International Sport and Diplomacy," *Sport in Society* 17, no. 9 (2014): 1098–1118; Heather L. Dichter and Andrew L. Johns, eds., *Diplomatic Games: Sport, Statecraft and International Relations since 1945* (Lexington: University Press of Kentucky, 2014).

3. Murray and Pigman, "Mapping the Relationship," 1099–1111; David Black, "Dreaming Big: The Pursuit of 'Second Order' Games as a Strategic Response to Globalization," *Sport in Society* 11, no. 4 (2008): 467–468.

4. Central Statistical Office, "T&T Population Reaches 1.4 million," February 15, 2016, https://cso.gov.tt/news/tt-population-reaches-1-4-million (accessed June 11, 2018); Alan Tomlinson, "Lord, Don't Stop the Carnival: Trinidad and Tobago at the 2006 FIFA World Cup," *Journal of Sport and Social Issues* 31, no. 3 (2007): 259–282; "FIFA/Coca-Cola World Ranking," https://www.fifa.com/fifa-world-ranking/ranking-table/men/ (accessed December 15, 2019); https://www.fifa.com/worldcup/news/germany-2006-the-final-ranking-21411 (accessed December 15, 2019).

5. Aviston Downes, "Forging Africa-Caribbean Solidarity within the Commonwealth," in *Diplomatic Games: Sport, Statecraft and International Relations since 1945,* ed. Dichter and Johns, 122. The discussion of foreign policy and diplomacy in the Caribbean is now framed by the notion or narrative of "small island states" and the peculiar issues of vulnerability (economic, environmental, and political), dependence, and marginalization in world affairs that have come to define this condition. See Jacqueline Anne Braveboy-Wagner, *Small States in Global Affairs: The Foreign Policies of the Caribbean Community (CARICOM)* (New York: Palgrave MacMillan, 2008).

6. Downes, "Forging Africa-Caribbean Solidarity," 122.

7. "History," http://www.concacaf.com/concacaf/history (accessed November 1, 2016); Tomlinson, "Lord Don't Stop the Carnival," 262.

8. "About the CFU," June 22, 2013, http://www.cfufootball.org/index.php/the-cfu/about-the-cfu (accessed November 1, 2016); Roy McCree, "Professionalism and the Development of Club Football in Trinidad and Tobago" (MSc diss., University of the West Indies, St. Augustine, Trinidad and Tobago, 1995); FIFA, Report on the Inquiry into the 2018/2022 FIFA World Cup Bidding Process, 235, https://img.fifa.com/image/upload/wnr43dgn3yysafypuq8r.pdf (accessed August 1, 2017); Valentino Singh, *Jack Warner: Zero to Hero* (Port of Spain: Medianet Ltd., 2006), 153–154; FIFA, Report on the Inquiry, 351.

9. "FIFA/Coca-Cola World Ranking," http://www.fifa.com/fifa-world-ranking/ranking-table/men/ (accessed June 11, 2018); Tomlinson, "Lord Don't Stop," 262–263; Alan Tomlinson, *FIFA: The Men, The Money, The Myths* (London: Routledge, 2014), 26–50, 133–135; Tomlinson, "Lord Don't Stop," 262–263; FIFA, Report on the Inquiry into the 2018/2022 FIFA World Cup Bidding Process, 8; Singh, *Jack Warner*, 186–188; Andrew Jennings, *FOUL!: The Secret World of FIFA: Bribes, Vote Rigging and Ticket Scandals* (London: Harper Collins, 2006), 74–94.

10. Tomlinson, "Lord Don't Stop," 266; Singh, *Jack Warner*, 183; FIFA, Report on the Inquiry into the 2018/2022 FIFA World Cup Bidding Process, 8–11.

11. McCree, "Professionalism and the Development"; Basil Matthews, "The Evolution of Football in Trinidad and Tobago, 1908–1962" (address delivered at Hotel Normandie, Port of Spain, December 12, 1965); Jennings, *FOUL!*, 136–138; Singh, *Jack Warner*; Valentino Singh, *Upwards Through the Night: The Biography of Austin Jack Warner* (Port of Spain: Lexicon, 1998); Tomlinson, "Lord Don't Stop," 269; FIFA, Report on the Inquiry, 109; Tomlinson, *FIFA: The Men*. Warner's resignation was precipitated by a "vote for cash" scandal; in which it was alleged that he acted in concert with the former president of the Asian soccer federation (Mohammed Bin Hammam) to buy the votes of CONCACAF member countries for US$40,000.00 each so that they would vote for him in FIFA's presidential elections. "World Governing Body Drops Probe: Jack Quits FIFA," *Trinidad and Tobago Newsday*, June 21, 2011, 1, 3; "JACK SHOCKER: Warner Resigns from FIFA; Football Body Drops Bribery Probe," *Trinidad Express*, June 21, 2011, 1, 3.

12. The investigative report, spearheaded by Caribbean jurist Sir Kennedy Simmons, found that Warner and former CONCACAF secretary Chuck Blazer "together and individually, used their official positions to promote their own self-interests . . . with disdain for the rules that governed their conduct." Singh, *Jack Warner*; Selwyn Ryan, *Selwyn Ryan: Selected Writings on Race, Class and Gender in Trinidad and Tobago: The Struggle for Hegemony* (Trinidad: Multimedia Production Centre, 2016), 123–162; Republic of Trinidad and Tobago, Members of Past Parliaments, http://www.ttparliament.org/members.php?mid=26&pid=25&id=JWA01 (accessed August 1, 2017); Jennings, *FOUL!*; "Jack Resigns as MP Today," *Trinidad Newsday*, April 26, 2013, 1, 3; "Warner in Destabilising Role of Insider/Outsider," editorial, *Sunday Express*, April 28, 2013, 12; "I Come to Deliver the Truth," *Trinidad Newsday*, April 28, 2016, 23; United States Department of Justice, "Nine FIFA Officials and Five Corporate Executives Indicted for Racketeering, Conspiracy and

Corruption," May 27, 2015, https://www.justice.gov/opa/pr/nine-fifa-officials-and-five-corporate-executives-indicted-racketeering-conspiracy-and (accessed November 20, 2016); Gail Alexander, "Jack on Interpol Wanted List," *Trinidad Guardian*, June 4, 2015, http://www.guardian.co.tt/news/2015-06-03/jack-interpol-wanted-list (accessed November 16, 2015); Jada Loutoo, "Jack Warner Extradition on Hold," *Newsday*, February 20, 2018, https://newsday.co.tt/2018/02/20/jack-warner-extradition-on-hold/ (accessed June 20, 2018); "Warner Loses Fight against US Extradition," *Jamaica Observer*, September 28. 2017, http://www.jamaicaobserver.com/latestnews/Warner_loses_fight_against_US_extradition?profile=1228orruption (accessed June 20, 2018). In September 2019, Warner won his appeal to have his case taken to the London Privy Council, which is the final court of appeal for this former British colony. Derek Achong, "Jack Gets Green Light for Final Appeal in Extradition Case," *Trinidad Guardian*, September 23, 2019, https://www.guardian.co.tt/news/jack-gets-green-light-for-final-appeal-in-extradition-case-6.2.943283.c7836106a8 (accessed December 15, 2019).

13. FIFA, Report on the Inquiry, 99.

14. David Black, "Dreaming Big: The Pursuit of 'Second Order' Games as a Strategic Response to Globalization," *Sport in Society* 11, no. 4 (2008): 467–468.

15. Jennings, *FOUL!*, 151; Republic of Trinidad and Tobago, House of Representatives, Parliamentary Debates, October 18, 1999; "Blatter Supports T&T 2007 U-20 World Cup Bid," *Trinidad Express*, September 25, 2001, 62.

16. Jennings, *FOUL!*, 151.

17. FIFA had also sold Warner the regional TV rights for the 1990, 1994, 1998, and 2002 World Cups for the price of US$1.00. Singh, *Jack Warner*, 163, 187–189, 211, 213–215; Jennings, *FOUL!*, 151–152; Republic of Trinidad and Tobago, House of Representatives, FIFA Youth Championship-Stadia, March 31, 2000, 2, Hansard, Parliamentary Library of Trinidad and Tobago, Port of Spain, Trinidad and Tobago; Tomlinson, "Lord Don't Stop," 272; Mark Pouchet, "Media Row Threatens Under-17s," *Trinidad Express*, August 18, 2001, 80; Mark Pouchet, "CSTN Tell Lawyers to Act," *Trinidad Express*, August 19, 2001, 48; Lasana Liburd, "Warner Grilled on Conflict of Interest," *Sunday Express*, September 30, 2001, 54.

18. Ian Prescott, "More $$ for Warners," *Trinidad Express*, September 10, 2001, 64; "A Question of Contracts," editorial, *Trinidad Express*, September 11, 2001, 10; Lasana Liburd, "Warner Grilled on Conflict of Interest," *Sunday Express*, September 30, 2001, 54; Jennings, *FOUL!*, 150–163; Tomlinson, "Lord Don't Stop," 271–273.

19. Tomlinson, "Lord Don't Stop," 272; Singh, *Jack Warner*, 188; Andrew Jennings, "Caribbean Question Turns Sepp into Silent Type," Trinidad and Tobago News Bulletin Board, October 7 2002, http://www.trinidadandtobagonews.com/forum/webbbs_config.pl?md=read;id=388 (accessed July 11, 2017); "Our Opinion: A Question of Contracts," *Trinidad Express*, September 11, 2001, 10.

20. "Our Opinion: A Question of Contracts"; Jennings, *FOUL!*, 152–153; 159–161; Singh, *Jack Warner*, 187–189; Garth Wattle, "Smoking Out the Truth," *Trinidad Express*, October 3, 2001, 70.

21. "Blatter Supports T&T 2007 U-20 World Cup Bid," *Trinidad Express*, September 25, 2001, 62.

22. "Warner Guarantees Safety," *Trinidad Express*, September 13, 2001, 62; Jennings, *FOUL!*, 152–153; 159–161; Singh, *Jack Warner*, 187–189.

23. Stuart Murray and Geoffrey Pitman, "Mapping the Relationship between International Sport and Diplomacy," *Sport in Society* 17, no. 9 (2014): 1098–1118.

24. As part of the reform process within FIFA, the decision on World Cup hosts is no longer made by its executive but its entire membership as shown recently in the award for the 2026 World Cup. Martha Kellner, "US, Canada and Mexico Beat Morocco in Vote to Host 2026 World Cup," June 13, 2018, https://www.theguardian.com/football/2018/jun/13/world-cup-2026-vote-north-america-morocco (accessed June 15, 2018); John Sugden and Alan Tomlinson, *Bedfellows: FIFA Family at War* (Edinburgh, Scotland: Mainstream, 2003), 251; Tomlinson, *FIFA: The Men*, 129–132.

25. "English Lions Maul Warriors," *Trinidad and Tobago Newsday*, June 2, 2008, 1, 3; "Trinidad & Tobago 0–3 England," BBC Sport, http://news.bbc.co.uk/sport2/hi/football/internationals/7425208.stm, June 1, 2008 (accessed November 1, 2016); "England, Soda Warriors' Tickets Sold Out," *Trinidad Newsday*, May 7, 2008, 8; "A Score to Settle: Soda Warriors, England Match Sold Out in 24 Hours," *Trinidad Guardian*, May 7, 2008, 78; "Dear Minister Hunt," *Trinidad Newsday*, May 21, 2008, 14.

26. "English FA Gets TV Rights," *Trinidad Express*, May 22, 2008, 6; "British Press: Warner Dictating Financial Terms," *Saturday Express*, May 24, 2008, 64; "Late Evening Court Sitting: T&T-England Match On," *Trinidad Guardian*, May 24, 2008, 7; "TTFF, Ministry of Sport Lawyers Settle Stadium Row: Match Gets Green Light," *Trinidad Express*, May 24, 2008, 78; "Late Evening Court Sitting: T&T-England Match On," *Trinidad Guardian*, May 24, 2008, 7.

27. England actually submitted its bid documents to FIFA on May 14, 2010. "David Beckham Goes World Cup Vote Hunting for England in Trinidad," *Guardian*, September 26, 2010, https://www.theguardian.com/football/2010/sep/26/david-beckham-england-world-cup-bid (accessed August 1, 2017); 2018 FIFA World Cup: Bid Evaluation Report: England, November 17, 2010, http://www.fifa.com/mm/document/tournament/competition/01/33/74/53/b6enge.pdf (accessed November 1, 2016).

28. FIFA, Report on the Inquiry into the 2018/2022 FIFA World Cup Bidding Process, 17; FIFA, 2018 FIFA World Cup: Bid Evaluation Report: England, 2010, 9, http://www.fifa.com/mm/document/tournament/competition/01/33/74/53/b6enge.pdf (accessed August 1, 2017).

29. Alan Tomlinson, *FIFA: The Men*, 131–132.

30. FIFA, Report on the Inquiry, 15–25, 38, 130, 139.

31. FIFA, Report on the Inquiry, 99–117.

32. Ibid., 107, 111.

33. Murray and Pitman, "Mapping the Relationship." For rather vivid insights into this culture of self-enrichment and narcissism, see FIFA, Report on the Inquiry.

The World Cup Is Ours!

The Myth of Brazilianness in Lula's Diplomatic Rhetoric, 2007–2014

Euclides de Freitas Couto and Alan Castellano Valente

In his 2007 speech in Zurich, Switzerland, at the ceremony when FIFA officially announced Brazil as the host of the 2014 FIFA World Cup, President Luiz Inácio Lula da Silva (Lula) celebrated another achievement of the Brazilian diplomatic efforts that had been under way since 2003. President Lula, a former laborer and union leader, had become one of the most prominent figures on the world scene as he sought to enhance the country's standing through political and economic projects. President Lula incorporated in his speech mythological narratives that, in turn, confirmed the dominant discourses on national identity: "Football is not a sport for us. It's more! It's a national passion!" Like carnival, football is one of the abstract bonds providing Brazilians with a sense of national community beyond local identification. According to sociologist Jessé Souza, in order to reach ordinary people who are highly sensitive to the protection of local ties, the nation, to constitute itself as such, provides a powerful "symbolic arsenal" to counteract local bonds, in competition with "other external" factors. These external factors are perhaps what Joseph Nye called "soft power"—the ability of a country, or in this case of Lula himself, to persuade others to do what he wants without force or coercion. Lula's arguments for his diplomatic ventures were based on the idea of delivering green mega-events to serve as a benchmark for the next generation of mega-events and also on the idea of infrastructure legacy. He highlighted the simple fact that hosting such events both signaled and promised further opportunities to enhance the agency of large developing countries in global affairs, and certainly beyond their regional bases. Lula even joked about Brazil's longtime football rivalry with Argentina, saying that they would be jealous of Brazil's success in hosting the event.[1]

Although Lula's speech may have sounded spontaneous and a bit naive at first, his discursive strategy in mobilizing the specters of national tradition was aimed, even if unconsciously, at finding a common good to secure a moral justification for public investment. Thus, holding the World Cup in Brazil would represent not only the country's organizational capacity but also the symbolic crowning of the tradition of the "soccer country"; that is, a selective reconstruction of the past was used to express the aspirations of hegemonic groups.[2] Lula's political goal with hosting sports mega-events—first the World Cup and then the Olympics—was to use his public diplomacy to attract business and enhance his own global reach using the world's media. He had in mind, of course, that these efforts would be a quick way to achieve international credibility and diplomatic status for himself and, by extension, for the country.

The myth of Brazilianness, on which the sociological formulations of the Brazilian passion for soccer are based, has gained sway because it has been disseminated by state policies and is, in some way, sympathetic to dominant interests. Interpretations of the "Brazilian nation" have become the foundation of a "selective tradition," as defined by Raymond Williams, through which some social practices are seen as guarding cultural values. The ground for the emergence of this tradition or an "imagined community," in the sense proposed by Anderson, began to be prepared in Brazil during the period called Estado Novo (1937–1945). In this period, a combination of efforts were undertaken by the state, intellectuals, radio, sports journalists, and newspapers that aimed to integrate soccer with a feeling of nationality based on assumptions about miscegenation. The works of Brazilian sociologist Gilberto Freyre, especially in *Casa-Grande & Senzala* (1933), unveiled the national myth. The discourse of miscegenation anchored the chorus among the journalists at that time. The famous journalist and writer Mário Filho published many articles that conveyed Freyre's thoughts about the national myth. In Mário Filho's work, the components of miscegenation furnished the texts published in newspapers during the 1920s and 1930s and later composed his masterpiece: *O Negro no Futebol Brasileiro*, first published in 1947 and then in an enlarged edition in 1964. Some historians today are intensely critical of his works, saying that they overestimate the attributes of race and ascribe to soccer the role of balancing socio-racial tensions in Brazil. Critics consider Mário Filho to be one of the "organic intellectuals" of the Estado Novo because of the instrumental character of his literary output, which was directly associated with the cultural policy guidelines outlined by President Getúlio Vargas's office (1934–1945 and 1951–1954). Conversely, among intellectuals linked to the culturalist tradition, Mário Filho's work is at the forefront of Brazilian sport literature, since, in addition to representing the aesthetic and conceptual renewal of the soccer chronicle narrative, his texts—supplemented by vivid oral reports—are paradigmatic in understanding the history of Brazilian soccer.[3]

Out of this conflicting context, the Brazilian sport chronicle emerged; the "founding myth" of the Freyrean tradition, it has been explored exhaustively by scholars and appears in the works of Mário Filho, Nelson Rodrigues, and José Lins do Rego, as well as in some of the few soccer articles written by Gilberto Freyre himself. Sportswriters, as well as some intellectuals who occasionally wrote for the sport pages, appropriated the "Freyrean symbolic arsenal" to turn the time around the World Cups into moments of nationalistic exaltation. These narratives, widely disseminated and publicized in the form of propaganda in sport programs and amplified in the very language of the sport commentators, bring forth the symbolic arsenals of the past, promoting the exaltation of national identity by taking as a background the sport performance that particularly stimulates Freyrean rereadings of the nation. This work, therefore, constitutes what sociologist Antônio Jorge Soares called "popular Freyrism." Freyrean interpretations of the Brazilian myth are based on the assumption that the success of Brazilian soccer can be directly associated with the psychosocial characteristics of the people: wicked, streetwise, samba-like, able to improvise, and artistic. Combined with common sense, these traits shape the essentialist readings about the nation that have become hegemonic since the cultural project was started by President Vargas during the Estado Novo: during his dictatorship and afterward, when he was elected president.[4]

Memories of the project of the nation as idealized by President Vargas resurfaced in October 2007 during the ceremony in which FIFA officially selected Brazil as the host country of the 2014 World Cup. By highlighting the Brazilian passion for soccer, the discursive pillars in president Lula's speech were designed to incorporate the rhetorical symbolic arsenal present in popular culture. In his speech, he was able to connect commonplaces to this solemn moment, using the occasion to evoke the whole project of nation as a constant work in progress that had been under way since the 1930s. Consciously or unconsciously, the presidential rhetoric used descriptions and interpretations inscribed in a tradition that is part of the way of thinking about the singularities of Brazilian culture and identity; by extension, the Brazilian way of playing soccer was used as a metaphor for his diplomatic efforts.[5]

Lula's Brazilian rhetoric seduced the international media and diplomats. Domestically, however, Lula had to devise a more pragmatic discursive expedient to offer answers to social demands and simultaneously to attend to the wishes of the hegemonic actors, despite all the feelings aroused by soccer. Lula, by that time, did not innovate, preferring instead to use a well-known rhetorical formula for both Brazilians and the international public regarding mega-events and their legacies. Rio de Janeiro had hosted the 2007 Pan American Games. The initial estimated cost for the event was $196 million (US), but the final expenditures were about ten times the initial budget, becoming an object of intense criticism in the Brazilian press. In spite of the political image damage caused by the preparations for the Pan American Games, due to a series of structural problems and extremely high costs, Lula and the local leaders of Rio de Janeiro used the rhetoric of legacy, portraying the whole enterprise as a "great achievement," a kind of rehearsal for the several mega-events that Brazil would host in the near future. The president thus convinced a skeptical public that hosting the mega-event would generate economic profit and would leave great infrastructure as a legacy.[6]

As part of his broader efforts to improve Brazil's position within the international system, President Lula frequently invoked a rhetoric about Brazilian national identity that relied heavily on football. These efforts helped Brazil win the right to host the 2014 World Cup, and Lula and his successor, Dilma Rousseff, continued to utilize rhetoric that emphasized a mythical Brazilian identity as well as the valuable legacies for the country from hosting this mega-event. Whereas this language may have helped achieve the diplomatic goals of the Workers' Party presidents within the international system and FIFA, it failed to persuade the domestic population, resulting in widespread protests and significant challenges inside the country. Nonetheless, by evoking rhetorical myth and elevating it within diplomatic endeavors, presidents Lula and Rousseff used football and the hosting of the 2014 FIFA World Cup as a representation of identity and national policy, projecting a specific image of Brazil abroad to help achieve the goals of expanding and enhancing the country's status.

Lula's Soccer Diplomacy Strategies

Beginning in 2003 under Lula, a new paradigm of Brazilian foreign policy was developed. The broad diplomatic effort promoted by Lula's government enabled the signing of a series of extremely positive international agreements and commercial partnerships, especially for the projection of the image of the country on the international scene. During Lula's administration, besides hosting numerous commercial events, Brazil hosted the Pan American Games in 2007 and was selected to host the 2014 FIFA World Cup and the 2016 Olympic and Paralympic Games, the two most important sporting mega-events in the world. Through the frequent emphasis on sport within his public statements and the efforts to win and organize these events, Lula helped revitalize the "Brazilian myth" with respect to football, especially in the field of international relations.

During his seven years in office, President Lula became one of the most prominent figures on the global political stage. In his 2003 speech at the World Economic Forum in Davos, he defended the project of a fairer and more democratic new international economic order by reducing the protectionist barriers to trade imposed by the rich countries. Similar to his speech at the October 2007 ceremony in Zurich at which Brazil was officially named the host of the 2014 FIFA World Cup, in Davos, Lula raised sympathy with emerging countries. In addition to Lula's general charismatic appeal, his government's diplomacy must also be assessed on his ability to enhance soft power by projecting a dynamic image of Brazil to the world. In particular, his use of sport mega-events to catalyze diplomatic goals placed the country at the forefront of diplomacy that shaped long-term attitudes and preferences worldwide. Despite the undeniable economic projection achieved after the stabilization of the economy during the Fernando Henrique Cardoso administration (1995–2002), and especially after the "Lula Era" (2003–2010), Brazil became one of the primary actors influencing the world political agenda. Lula's personal image was even more widely known than the country itself, which confirms, in theory, the true success of his diplomacy in projecting his own image as the embodiment of Brazil. The former president was well-known for constantly breaking diplomatic protocols and addressing his political agenda via soccer metaphors. The media frequently criticized his discursive strategies, commenting that his lack of formality had even contaminated the state ministers, who perhaps should not address the media or the people in such an informal tone.[7]

Brazilian diplomacy made great efforts to insert the country in a more democratic way in the process of globalization. With the support of the moral discourse of the fight against poverty and hunger and within the framework of Brazilian foreign policy, different strategies were used to realign the country on the international agenda. Brazil acted as a protagonist in international negotiations (in commercial trading, war conflicts, and humanitarian matters), aligned with emerging countries in South America, expanded the country's participation in multilateral trading organizations, and increased the number of Brazilian diplomatic missions abroad by 30 percent. The extensive program of presidential diplomacy resulted in a record number of trips for diplomatic purposes and participation in a complex circuit of meetings with foreign leaders, something never previously achieved in the history of Brazil's diplomatic staff in Itamaraty. Another of Lula's diplomatic goals was for Brazil to occupy a permanent seat in the UN Security Council. However, Brazil will have to wait for at least two decades, due to the lack of interest of the present government and, more importantly, due to the global powers' perception that the country does not fit the objective factors—connected to economic stability, technological endowments, and military capabilities—to claim a permanent seat alongside the United Kingdom, the United States, Russia, France, and China.[8]

Lula's diplomatic policy was aimed at calling the attention of the international powers to Brazil's ascending leadership in South America. Thus, as part of the coordinating strategy for the July 2004 UN peacekeeping mission in Haiti, the poorest country in the Americas and a country plagued by a serious economic and political crisis, Brazil promoted a friendly match against local soccer players. The participation of the Brazilian national soccer team in this game scored a great point for Lula's diplomacy. The so-called "Peace Game" was not just a soccer match, but a metaphor for an emerging and unified country filled with a passion for soccer and life itself, ready to help the poorest peoples to build a better world for all. This match alone was not enough to win Brazil a permanent seat in the UN Security Council, but Lula's diplomatic efforts were nonetheless able to present Brazil as an emerging economy and a power broker with great prospects for the medium term.[9]

In addition to formal diplomatic efforts via the United Nations, nongovernmental organizations and international private agencies such as FIFA and the International Olympic Committee (IOC) also act in an organized and pragmatic way as they defend interests they share with business partners and state agents, or, in other cases, as they act autonomously. To strengthen their international prestige, emerging countries have taken advantage of the strategy of hosting sport mega-events. In an attempt to understand the current forms of the relationship between diplomacy and sport, Stuart Murray and Geoffrey Pigman chose the category "sport as international diplomacy" to differentiate this from the conventional idea of "sport as a diplomacy instrument." The relationship between sport and diplomacy from the point of view of this taxonomy encompasses both the effects of international sport on diplomacy and the effects of diplomacy on international sport. Driven by a dialogical relationship, different configurations of diplomacy are formulated and settled, in which actors such as FIFA, the IOC, and large transnational corporations present themselves as protagonists in negotiations with governments. The impact of these relationships may be even greater than of conventional diplomacy, as the economic interests underlying them materialize, for example, in the implementation of sporting mega-events where emotional and commercial appeal is able to reach the public on a global scale.[10]

Drawing on these concepts, President Lula simultaneously promoted assumptions that defined the Brazilian people in the efforts to win the bid to host the 2014 World Cup. Lula especially emphasized Brazilians' "innate empathy and hospitality" and their role as the greatest lovers of football in the world. By nurturing the broad cultural heritage of Brazil in which football plays a central role, Lula presented the project of holding an event such as the FIFA World Cup in Brazil strategically to gain international visibility. His references to the "land of football" appealed to both Brazilian national self-image and to international public opinion. Because Brazil had won five of FIFA's World Cups, and based on the country's supposed superiority in the game, the argument ran, hosting the World Cup would surely bring another title to the country.[11]

Taking as a moral foundation the "myth of Brazilianness" in which football is viewed as the cultural patrimony of the country, Lula's foreign policy followed the principles of neoliberalism. His administration prioritized the hosting of sport mega-events because in the heart of this rhetoric such events appear to be potential catalysts for sustainable economic development in emerging countries. Promoters stress that, in addition to providing moments of national and intercultural celebration, these events have become increasingly efficient instruments to disseminate capitalist values, reproduced in the form of tourism, consumerization, and modernization of cities and sporting arenas. However, recent research shows that the main function of mega-events is to attract flows of international capital, making it possible to integrate emerging countries into the transnational investment route—through the complex repertoire of urban commodification represented by instruments such as public–private partnerships, tax exemption and corporate management of cities, and the increase in advanced telecommunication, tourism, and commercial services.[12]

Lula's rhetoric encompassed the argument of legacy and of football as a national passion, giving the idea that the government was fulfilling a long-time dream of the people. In this way Lula's comments diminished the negative criticism against this huge investment. The rhetoric of the legacy associated with the Brazilian myth therefore fulfilled a dual function in President Lula's official speech. First, it sought to convince the public that it was feasible to host the sport mega-event. Second, in the sphere of foreign relations, it served to project the country on the international scene by exalting its cultural and multiethnic tradition synthesized by the supposed unconditional adherence of its people to football. This symbiosis, coupled with the president's own sympathy, set the tone of Lula's diplomacy in the years leading up to the preparations for the 2014 World Cup.

FIFA's Demands

After the 2007 announcement of Brazil's selection as the host country for the 2014 World Cup, a set of discursive practices were used to justify the need to fulfill FIFA requirements and to allocate large public investments to build infrastructure for the event. The same arguments gained emphasis in the discursive practice of President Rousseff and the other political leaders of the country who, at that moment, united to legitimize the continually increasing World Cup budget with Brazilian public opinion. The presidential campaign of the Workers' Party (Partido dos Trabalhadores) promised to set a political agenda to follow Lula's goals and to keep the deals his administration had made. In the wake of hosting this mega-event, the Brazilian parliament approved the General Law of the Cup in June 2012. This new legislation enabled local and regional political powers to work together to organize the World Cup. The entire foreign ministry also worked to implement public diplomacy efforts and use global media to attract attendees from around the world and, most of all, investors. Contractors, banks, hotel chains, and municipal and state governments began a broad political and media movement to get parliament to approve the allocation of public resources and to legitimize this spending in the public eye.[13]

Congressmen showed their political goodwill by approving the General Law of the Cup with only minor conflicts in the Brazilian parliament, creating, according to some experts, a "state of temporary exception." This law established the norms governing FIFA Confederations Cup 2013, FIFA World Cup 2014, and World Youth Journey 2013, which took place in Brazil. In an effort to meet FIFA's requirements, the Brazilian Parliament actually violated the basic principles of sovereignty to pass the General Law of the Cup. FIFA demanded vehicle restrictions on local traffic in the so-called FIFA exclusive areas within a two-kilometer perimeter of the venues, licenses for selling alcohol at the venues, and restrictions on ambush marketing. These changes and other requirements regarding concessionary tickets and the activities of street vendors surrounding the venues triggered a loud negative response from the Brazilian public. Across social media and traditional media outlets, Brazilians shouted out their criticism: "Mega-events and Human Rights Violations in Rio de Janeiro, People's Cup Committee shows that there is little to celebrate." Simultaneously with the federal government's effort to legitimize these actions, several nationwide protests broke out. Most of these protests included people affected by work related to the World Cup, and many people grounded their revolt around crucial issues such as the poor condition of public health, transport systems, and education in the country.[14]

Lula's foreign policy, with the massive support of Brazilian political leaders and the supreme court, formed a coalition between the hegemonic groups—FIFA itself, the World Cup sponsors, and the government of the Brazilian states hosting the event—to promote the supposed legacies of the World Cup to the country. The political rivalry between the Workers' Party and the opposition parties, especially the Brazilian Social Democracy Party (PSDB) and the Democrats (DEM), created additional challenges. The realization of the World Cup involved a complex political articulation between the federal government and state governments because the possibility of distributing public resources to traditional private partners—especially contractors—had become an obsession for the governors of several Brazilian states. Although the FIFA booklet of demands required the provision of eight host cities for the event, Brazil hosted the World Cup in twelve cities. Having so many host venues was an important part of the coalition policy of the Workers' Party, which wanted to meet the political and economic aspirations of the largest possible number of partners. Manaus, Cuiabá, Natal, and Brasilia—unimportant football cities where the average attendance for local championships does not exceed a thousand spectators—had new stadiums built, at a total cost of over 300 percent of the initial budget, according to official data provided by the Brazilian government.[15]

In addition, using a legal breach in the general law for mega-events taking place in Brazil after 2011, governors could fulfill special demands in hiring services without a public tender process. This law of exception, meant to accelerate the process of allocating public funding, would guarantee, in theory, compliance with the schedule of works imposed by FIFA's charter. The government largely took these actions without public notice, which further reduced the transparency of public bidding processes for the work to facilitate cartel activities. Thus, Brazilian officials privileged the interests of large Brazilian multinationals, such as the construction companies Odebrecht, Andrade Gutierrez, OAS, and Camargo Correa, all of which traditionally fund political campaigns for all political parties. At the heart of this redistribution of public resources to the private sector, the government financed approximately 80 percent of the total cost of the World Cup, most of which came from the state banks Banco Nacional de Desenvolvimento Econômico e Social (BNDES) and Caixa Econômica Federal (CEF). Public funding was used even for the building or remodeling of private sports arenas after the event, such as the Arena Corinthians (São Paulo), Beira Rio (Porto Alegre), and Arena da Baixada (Curitiba). In 2007, in the first in situ survey conducted by FIFA, consultant Hugo Salcedo stated that the Brazilian Football Confederation "currently estimates that investments in the construction and remodeling of stadiums would be $1.1 billion." The day before the opening of the 2014 mega-event, the transparency portal of the federal government released data that revealed that investments from the federal coffers alone for the construction and renovation of stadiums exceeded $2 billion (US). In addition to the investments made by the state governments, the stadium expenses cost approximately $3 billion (US). Notably, the 2014 World Cup was the most expensive in the history of football mega-events. Germany had invested about €3 billion for the 2006 event, South Africa €4 billion for 2010; in Brazil, available data show that investments exceeded €9 billion when the costs of urban mobility works, airports, training, tourism development, public safety, and others are tallied.[16]

In emerging countries, where fragile representative democratic systems are obscured by the interests of hegemonic groups, political alliances and trade pacts overlap in their collective interests. The articulation between public and private actors thus promotes the shift of public resources to the private partnership, generating direct profits through the promotion of sport mega-events. The 2014 World Cup was not only the event with the highest public investments but it also filled FIFA's coffers, with profit of over $4 billion (US)—66 percent more than the tournament in South Africa had earned the international federation. By the time the 2014 World Cup took place, Lula had not been president for years. Yet, the organizers frequently invoked the former president and his rhetoric to counter key questions about transparency, legacy, and criticism of the preparations. According to the executive secretary of the Ministry of Sports, Luís Fernandes, "The great legacy of the World Cup was another step taken towards the development of the country. Brazil is a developing country and from the first moment we saw that the opportunity to host the World Cup was a historic window to leverage infrastructure investment that the country needed."[17]

Thus, the official discourse of the Brazilian government was very close to that of the market, two actors with a great interest in holding the World Cup in the country. If Lula saw a way to expand his political capital by projecting the image of his government's prosperity domestically and abroad, economic agents (banks, contractors, and the media) saw a chance to expand their investments in a country considered a major emerging power.

The Political Scenario in Brazil: World Cup for Whom?

The political and economic developments resulting from Brazil's international policies in the years prior to the 2014 World Cup affected the performance of Brazilian diplomacy and the execution of mega-events between 2007 and 2014. During this period, the country experienced ambivalent situations under presidents Lula and Rousseff, both elected by the leftist Workers' Party. Social policies reduced poverty, which fulfilled the United Nations' Millennium Goals as well as the party's own campaign promises. The alignment of the Workers' Party with the neoliberal agenda contributed, in part, to the rise of the country's image internationally; however, it pressed the government, especially during Rousseff's time in office, to work on a tight budget and cut social investments exponentially. The government failed to follow this tight budget, which led to a series of poor economic decisions and aroused the media against Rousseff and her policies. The dream of making the best World Cup ever began to turn into a nightmare, as the traditional political opponents of the Workers' Party commenced a major media campaign seeking to denounce and expose the misuse of public resources by the federal government.[18]

At the same time, during preparations for the World Cup, the media explored problems related to the organization of the event, especially social issues and unmet basic needs that could be associated with the federal government: health, education, and transport. Social networks, fueled largely by opposition to the federal government, soon invited people to occupy the streets of the main Brazilian cities, promoting one of the largest protests witnessed in Brazilian history. The protesters carried signs with messages such as "We Want Education / Health in FIFA standards," in reaction against the vilified FIFA-standard stadiums often evoked in official discourses to justify the spending on infrastructure venues. The protesters signaled that the World Cup was no longer a priority; instead, the tournament became a motive for questioning the resource management model, especially the ever-rising budget for the event. These protests convinced the Brazilian parliament to approve FIFA's general set of laws related to organizing the event, but this legislation then triggered a series of heated debates nationwide, causing further problems for the government.[19]

The movement, known as the June Days (*Jornadas de Junho*), began protesting Rousseff's government in the streets of the main Brazilian cities in June 2013 on the eve of the Confederations Cup (the test event held one year before the World Cup in some of the same venues). Although it had a diffuse agenda, the June Days put in check the model of public resources management in recent years. In the midst of the debate about the bankruptcy of the welfare state, a demonstration in the city of São Paulo against the increase of bus fares triggered a series of large protests across Brazil. Engendered in a new socio-communicational dynamic, a complex network phenomenon organized via Facebook ended up with thousands of people in the streets, leading to a heterogeneous set of protests against the neglected public policies.[20]

In addition, the final stages of preparation for the 2014 World Cup were plagued by numerous delays in the work schedule, cost overruns, fatalities, and nationwide protests, adding to the various problems related to the organization of the mega-event. These problems created a series of embarrassments for Brazilian diplomacy, often requiring the direct intervention of President Dilma Rousseff to mediate conflicts with FIFA, especially with FIFA's secretary general, Jérôme Valcke. Since 2012 Valcke's statements regarding delays in the mega-event's preparation had contributed to increasingly contentious relations between the Brazilian government and FIFA. After Rousseff's intervention, the FIFA president and secretary general publicly apologized for the inconvenience caused by what they called "a series of misunderstandings in communication between the parties." FIFA president Joseph "Sepp" Blatter himself spoke with President Rousseff to reaffirm his confidence that everything was under control in Brazil and on schedule.[21]

Under Rousseff, in the months before the World Cup, the recent years of growth under the direction of the Workers' Party and especially President Lula appeared to be over. The voices of those citizens directly harmed by the works of the sports spectacle joined the chorus of people not content with the direction state management was taking. Following the perverse logic of "ad hoc urbanism," in the process of urban redevelopment and construction of stadiums for hosting the World Cup, thousands of people had been expropriated and removed from their homes, and self-employed street vendors around the stadiums found that their work had been made impossible. These actions also contributed to the elitism of the stadiums. In the name of safety and comfort, architectural changes modify the experience of the use of sport venues, developing a spatial practice that transforms the fan into a passive consumer and viewer and the public stadiums into private sport arenas controlled by transnational corporations. Thus, to the detriment of the collective interest, urban operations linked to sport mega-events have been designed to favor urban speculation, benefit contractors, promote land valuation, implement modern telecommunications infrastructure in prime areas, and increase the hotel industry and cultural businesses. Furthermore, Rousseff's office proved to be inept at communicating and providing quick responses as these problems arose at the time. She had neither the charisma of her predecessor nor the ability to convince the public of the benefits of mega-events for Brazil in terms of geopolitics and internal growth.[22]

Preparation for the 2014 World Cup therefore took place during a period of great political instability in which most media reports worked to the detriment of President Rousseff's image. While sport journalism typically promotes an event and its positive aspects, other editorials published by the media criticized the government for delays in the scheduled construction of works, mobility, and infrastructure. In one example, construction of the BRT (bus rapid transit) in one of the host cities, Belo Horizonte, was investigated by the Department of Treasury and Finance because this project alone overran the budget by R$115 million and was 20 months late. Since the beginning of 2010, when most of the stadium construction and renovations began, two trends predominated in the Brazilian media: on the one hand, criticism of public spending on the whole works for the mega-events; on the other hand, praise for the country's marketing competition, which reproduced the official rhetoric of the legacy. As Rousseff commented: "I personally think that no legacy is the World Cup, all the legacies are for the Brazilian people. For example, we are not building airports for the World Cup, we are making airports for all Brazilians, they will happen to be used for the World Cup."[23]

Skepticism related to suspicions of overbilling in the budgets of the World Cup began in earnest in June 2013. Police repression during the June Days protests, which turned violent in some instances, aroused a sense of indignation and revolt among a large part of the population, which was now divided on the issue of the country hosting the World Cup. Whereas the rhetoric of Brazilianness mobilized by the government and amplified by the media in 2007 had helped bring the World Cup to Brazil, by 2013 the same media outlets could no longer hide the essence of the operation that had, in fact, enabled the mega-event to take place in the country. The simple discourse of "the nation on soccer shoes" or "the Brazilian passion for football" appropriated by Lula in his speeches no longer worked to arouse a unified public sentiment. A survey conducted on the eve of the 2014 World Cup by IBOPE, one of the largest opinion polling institutes in Brazil, indicated that 42 percent of the Brazilian population was against holding the event in the country. The series of protests in 2013 showed that the people's priorities had moved in the opposite direction.[24]

This fanciful image of an emerging country began to wear off just as the international economic crisis began in 2008 during Lula's administration; the value of commodities plunged, compromising Brazil's trade balance and the federal government's economic planning. Until 2008, in most of Latin America, high commodity prices and strong economic growth hid economic and social problems. During Lula's first years in office, there was significant growth, and revenues from commodities led to an expansion of consumption, a general increase in living standards, and a decline in economic inequality but did not substantially alter the social structure. The minimal investments in Brazil in the areas of health, education, and technology were not enough to alter the country's complex social stratification framework.[25]

When protests against the government began in 2013 during the Confederations Cup, Brazil, far from being an island of prosperity, showed discouraging economic indicators that signaled the economy was on the verge of a recession. In the previous year, the economy had grown only 0.9 percent and the unemployment rate had increased to 6.5 percent, indicating that the growth model of the Lula era—from 2003 to 2010—had ended its cycle. At the same time, the media highlighted the continuous corruption scandals that had tainted national politics and Rousseff's (and Lula's) Workers' Party, particularly in relation to the high costs of World Cup's infrastructure. President Rousseff tried to legitimize the massive public funding by emphasizing the legacies originally developed by Lula's government. The rhetoric of the legacy adopted by the Workers' Party presidents reasoned that the country could not afford to miss the opportunity to gain status as a powerful leader and to increase its economic growth and social development. The populist discourse about the legacy and the essential goodness of sport led many people to assume that the costs and benefits were worth the trouble. However, the changes in Brazil's economy combined with the national protests forced Rousseff's government to change the nature and tone of the rhetoric about the World Cup. The government no longer connected diplomatic matters, FIFA, football, and Brazilian identity in its official communications.[26]

The news about the atmosphere of insecurity that had overtaken Brazil quickly spread throughout the world, prompting FIFA officials to consider canceling the Confederations Cup. In June 2013 FIFA gave an ultimatum to the Brazilian government, forcing President Rousseff to formalize assurances that the competition could be held safely. The president assembled an urgent ministerial meeting to respond to FIFA's concern, during which the Ministry of Justice and the country's security forces pledged to guarantee the necessary order for the event. The same week, Rousseff read an official statement on live television, in which she expressed her concern about the demonstrations and sought to minimize criticisms about the situation and about the issues of health, education, and transport in the country. Again, the rhetoric of the legacy and the consistent denial of the government's participation in the financing of the World Cup preparation were at stake. Rousseff asked Brazilians to stop protesting so that order and peace could return to the country. In her words: "Let's treat our guests with respect and make a great World Cup."[27]

The events surrounding the 2013 Confederations Cup were emblematic since they brought forth the complex framework around which current diplomatic relations are based. The presence of non-state actors as partners of the state suggests the reshaping of the strategies of negotiation and action of governments. Particularly in the case of the Confederations Cup, the Brazilian government fully complied with FIFA's demands, even taking unpopular measures such as allowing the police force to use violence against protesters. In addition, when a party controls the office for three terms, it typically loses political power elsewhere. The neglected state of public services and the constant media coverage ultimately collided with the agenda imposed by the interests of the hegemonic groups.

Amid this social turbulence, the organization of the World Cup in Brazil, far from being seen as a landmark of the achievements of the governments of the Workers' Party, ultimately became a moment for the public to question President Dilma Rousseff's decision making domestically, as she dealt with internal problems, and in the diplomatic field with FIFA's representatives. Although her reelection in November 2014 might indicate that the political fallout from the protests could have diminished, the extensive media campaign led by opposition groups against her in the ensuing years resulted in her impeachment, seen within Brazilian historiography as a coup d'état. If the whole idea designed by Lula and the Workers' Party for bidding and hosting such mega-events was to increase global reach to quickly gain international credibility and status, as well as to project the country's image abroad through the discursive praxis of public diplomacy, the costs were too high for an emerging economy with such a weak internal political basis. President Lula's attempts to enhance soft power collapsed right before the mega-events took place, which jeopardized the image he had constructed of himself as a world leader and helped to undermine the political forces of the Workers' Party.[28]

Under Lula, Brazil's image was an important part of the country's foreign policy and was used to convert the country's cultural capital into political and economic capital. Diplomacy sought to promote the country's brand through closer multilateral relations with other countries around the globe and with nongovernmental actors. To this end, President Lula envisioned that sport diplomacy would provide a shortcut to achieve his goals, which resulted in the hosting of such mega-events as the 2007 Pan American Games, the FIFA World Cup in 2014, and the 2016 Olympics. These events were part of the repertoire of political actions outlined by the Brazilian government under the Workers' Party presidents.

As it amplified the meanings of an imagined community, Brazilian diplomacy personified Lula's free way of conventional thinking, perhaps involuntarily or unconsciously, and it harmonized with traditional images of Brazil as it was seen by the rest of the world: the land of samba, soccer, capoeira swing, art improvisation, and exotic food. The symbolic architecture of the land of soccer, initiated in the 1930s and reinvented during the military dictatorships, provided Lula's discourse with the necessary components to foster a cultural texture to sublimate social dissensions of every order. This rhetoric offered an idealized view of the nation to sway national and international public opinion. Joy, sympathy, beauty, and racial harmony—fruits of the aphrodisiac victory of miscegenation—were presented as essential features of the Brazilian people. Their Brazilianness, when placed onto the football pitch, created a sui generis style of play, commonly known as "soccer art" since the 1960s, in contrast to the "football force" practiced by Europeans.[29]

In addition to these representations of the nation, Lula used the rhetoric of the World Cup's legacies to achieve his goals with the public at home and the concept of the green mega-event to appeal to the international crowd. Mega-event legacy rhetoric is extremely seductive because it reaffirms common sense: large urban equipment, monumental works, and improved public transportation are components of the "spectacle of urbanism," the essence of which is nothing more than the reproduction of international capital.[30] At first glance, the discursive strategies adopted by Lula's diplomacy seduced the international community and appeased the conflicts among local actors: media, contractors, local governments. By contrast, after the 2010 elections, Rousseff's presidency had to contend with the consequences of the international economic crisis, the political losses of the allied base of government in the parliament, the complex framework of the ongoing political disputes, and, most of all, the recurrent reports of corruption scandals related to the ever-rising budget for the World Cup, which led to an open campaign against the federal government. Increased unemployment and lower consumption rates, on top of media and parliamentary campaigns against Rousseff, culminated in wearing down the image of the federal government as well as of the Workers' Party. This situation jeopardized the viability of the World Cup.

In this ambivalent scenario in which the interests of nongovernmental actors overlapped collective interests, what architect and urban planner Raquel Rolnik called the "June Days" disturbed the order in a country that had seemed to live in a kind of "benign vertigo of prosperity and peace," and brought forth not one but a myriad of ill-resolved agendas, contradictions, and paradoxes. These events, related to domestic problems, came about just when the world turned its eyes toward Brazil. Expecting to find the images traditionally associated with Brazil—the exuberant natural landscapes and beautiful women—journalists from all over the world, who came to cover the Confederations Cup, instead faced a chaos never seen before in the country. Mass protests, burning vehicles, and military troops scattered through the streets showed a global audience the social contradictions instead of the image Lula had desired: a strong new power in international relations and a "nation deeply identified with soccer."[31]

Although sport served as an important platform for Lula's diplomacy, the internal political contradictions associated with the imbalance of the international economy provoked the questioning of the political-economic model adopted by the Workers' Party government and contributed to its weakened position in the country at the end. The neoliberal adventures undertaken with sport mega-events in the decade under Lula and Rousseff did not turn out quite as the Lula administration had envisioned. Instead of accelerating the country's sustainable development or helping to achieve the country's geopolitical goals, the organization of these events—especially the 2014 FIFA World Cup—triggered major political and economic problems that will need a great deal of diplomacy to mend. Lula pointed to "the passion of the nation for football" as an argument to host the games in Brazil and as an identity that unified the country. At the end, not without an ironic twist, the people's priorities proved stronger than the politicians' goals.[32]

Notes

1. Gabriel Peters, "Admirável Senso Comum? Notas sobre Schutz, Garfinkel e o Problema da Relação Agência / Estrutura na Teoria Social," *Anais do 34º Encontro Anual da Anpoc (*2010): 15; "Brasil é Sede da Copa de 2014," October 30, 2007, http://www.youtube.com/watch?v=oHDpugDHF7M&feature=relmfu (accessed February 6, 2017); Jessé Souza, "A Construção do Mito da 'Brasilidade,'" in *A Ralé Brasileira: Quem é e Como vive,* ed. Jessé Souza (Belo Horizonte: UFMG, 2011), 29–40; Joseph S. Nye, "Public Diplomacy and Soft Power," *Annals of the American*

Academy of Political and Social Science 616 (2008): 94–109; Pablo Uchôa, "Lula Promove Copa de 2014 e Faz Promessa de Transparência," BBC News Brasil, https://www.bbc.com/portuguese/noticias/2010/07/100708_brasil2014_pu_rc (accessed June 13, 2018).

2. Raymond Willians, *Marxism and Literature* (New York: Oxford, 1977), 115.

3. Ibid., 115; Benedict Anderson, *Imagined Communities: Reflections on the Origin and Spread of Nationalism* (New York: Verso, 2006), 5–6; "Freyre, Gilberto," United Architects—Essays, n.d., https://danassays.wordpress.com/encyclopedia-of-the-essay/freyre-gilberto/ (accessed June 28, 2018); Gilberto Freyre, *Casa-Grande & Senzala*, 46th ed. (Rio de Janeiro: Record, 2002); Mário Filho, *O Negro no Futebol Brasileiro* (Rio de Janeiro: Irmãos Pongetti Editores, 1947); José Sérgio Leite Lopes, "A Vitória do Futebol que Incorporou a Pelada: A Invenção do Jornalismo Esportivo e a Entrada dos Negros no Futebol Brasileiro," *Revista USP* 22 (1994): 64–83; Marcelino Rodrigues da Silva, *Mil e Uma Noites de Futebol: O Brasil Moderno de Mário Filho* (Belo Horizonte: UFMG, 2006); Antônio Jorge Soares,"Futebol Brasileiro e Sociedade: A Interpretação Culturalista de Gilberto Freyre,"in *Futbologías: Fútbol, Identidad y Violência em América Latina*, ed. Pablo Alabarces (Buenos Aires: Clacso, 2003); Euclides de Freitas Couto and Alan Castelano Valente, "Do Viralatismo à Crítica Engajada: Ambivalências das Crônicas de Juca Kfouri em Tempos de Megaeventos Esportivos,"*Aletria* 26, no. 3 (2016): 141–156.

4. The exception to this rule occurred in the 1960s and 1970s when intellectuals affiliated with the Marxist tradition appointed soccer as one of the instruments of alienation of the masses, since its symbolic capital would be at the service of the hegemonic groups. Published in alternative journals, these criticisms constituted a counterpoint to the culturalist interpretation. Euclides de Freitas Couto, *Da Ditadura à Ditadura: Uma História Política do Futebol Brasileiro (1930–1978)* (Niterói: UFF, 2014), 118; Antônio Jorge Soares, "Futebol Brasileiro e Sociedade: A Interpretação Culturalista de Gilberto Freyre," in *Futbologías: Fútbol, Identidad y Violência em América Latina*, ed. Pablo Alabarces (Buenos Aires: Clacso, 2003), 150.

5. Rodrigues da Silva, *Mil e Uma Noites de Futebol.*

6. "PAN-2007 Custa dez Vezes Mais do Que o Orçamento Inicial," n.d., http://inverta.org/jornal/edicao-impressa/411/Economia/411PAN (accessed March 10, 2017); Arlei Sander Damo, "O Desejo, o Direito e o Dever: A Trama Que Trouxe a Copa para o Brasil," *Movimento* 18, no. 2 (2012): 45–81.

7. *Time* nominated President Lula in 2010 as one of the hundred people who most affect the world. "Discurso de Lula em Davos," BBC Brasil.com, January 26, 2003, https://www.bbc.com/portuguese/noticias/2003/030126_integraamt.shtml (accessed February 9, 2017); "Brasil é Sede da Copa de 2014," http://www.youtube.com/watch?v=oHDpugDHF7M&feature=relmfu (accessed February 6, 2017); Michael Moore, "Luiz Inácio Lula da Silva," *Time*, April 29, 2010, http://content.time.com/time/specials/packages/article/0,28804,1984685_1984864_1984866,00.html (accessed February 9, 2017); Paulo Roberto de Almeida, "Never Before Seen in Brazil: Luis Inácio Lula da Silva's Grand Diplomacy," *Revista Brasileira de Política*

Internacional 53, no. 2 (2010): 177; Virgilio Abranches, "Metáforas do Presidente Contaminam Fala dos Ministros," December 28, 2003, https://www1.folha.uol.com.br/fsp/brasil/fc2812200309.htm (accessed June 15, 2018).

8. This expression, which has been used in diplomatic discourse for a long time, comes from the United Nations' "Goals for the Millennium Development." From his election in 2002 through 2004, Lula took a hundred national and international trips for exclusively diplomatic purposes. United Nations, "Transforming Our World: The 2030 Agenda for Sustainable Development," September 25, 2015, https://sustainabledevelopment.un.org/post2015/transformingourworld (accessed July 13, 2018); Amado Luiz Cervo, "Brazil's Rise on the International Scene: Brazil and the World," *Revista Brasileira de Política Internacional* 53 (2010): 9; Paulo Roberto de Almeida, "Uma Política Externa Engajada: A Diplomacia no Governo Lula," *Brasília: Revista Brasileira de Política Internacional* 47, no. 1 (2004): 164–165.

9. Steve Kingstone, "Brazil Takes On Football-Crazy Haiti," August 19, 2004, http://news.bbc.co.uk/2/hi/americas/3575292.stm (accessed July 13, 2018).

10. Stuart Murray and Geoffrey Allen Pigman, "Mapping the Relationship between International Sport and Diplomacy," *Sport in Society* 17, no. 9 (2014): 1098–1118.

11. Mariângela Ribeiro dos Santos, "O Futebol na Agenda do Governo Lula: Um Salto de Modernização Conservadora Rumo à Copa do Mundo FIFA 2014" (MA diss., Universidade de Brasilia, 2011).

12. John Horne, "A Construção dos BRICS por Meio da Construção de Estádios: Reflexões Preliminares sobre os Recentes e Futuros Megaeventos Esportivos em Quatro Economias Emergentes," in *A Copa do Mundo e as Cidades: Políticas, Projetos e Resistências*, ed. Fernanda Sánchez, Glauco Bienenstein, Fabrício Leal de Oliveira, and Pedro Novais (Rio de Janeiro: Editora da UFF, 2014), 42; Carlos Vainer, preface to *O Jogo Continua: Megaeventos Esportivos e Cidades*, ed. Gilmar Mascarenhas, Glauco Bienestein, and Fernanda Sánchez (Rio de Janeiro: UERJ, 2011), 13.

13. Rafael Fortes, "O Mundial de 2014 no Imaginário Popular Brasileiro," in *A Copa das Copas? Reflexões sobre o Mundial de Futebol no Brasil*, ed. José Carlos Marques (São Paulo: Ludens, 2015), 43.

14. Silvano Andrade do Bomfim, "Lei Geral da Copa, Soberania Nacional e Constituição," *Revista Brasileira de Direito Constitucional* 19 (2012): 236; Brasil. Presidência da República. Lei Geral da Copa, Cap. II, Seção II, § 1°. February 20, 2017, http://www.planalto.gov.br/ccivil_03/_ato2011–2014/2012/Lei/L12663.htm (accessed April 1, 2017); "O Rio Que Viola os Direitos Humanos," *Carta Capital*, May 13, 2013, https://www.cartacapital.com.br/sociedade/o-rio-que-viola-os-direitos-humanos (accessed June 10, 2018).

15. "STF Julga Improcedente ADI contra Dispositivos da Lei Geral da Copa," May 7, 2014, http://www.stf.jus.br/portal/cms/verNoticiaDetalhe.asp?idConteudo=266270 (Accessed June 10, 2018); "2014 Fifa World Cup: Where Are the 12 Host Stadiums in Brazil?" BBC Sport, June 6, 2014, https://www.bbc.com/sport/football/24897388 (accessed July 9, 2018); Portal da Transparência, http://www

.portaltransparencia.gov.br/copa2014/financiamentos/assunto.seam?assunto=tema (accessed March 1, 2017).

16. Law 12.462/2011 formalized "the differentiated contracting regime" in 2011. The federal level regulation also passed in 2011 with decree 7.581. Initially, the simplified rules were directed to the contracting of goods and services for the Confederations Cup (2013), World Cup (2014), and Olympic Games (2016). Presidência da República—Casa Civil, Institui o Regime Diferenciado de Contratações Públicas—RDC. 2011, Lei 12.462/2011 de 4 de agosto, http://www.planalto.gov.br/ccivil_03/_ato2011–2014/2011/lei/l12462.htm (accessed September 2017); Gláucia Marinho, "Brasil," in *Copa para Quem e para Quê?Um Olhar sobre os Legados dos Mundiais de Futebol no Brasil, África do Sul e Alemanha*, ed. Marilene de Paula and Dawid Danilo Bartelt (Rio de Janeiro: Fundação Heinrick Böll, 2014), 11, 19; Mariana Bastos and Rodrigo Mattos, "Um País para a Copa/Estádios. Na Média, Custo de Arenas Cresce 67%," May 27, 2009, http://www1.folha.uol.com.br/fsp/esporte/fk2705200922.htm (accessed June 11, 2018); Portal Transparência. Financiamento Copa 2014, http://www.portaltransparencia.gov.br/copa2014/financiamentos/assunto.seam?assunto=tema (accessed June 12, 2018); Tony Manfred, "Brazil's $3 Billion World Cup Stadiums Are Becoming White Elephants a Year Later," *Business Insider*, May 13, 2015, http://www.businessinsider.com/brazil-world-cup-stadiums-one-year-later-2015–5 (accessed August 17, 2017).

17. Mike Ozanian, "World Cup Brazil Will Generate $4 Billion for FIFA, 66% More Than 2010 Tournament," *Forbes*, June 5, 2014, https://www.forbes.com/sites/mikeozanian/2014/06/05/the-billion-dollar-business-of-the-world-cup/#20760fb5641a (accessed June 22, 2017); Flávio de Campos, "A Copa da Política em um País do Futebol," in *A Copa das Copas? Reflexões sobre o Mundial de Futebol no Brasil*, ed. Flávio Campos (São Paulo: Ludens, 2014), 31–38; CBF, Organizadores Destacam Sucesso da Copa do Mundo e Investimentos no Brasil, January 20, 2015, https://www.cbf.com.br/a-cbf/informes/index/organizadores-destacam-sucesso-da-copa-do-mundo-e-investimentos-no-brasil (accessed July 28, 2018).

18. Júlia Dias Carneiro, "Para Copa, Olimpíada ou Quando? O Museu 'Elefante Branco' Parado Há Mais de Dois Anos no Rio," BBC News Brasil, July 2, 2018, https://www.bbc.com/portuguese/brasil-44638797 (accessed July 2, 2018).

19. "Brazil Erupts in Protest: More Than a Million on the Streets" *Guardian*, June 21, 2013, https://www.theguardian.com/world/2013/jun/21/brazil-police-crowds-rio-protest (accessed July 13, 2018); Alan Gripp, "Retrospectiva: Manifestações não Foram Pelos 20 Centavos," *Folha de S.Paulo*, December 27, 2013, https://www1.folha.uol.com.br/poder/2013/12/1390207-manifestacoes-nao-foram-pelos-20-centavos.shtml (accessed June 18, 2018).

20. Geane Alzamora, Tacyana Arce, and Raquel Utsch Carvalho, "Acontecimentos Agenciados em Rede: Os Eventos do Facebook no Dispositivo Protesto," *Ruas e Redes: Dinâmicas dos Protestos BR*, ed. Regina Helena Alves Silva (Belo Horizonte: Autêntica, 2015), 41.

21. Daniela Moreira, "Aldo Rebelo Oficializa Pedido de Novo Interlocutor à Fifa," *Exame*, March 5, 2012, https://exame.abril.com.br/brasil/aldo-rebelo-oficializa

-pedido-de-novo-interlocutor-a-fifa/ (accessed June 22, 2018); "World Cup 2014: Fifa's Valcke Apologises to Brazil," BBC News, March 6, 2012, https://www.bbc.co.uk/news/world-latin-america-17267547 (accessed July 13, 2018).

22. Expression coined by the French sociologist François Ascher at the end of the twentieth century, which means a model of urban management that privileges the interests of private and governmental actors to the detriment of collective well-being. François Ascher, *Os Novos Princípios do Urbanismo* (São Paulo: Romano Guerra Editora, 2010), 57; Gustavo Prieto and Juliana Viana, "No Templo do Futebol, a Privatização da Vida Cotidiana: Da Festa para a Elitização da Cidade do Espetáculo," in *A Copa do Mundo e as Cidades: Políticas, Projetos e Resistências,* ed. Fernanda Sánchez, Glauco Bienenstein, Fabrício Leal de Oliveira, and Pedro Novais (Rio de Janeiro: Editora da UFF, 2014), 170; Fernanda Sánchez, "Copa do Mundo, Megaeventos e Projeto de Cidade: Atores, Escalas de Ação e Conflitos no Rio de Janeiro," in *A Copa do Mundo e as Cidades,* 51.

23. Fortes, "O Mundial de 2014 no Imaginário Popular Brasileiro," 54; Aiuri Rebello, "Obra da Copa em BH Tem Suspeita de Superfaturamento de R$ 23 mi. Uol. Brasília," August 22, 2013, https://copadomundo.uol.com.br/noticias/redacao/2013/08/22/obra-da-copa-em-bh-tem-suspeita-de-desvio-de-r-23-milhoes.htm?mobile&width=280&cmpid=copiaecola (accessed July 27, 2018); Redação Época com Estadão Conteúdo, "Dilma: 'Nenhum Legado é da Copa do Mundo. É para o Povo Brasileiro,'" *Época,* June 1, 2014, https://epoca.globo.com/vida/copa-do-mundo-2014/noticia/2014/06/bdilmab-nenhum-legado-e-da-copa-do-mundo-e-para-o-povo-brasileiro.html (accessed June 20, 2018).

Edson Sardinha, "Ibope: Diminui Apoio de Brasileiros à Copa no País,"

24. Congresso em Foco, June 3, 2014, https://congressoemfoco.uol.com.br/especial/noticias/ibope-diminui-apoio-de-brasileiros-a-copa-no-pais/ (accessed September 4, 2017).

25. Neil Pyper, "Why the Commodities Crunch Could Hurt Stability in Latin America," The Conversation, January 14, 2016, http://theconversation.com/why-the-commodities-crunch-could-hurt-stability-in-latin-america-53149 (accessed July 5, 2017); Jessé Souza, "Uma Nova Classe Trabalhadora Brasileira," in *Os Batalhadores Brasileiros: Nova Classe Média ou Nova Classe Trabalhadora?,* ed. Jessé Souza (Belo Horizonte: UFMG, 2012), 19–60.

26. "Has Brazil Blown It?" *Economist,* September 27, 2013, http://www.economist.com/news/leaders/21586833-stagnant-economy-bloated-state-and-mass-protests-mean-dilma-rousseff-must-change-course-has (accessed March 11, 2017); "Após Protestos, Dilma Mudará Discurso de 'Legado da Copa' para Ufanismo do 'País do Futebol,'" Política na Rede, February 11, 2014, http://www.politicanarede.com/2014/02/apos-protestos-dilma-mudara-discurso-de.html (accessed July 5, 2017).

27. "Brazil into Chaos, Tension Rises. FIFA Threatens to Suspend," *Magazine Football,* June 22, 2013, http://www.football-magazine.it/en/brasile-nel-caos-sale-la-tensione-la-fifa-minaccia-la-sospensione (accessed March 8, 2017); "Brazil Protests: Dilma Rousseff Unveils Reforms," BBC News, June 22, 2013, http://www.bbc.com/news/world-latin-america-23012547 (accessed March 9, 2017).

28. For a detailed analysis of the political coup that toppled President Dilma Rousseff, see Hebe Mattos, Tânia Bessone, and Beatriz Mamigonian, eds., *Historiadores Pela Democracia—O Golpe de 2016: A Força do Passado* (São Paulo: Alameda, 2016); Rodrigo Patto Sá Motta, "Brazil on the Edge of the Abyss Again," in *Historiadores Pela Democracia*, 93.

29. Anderson, *Imagined Communities*, 5–6.

30. David Harvey, "The Right to the City," *New Left Review* 53 (2008): 24.

31. Raquel Rolnik, "A Vozes das Ruas: As Revoltas de Junho e Suas Interpretações," in *Cidades Rebeldes: Passe Livre e as Manifestações que Tomaram o Brasil*, ed. David Harvey, Ermínia Maricato, Slavoj Žižek, Mike Davis, and Carlos Vainer (São Paulo: Boitempo/CartaMaior, 2016), 6; Fortes, "O Mundial de 2014 no Imaginário Popular Brasileiro," 40.

32. Roberto Damatta, "Esporte na Sociedade: Um Ensaio sobre o Futebol Brasileiro," in *Universo do Futebol: Esporte e Sociedade Brasileira*, ed. Roberto Damatta (Rio de Janeiro: Pinakotheke, 1982), 24–25.

Conclusion

"Good Kicking" Is Not Only "Good Politics" but Also "Good Diplomacy"

Peter J. Beck

On July 4, 1954, West Germany, the Federal Republic of Germany (FRG), celebrated two notable sporting achievements. At Rheims, Mercedes Benz cars, marking the company's postwar return to the sport, took the first two places in the French Grand Prix motor race. At Bern, Switzerland, a late goal gave the West German soccer team a 3–2 victory over the hitherto invincible Hungarians in the World Cup final. Both events were celebrated as far more than sporting successes. As the world media recorded, they were welcomed as political and diplomatic triumphs for a nation defeated in war and then treated initially as a second-rate power subject to a range of postwar restrictions that extended to the sphere of sport. Victory on the football field, after defeat on the Second World War battlefield, touched every West German, even non-soccer fans. Fostering strong feelings of national community, even—to quote Diethelm Blecking—a kind of "communal intoxication," the *Wunder von Bern* (Miracle of Bern) became a reference point for German national identity, as articulated vividly by the 2003 film *Das Wunder von Bern.*[1]

Inevitably the West German team received a rapturous welcome upon its return home. In Berlin's Olympic Stadium, a large crowd saw President Theodor Heuss present each player with a silver laurel, the country's highest sporting award. Significantly, Heuss, in response to foreign media concerns that excessive German triumphalism and ultranationalist rhetoric suggested continuities with Adolf Hitler's Third Reich, adopted an overtly apolitical approach, especially given the stadium's use for the infamous 1936 Nazi

Olympics: "We can all rejoice about the German victory but nobody should believe that good kicking was good politics." Unsurprisingly Gerhard Schröder, the minister of the Interior, echoed Heuss's line when greeting the team in Bonn: thus, he asserted that "the victories and defeats of a team could have no influence on positive or negative evaluation of the nation to which they happen to belong."[2]

Sport and Diplomacy in a Fast-Changing World

Regardless of the efforts of Heuss and Schröder, among other politicians, to defuse adverse foreign media commentaries by separating sport from diplomacy and politics, it was difficult to accept that the World Cup final was viewed in West Germany as—to quote Peco Bauwens, the president of the Deutscher Fussball-Bund—"just a game." Paradoxically, it was a speech, delivered by Bauwens—the *Times*'s correspondent critiqued his employment of the vocabulary of Hitler's Third Reich—at Munich and broadcast across Germany, that caused most opprobrium. In reality "good kicking" was regarded within and outside West Germany as "good politics," even if subsequent nationalist excesses risked derailing the positive global effects of the *Wunder von Bern*. Sport, it appeared, was capable of exerting not only positive but also negative impacts upon a nation's image in the world. "Good kicking" proved also "good diplomacy," even if at the time soccer tended to be discussed in government, the media, and academia more in terms of politics than diplomacy. By contrast, as evidenced by this book, today the soccer and diplomacy link has moved from the wings to center stage.[3]

This book reflects the recent surge of academic interest in sport and diplomacy, and particularly the impact made by diplomacy specialists upon the study of sport, as reflected by Sarah Snyder's insightful contribution to this book. Within this context, contributors explore, define, and debate the nature and parameters of this relatively underexplored and undertheorized focus for study, especially as compared to the more established and better understood relationship between sport and politics. A central theme running through the whole volume is the need for greater clarity and precision, particularly in the use of such terms as *sport diplomacy* and *sport-as-diplomacy* and their soccer variants. J. Simon Rofe has pointed out elsewhere the need to differentiate more sharply between diplomacy and politics, given the frequent tendency either to treat the terms as interchangeable or to use the term *politico-diplomatic*: "diplomacy needs to be distinct from politics. The latter, politics, concerns the message; the former, diplomacy, the mode of the message." From this perspective, sport, though central for players and spectators, proves merely a means to an end, not an end in itself.[4]

Traditional diplomacy, working with other parties through dialogue, negotiation, influence, persuasion, and pressure, conducted through governments, foreign offices, embassies, and diplomats, helps states pursue, promote, and protect their respective national interests without resorting to conflict, sanctions, and force. However, in recent decades the advent of new digital technologies has radically transformed international relations and modes of diplomacy, as exemplified by the dramatic rise of public diplomacy as an essential tool of statecraft seeking to engage foreign governments, media, and opinion. Indeed, for Simon Anholt, who coined the term *nation brand* and created the nation branding index, public diplomacy's emergence has made public opinion a global superpower.[5]

Arguably cultural forms of diplomacy—these include sport—provide the most vibrant and effective examples of public diplomacy, one way of exerting what is represented as soft power. Indeed, a 2005 United States State Department report depicted cultural diplomacy as "the linchpin of public diplomacy": "It is in cultural activities that a nation's idea of itself is best represented. And cultural diplomacy can enhance our national security in subtle, wide-ranging, and sustainable ways." Traditionally, states have been ranked as superpowers, great powers, middling powers, minor powers, emerging powers, and so on by reference to hard power criteria, most notably demographic, economic, military, nuclear, and technological factors. Such power gradations continue, but today global rankings based upon soft power and nation brands are not lacking in politico-diplomatic significance. For some states—they include France, Germany, the United Kingdom (UK), and the United States—considerable kudos and international prestige are attached to being described as cultural superpowers that achieve policy goals through admiration of their cultural values and achievements and the resulting aspiration of other states to emulate their example. Generally speaking, cultural diplomacy, like other forms of public diplomacy, is represented as concerned basically with foreign audiences, but is frequently targeted also at domestic audiences, such as in terms of taking credit for foreign successes, selling a change of foreign policy direction to the electorate, or diverting attention from current controversies.[6]

Stressing the impact of attraction rather than coercion, Joseph Nye Jr.'s take on soft power features prominently throughout this book. Several chapters, set in the post-1945 period, impart relevance to Nye's claims about public diplomacy's role in winning the Cold War. In this vein, David Caute's descriptor, the "Cultural Olympics," captures well the constant efforts of rival Cold War camps to outdo each other through cultural offensives designed to demonstrate to both domestic and external audiences their respective supremacy in the arts, education, and sport.[7]

In Britain, the Foreign and Commonwealth Office (FCO) once described cultural diplomacy as "a Humpty Dumpty term" meaning "more or less what one wants it to mean." By contrast, today cultural diplomacy has become more clearly defined as a subset of public diplomacy, that is, an activity intended to alter the attitudes and behavior of governments, media, and people in other states through sport and other cultural activities. Cultural diplomacy describes attempts—to quote Nicholas Cull—"to manage the international environment through making its [the nation's] cultural resources and achievements known overseas and/or facilitating cultural transmission abroad." Whereas much of the diplomatic activity undertaken by governments takes place behind the scenes—despite critiques of secret diplomacy it is not easy to conduct traditional diplomacy in the public eye—cultural forms of diplomacy work by communicating messages *in public* to the target audience(s). Indeed, the more public attention an activity attracts globally the better its contribution as a cultural export. In effect, as recorded by a recent *Times* headline about British cultural diplomacy, "Books, Football and Gandalf Take Nation around the World."[8]

Echoing such sentiments, the late Nelson Mandela, the former president of South Africa (1994–1999), frequently articulated "*the power*" of sport, and especially its qualities in the sphere of communication and representation. For Mandela, sport, possessing the "power to change the world . . . to inspire . . . to unite people," often proved "more powerful than governments" and traditional diplomacy. This power, he asserted, rested basically upon sport's unique qualities in impacting upon people and societies in ways that extended far beyond the capability of traditional modes of diplomacy: "Sport is probably the most effective means of communication in the modern world, bypassing both verbal and written communication and reaching directly out to billions of people worldwide."[9]

The term "sport diplomacy," a high-profile variant of cultural diplomacy, describes how sport is consciously employed by governments as both an additional and an alternative instrument of diplomacy. Frequently sport diplomacy is used to complement and boost the impact of more traditional forms of diplomacy, such as by way of amplifying messages to decision makers, opinion formers, and people in other countries or by targeting specific audiences, such as by—to quote Paul Dietschy—"reaching other milieus than the elite." In certain circumstances, sport diplomacy might be deemed to provide a more promising modus operandi than traditional diplomacy, even perceived at times, as in Franco's Spain, as offering the only feasible foreign policy approach.[10]

Soccer and Diplomacy

The diplomatic potential and impact of different sports varies, but clearly soccer, the focus of this book, offers a sound basis for studying sport and diplomacy since it is widely acknowledged as the world game, whether measured in terms of participants, spectators, press coverage, television viewers, or online/mobile phone users. Few activities carry more public diplomacy weight or media visibility in present-day life than football. Soccer's undoubted ability to capture the popular imagination, inspire a strong belief in a shared cause, foster a sense of belonging and community, and provide an engaging unscripted narrative line enables the game to transmit, indeed amplify, messages for states to large audiences within and beyond their borders. Thus, a mutual love of the game overrides geographical, linguistic, and other boundaries to unite disparate peoples across the world. In turn, soccer's diplomatic reach, its communicative power as public diplomacy targeted at a global audience, has been accentuated by the ongoing revolution in digital communications technologies.[11]

The term "soccer diplomacy," a subset of sport diplomacy, describes how governments utilize soccer as a means of public diplomacy conducted principally through individual players, teams, matches, tours, tournaments, and governance structures. Like any form of public diplomacy, soccer diplomacy is a highly mediated form of diplomacy whose reach and effectiveness are, in many respects, functions of how and to what extent specific activities are recorded, described, and reported by the audiovisual, digital, and print media and then accessed by the target audiences. In this vein, soccer's World Cup tournament, like other mega-events, has acquired an ever-increasing cultural diplomatic role offering—to quote Cull—"unique opportunities" for host and participating nations to reach out to global audiences. Over one billion people watched the 2018 World Cup final, with the tournament reaching a global television audience of 3.57 billion people. More significantly, the growing use of new technology and social media platforms for sport meant that an estimated 309 million people around the world watched World Cup matches online or on a mobile device.[12]

Likewise, each season the leading soccer leagues claim a substantial global politico-diplomatic reach. Thus, Britain's Premier League, whose games are broadcast to a massive global audience to view on television, online, or a mobile device, looms large as a leading British brand. Indeed, according to Populus polling data (2018), today the Premier League proves Britain's top globally recognized brand, scoring strongly among younger affluent groups in the developing economies of Asia and Africa. Moreover, "Our analysis shows that the Premier League's impact as an icon does not rely on favourability towards the UK. Instead, it shows that the League has the power to 'pull' people towards the UK." Recording how soccer exerts positive impacts upon international audiences' perception of the UK as "modern," "exciting," "successful" and so on, Populus data establish that—to quote McClory—"the Premier League is an important contributing resource of British soft power."[13]

Unsurprisingly, over time governments have sought to articulate, albeit to varying degrees, the nature, role, and value of cultural diplomacy as one element of their public diplomacy portfolio furthering specific policy objectives. However, as Murray and Pigman have pointed out, "most international sport is organized for purposes officially unrelated to diplomacy." Such activities, though often framed and supported, possibly even partially funded, by governments and/or official agencies, feature nongovernmental actors, take place through civil-societal relationships, and frequently appear on the surface at first sight to be relatively autonomous from the state. Within this context, soccer's diplomatic role arises primarily from the manner in which states bask in the reflective glory of their soccer players and teams, which are identified by spectators, newspaper readers, television viewers, governments, and the media as representing the nation, but perhaps also a government or a political regime. From this perspective, soccer diplomacy assigns an extra-sporting role to individual players who may not necessarily wish to be seen as acting upon behalf of a particular state. For example, during the late 1950s did Real Madrid's players, especially those from outside Spain, relish being treated as a propaganda tool for Franco's Spain? Do Algerians, Argentineans, Brazilians, Egyptians, or Germans playing today in Britain's Premier League, particularly players who possess image rights contracts, wish to be exploited as instruments of *British* soccer diplomacy? The diplomatization and politicization of their role as high-profile soccer players is often far from their desired career goals.[14]

Whereas soccer diplomacy is a relatively well-established feature of international society, soccer-as-diplomacy, another form of diplomacy foregrounded in this book, is still an emerging concept. In many respects, its rise proves a function of the manner in which public diplomacy brought about significant shifts in power between states and non-state actors, most notably national, regional, and international sport federations (ISFs). Representing the game's role in creating a wide range of diplomatic networks within and outside the sport, this descriptor refers to the manner in which non-state actors, most notably the game's national associations and ISFs, interact with the state, business, and industry as a result of ongoing international contacts and competition. Whereas soccer diplomacy stresses the role of communication and representation, soccer-as-diplomacy, though involving both communication and representation, centers upon negotiation, the third element of this book's diplomatic triumvirate.

Rather than summarizing individual chapters one by one, the remainder of this conclusion seeks to codify and assess what contributors write about the nature and impact of soccer diplomacy and/or soccer-as-diplomacy by way of providing readers with a sound basis for discussion and future study. This book is structured around what Heather Dichter represents in her introduction as three defining diplomatic themes: communication, representation, and negotiation. Although each theme can be discussed separately, in practice, as evidenced by the chapters in this book, their distinctiveness tends to become blurred. As a result, contributors tend to offer insights relevant to more than one section of this conclusion, and hence to figure in several sections of the following text.

Writing about Soccer Diplomacy

Drawing upon a wide range of countries and a lengthy time period, contributors highlight the role of soccer diplomacy as a means of place branding, that is, selling images of a nation to win hearts and minds across the globe. They argue that allowance needs to be made for the varying positions taken by governments in regard to sport diplomacy as well as the differing character of countries. Whereas certain governments, such as those in Franco's Spain, East Germany, apartheid South Africa, and the Soviet Union, overtly intervened in and controlled sport, others, most notably those in Australia, Britain, France, and the United States, have espoused a laissez-faire approach toward sport. Even so, in practice, the latter, though depicting their apolitical stance as a central liberal value, have often adopted, at least behind the scenes, a somewhat interventionist interpretation of nonintervention.

Despite an understandable unwillingness to challenge traditional images regarding what was represented publicly as the distinctive separation of diplomacy and politics from sport, over time many governments, apprised by diplomatic representatives stationed abroad about the extent of political intervention elsewhere, were forced to an equally reluctant acceptance of the fact that international football was far too important to be left entirely to sporting bodies. Matches and tournaments involving their respective nation's teams, it was clear, were interpreted elsewhere as diplomatically and politically significant regardless of their hands-off approach. Appreciating sport's potential and actual politico-diplomatic value, policymakers in such countries found it impossible to stand aside from events. Thus, their soccer diplomacy, albeit assuming a more subtle and occasional form than the more authoritarian variants found elsewhere, proved both more substantial and frequent than either claimed or assumed in public.

In this vein, this book's contributors show how football has been, and still is, valued by politicians, diplomats and government officials, the media, and people working in the game, among others, for its role in conveying to the target audience(s) positive images of the country represented by the players and/or countering and correcting erroneous, unfavorable, negative, or outdated impressions. In effect, soccer diplomacy takes the form of a charm offensive, a calculated campaign designed to gain admiration, favor, and support. Soccer is viewed as yet another cultural export that gives public visibility to a nation as a political, economic, social, and cultural model, a way of life to be respected, admired, trusted, and possibly emulated. The resulting goodwill, it is argued, promotes national politico-economic interests in the wider world by creating a climate conducive to better diplomatic relations and/or enhanced trade and investment. At the same time, politicians, diplomats, and officials have not always appreciated that in practice things might go wrong and in fact promote messages that lack clout or impact adversely upon the interests of their respective countries and governments. In part, this might prove a function of what Paul Dietschy represents as "the distance between the social background of the diplomatic milieu and the popular culture of football."[15]

Readers will see that the use of soccer diplomacy has proved common in both major (Brazil, France, Germany, Spain) and lesser (Chile, Iceland, South Africa, Trinidad and Tobago, Vietnam) footballing powers as well as in countries (Australia, the United States) in which soccer was not the principal domestic sport. Contributors draw upon a diverse range of primary and secondary sources that yield insights into the thinking, policy, and actions of governments and ISFs, even if restrictions on the release of allegedly sensitive files as well as the deliberate destruction of official records result in occasional gaps in the evidence. For any form of public diplomacy, the media plays a crucial role in carrying messages to domestic and global audiences; hence, newspapers and audiovisual sources figure prominently in the references throughout this book. By contrast, oral testimony based upon interviews with those involved in events is absent. Admittedly, it is difficult to see holders of high office in ISFs and leading soccer players making themselves readily available to academics, but interviews with politicians and government officials involved in policymaking can offer an additional research dimension.[16]

Contributors Address Soccer Diplomacy

Moving to specific topics, Paul Dietschy shows how the French government, albeit refraining from funding sport, used soccer diplomacy during the 1920s to project messages about a France full of vitality by way of not only publicizing "the good name" of French youth but also countering negative portrayals of a country "bled to death" by the First World War. Then during the 1930s, soccer in France was assigned a central propaganda role in responding to the challenge posed by the fascist powers. By contrast, Juan Antonio Simón points to the manner in which Fascist Italy became a model for Franco's Spain.[17]

During the late 1930s in Franco's Spain, sport became a "matter of the State," that is, an activity controlled centrally by the government through the Ministry of Foreign Affairs and a tool for ideological propaganda within and outside the country. Subsequently, the fall from power of Benito Mussolini and Hitler, Spain's chief international partners, led Franco's regime to treat soccer diplomacy as the principal way—indeed, as argued by Simón, the only way—to pursue a new course in foreign policy to break out of post-1945 international isolation and enhance national visibility. But fixtures were banned against teams from the Soviet bloc, Francoism's chief ideological enemy. During the 1950s Spain's international position was transformed through the gradual normalization of politico-diplomatic relationships, as reflected by entry to the United Nations (UN) and the removal of the ban on playing Soviet bloc teams. The most vivid manifestation of this transformation came on the football field when Spain not only hosted the 1964 European Nations Cup tournament but also beat the Soviet Union in the final. An even greater boost to Spain's global image came from the footballing achievements of Real Madrid, whose victories in the first five editions of the European Cup (1955–1960) gave Spain visibility on the world stage at a time when television was taking soccer to a global audience and showing the world a modern, cosmopolitan, and successful Spain. At a time when the presence of foreign players in European club sides was a rarity, Real Madrid—the team included Alfredo Di Stéfano (Argentina), Canário (Brazil), Ferenc Puskás (Hungary), José Santamaría (Uruguay), and Raymond Kopa (France)—possessed a distinctive cosmopolitan composition.[18]

In her wide-ranging H-Diplo review of the history of sport and diplomacy, Heather Dichter identified how the US State Department "consciously used sport" to support and enhance national interests and particularly "to promote the American way of life" in the East–West struggle for hearts and minds. In this vein, George Kioussis's study of footballing exchanges conducted by Iceland and the United States during the mid-1950s offers an excellent example of US Cold War soccer diplomacy. Thus, the US State Department sponsored the national soccer team's 1955 tour to Iceland for the prime purpose of building goodwill with the Icelandic people, media, and government so they would allow the continuation of the American military presence at the strategically valuable Keflavik airbase.[19]

Dichter shows how the German question also played a central role in the development of the Cold War. Within this context the two German states saw sport diplomacy in general, and soccer diplomacy in particular, as key to pursuit of their respective conflicting politico-diplomatic agendas. Whereas West Germany fostered images of a state no longer burdened by its Nazi past, a democratic peaceful country central to the NATO alliance, East Germany valued membership in sporting bodies and participation in international sporting events for reflecting its identity as a member of the Soviet bloc, most notably by offering opportunities to give visibility to the GDR symbol, flag, and anthem and to exploit sporting success as a function of the communist regime.

Looking to another Cold War theater, Erik Nielsen explores the Australian national soccer team's visit to Vietnam, a tour represented hitherto in the literature as an instrument of Australian soccer diplomacy. From this perspective, the team, viewed as "the perfect public relations vehicle," was sent to a war zone as part of an Australian government propaganda offensive designed to win over hearts and minds in South Vietnam. By contrast, Nielsen argues that archival evidence favors an alternative interpretation that treats the 1967 tour as an example of soccer-as-diplomacy, as detailed later in this conclusion. Whatever one's preferred approach, this episode is of interest as it illuminates Australia's emerging awareness of Asia's significance for the country's future and particularly as it indicates that soccer had a role to play in preparing the ground for a possible significant foreign policy shift, as prefaced in 2006 by the move of Football Federation Australia from the Oceania Football Confederation to join the Asian Football Confederation (AFC). More recently, in 2015 Australia, having finished as runners-up in 2011, not only hosted but also won the 2015 AFC Asian Cup tournament.[20]

For many governments, mega-events play a central role in soccer diplomacy; they can make a significant contribution in terms of image-building and reputation management by testing, confirming, and showcasing the country's ability to stage such events successfully. Euclides de Freitas Couto and Alan Castellano Valente highlight that Brazil's President Luiz Inácio "Lula" da Silva saw soccer diplomacy, complemented by Olympic diplomacy, as the principal way to project across the world images of Brazil as a dynamic global power. Lula viewed success in bidding for and hosting the 2014 FIFA World Cup and the 2016 Olympics as central to his desire to transform the country's international standing and to prove to the world that Brazil was a politically stable country with a growing economy. Furthermore, Lula represented soccer prowess and excellence as a key factor in providing the people with a strong sense of national community, or Brazilianness. Seeking to rebrand Brazil through mega-events, Lula "envisioned that sport diplomacy would provide a shortcut to achieve his goals" through what Couto and Valente describe as "the conversion of the country's cultural capital into political and economic capital."[21]

Normally only large wealthy states are seen as capable of hosting mega-events. However, there are exceptions, as evidenced by Brenda Elsey's chapter centered upon Chile, a country dwarfed by Brazil's territorial extent and population. For Chile, hosting the 1962 World Cup was viewed as offering an opportunity to transform its image from that of a faraway unknown country located at the "end of the world" to become recognized on the global stage as a stable, democratic, and modern state. As Elsey argues, "the prestige of football" was represented as Chile's "chance at greatness." Her chapter has strong contemporary relevance, since Qatar, the successful bidder for the 2022 World Cup tournament, is outstripped in both size and population even by Chile. However, large natural gas and oil reserves enable this small Gulf state to easily meet the financial and other demands of hosting a mega-event, seen as a central element in moving on from negative images focused upon its despotic regime and terrorist links. The World Cup bid was part of Qatar's soft power strategy to win friends and influence in the wider world, most notably boosting its efforts to reposition itself as not only a global sports hub but also a modern, open state.[22]

Writing about Soccer-as-Diplomacy

Moving on from Benedict Anderson's concept of the nation as an "imagined community," Barbara Keys has argued the case for treating international sport as an "imagined world," that is, a functioning international regime governed by distinctive laws and diplomatic practices that possesses a degree of autonomy from nation-states. Rooted in the principle of competition among individuals and teams representing nations, the world of international sport is seen to espouse an idealistic universalism that both unites and transcends nationalism. International sport has therefore developed what Murray and Pigman have termed a specialized, distinct "form of diplomacy in its own right" that enables ISFs, among others, to achieve their interests and objectives by creating a wide range of diplomatic networks within and outside the sport. ISFs have been forced to perform a diplomatic role as they engage in representation to and negotiation with governments, regional and national sports bodies, business, industry, and the media and as they manage and produce the resulting sporting events. Soccer-as-diplomacy has a different focus than soccer diplomacy. Admittedly both involve communication and representation, but soccer-as-diplomacy centers principally upon negotiation, this book's third diplomatic theme.[23]

Contributors Address Soccer-as-Diplomacy

One of the more interesting revelations about soccer-as-diplomacy is provided by Dietschy, in his claim that France, not Fascist Italy, Nazi Germany, or the Soviet Union, was the initiator of soccer-as-diplomacy. He points to France's "invention of a soccer diplomacy" in 1920, when the French Ministry of Foreign Affairs created the Service des œuvres Françaises à l'Étranger (SOFE), a new section for sport and tourism. According to Dietschy, SOFE used diplomacy to enhance French links and influence within ISFs, most notably FIFA and the IOC, as well as to support the organization of international matches and competitions. In the case of soccer, SOFE's global ambitions were helped, indeed reinforced, by Jules Rimet's role as president of FIFA (1921–1954) as well as by the absence of the four influential British football associations from FIFA for much of the interwar period.[24]

Obviously mega sporting events make extensive diplomatic demands upon host governments. Indeed, Couto and Valente illuminate well the diplomatic ramifications of hosting the 2014 World Cup tournament. Like the Olympics, its size and scope raised major issues—concerning infrastructure, media, security, sponsorship, transport, and visas, among other topics—for the Brazilian government, thereby forcing it to engage closely with FIFA and other footballing organizations, as well as their business and media partners. Thus, as they sought to underpin the infrastructural and other requirements of hosting a successful event, the Brazilian authorities created an extensive diplomatic network that involved not only FIFA and other ISFs but also a wide range of domestic bodies. As a result, in 2012 the General World Cup Law was passed to ensure that Brazilian municipal and state governments, building contractors, banks, hotel groups, and transport providers were fully behind the World Cup project.

Dichter shows that even lesser footballing events may generate a wide-ranging multilayered diplomatic network comprising international organizations, national governments, and nongovernmental actors. Thus, protracted and wide-ranging negotiations, framed by the Cold War in general and the two Germanies' issue in particular, were conducted about East German participation in the 1961 UEFA Junior Tournament hosted by Portugal and the 1964 UEFA youth football tournament held in the Netherlands. The resulting diplomatic networks included NATO; the British, East German, French, Netherlands, Portuguese, United States, and West German governments; the IOC; and national and international football federations. Even NATO, which disclaimed any competence in soccer matters, became a reluctant participant, given the Allied Travel Office's control over travel to and from the West by East Germans and concerns that any ban on the GDR's involvement in these tournaments would cause negative publicity for the NATO alliance during a tense phase of the Cold War. The episode shows how international sport both mirrored and had an impact on the post-1945 division of Germany. At times soccer seemed all-conquering, as suggested by one West German complaint that some people treated soccer as "more important than Berlin," typically the central Cold War tension point.[25]

Another enduring feature of the international scene during the mid to late twentieth century was the South African apartheid issue. Here also, sport proved a major element. Chris Bolsmann discusses the abortive diplomatic efforts of the Football Association of Southern Africa (FASA), formerly the South African Football Association (SAFA), to retain its membership in FIFA, and hence its eligibility to participate in international football tournaments, at a time when South Africa was increasingly treated as an international pariah. This episode offers yet another example of how over three decades an extensive diplomatic network was created within and outside South Africa to find an agreed way forward reconciling FIFA membership criteria with the increasingly rigid stance adopted by the South African apartheid government toward sport. In many respects, Bolsmann's chapter echoes Dichter's study of the GDR in terms of dealing with the impact of sporting ostracism and illustrating the limits of regimes' claims to control sport. Thus, the apartheid South African government was able to force FASA to organize domestic soccer on the basis of racism, segregation, and discrimination and to deny passports to members of a rival SASF (South African Soccer Federation) delegation that wished to attend FIFA congresses. But it failed to prevent restrictions being placed on South African membership in FIFA and the Confédération Africaine de Football or participation in international football tournaments.

Like most sport history studies, this book concentrates largely upon elite-level activities, which tend in the case of most sports, especially football, to figure most prominently in regard to diplomacy and politics. However, this elitist focus should not obscure the emerging significance of grassroots diplomacy centered on people-to-people interaction at a more popular level. Moreover, grassroots diplomacy fits well into a contemporary world in which social networking technologies are revolutionizing the possibilities for person-to-person communication across cultural, geographical, linguistic, national, religious, and other boundaries. The game's universal appeal enhances its ability to create meaningful diplomatic relationships at the grassroots level, most notably in the sphere of coach-to-coach and coach-to-player interactions.

Generally speaking, grassroots diplomacy is still under-researched in the sport history literature, while any publications tend to concentrate primarily upon the recent period. But there are exceptions. For instance, during the late 1930s one distinctive feature of the British Council's limited involvement in sport concerned the occasional recruitment and funding of British athletics, boxing, and football coaches to live and work overseas in such countries as Greece and Turkey. These foreign placements, though less visible than, say, an international football match, were valued for their long-term impacts, as they built durable mutual relationships, reinforced traditional images of Britain's sporting heritage and primacy, reached young people, and contained the propaganda of the Axis powers. As a result, these coaching posts, proving both relatively cheap and cost-effective, were adjudged as—to quote Britain's consul-general in Salonica—"a sound investment from the propaganda point of view."[26]

Moving on to the recent period, grassroots diplomacy through sport has emerged as an increasingly common form of public diplomacy. With its growing popularity, diplomacy, once the domain of the nation-state, has become more accessible to "the people" through a growing range of public diplomacy activities, particularly those centered upon sport. Despite its elitist nature, the Premier League's global impact, as discussed above, has been accentuated at the grassroots level by the Premier League skills development program for coaches and referees run in partnership with the British Council and British diplomatic missions overseas. Reportedly since 2007 more than twenty thousand men and women across twenty-nine countries have been trained as coaches and referees.[27]

Grassroots diplomacy also has a significant role in the sports-based activities of the US Department of State's Bureau of Educational and Cultural Affairs' (ECA). For example, between 2012 and 2014 its project Soccer for Peace and Understanding in Jordan (SPUJ), a peace-building and social development program based upon coach-to-coach interaction at the local community level, taught Jordanian coaches how to develop and instill citizenship, leadership, and other skills in young people through football. The SPUJ's impact benefited from the fact that "few things are closer to the Jordanian heart and psyche than the sport of football." Apart from proving low risk, cheap, and cost-effective, this project yielded long-term politico-diplomatic benefits for the United States. Although such objectives were deliberately downplayed publicly, the SPUJ program enhanced US–Jordanian relations through sport. In Lindsey Blom's words, such programs provide useful cultural propaganda for the United States because, "when properly facilitated," they are able to "transcend cultural differences and existing conflicts" and "bridge diverse groups of people within a country as well as across countries." More importantly, from the State Department's perspective, Blom claims that such grassroots diplomacy promoted "the cultural values, brand, and image that the United States wishes to impress on other countries."[28]

Normally, sport-as-diplomacy is discussed principally in regard to ISFs and external bodies. However, the term "diplomacy-as-sport" can be applied more broadly, most notably to take account of the role performed by individuals who operate, in effect, as part of their own diplomatic network. In this vein, Roy McCree examines how a soccer official representing a country that was a minor player in both the politico-economic and footballing worlds forged an extensive diplomatic network to exercise (and abuse) considerable commercial, diplomatic, and political influence and power nationally, regionally, and globally. Jack Warner moved successively from the Trinidad and Tobago Football Association to posts in the Caribbean Football Union, the Confederation of North, Central American and Caribbean Association Football (CONCACAF), and FIFA; along the way he acquired tremendous influence over such executive matters as the election of FIFA presidents, the membership of key committees, the selection of host countries for the World Cup and other tournaments, and the sale of valuable media rights. As McCree observes, his rise was facilitated by the fact that FIFA's overly democratic structure—one member, one vote—works in favor of lesser footballing powers. Lacking diplomatic, political, military, or economic clout, small countries can employ soft power through sport not only to attract global visibility but also to exert significant impacts upon the major footballing powers, as evidenced by Warner, who used his position to exercise power over, make excessive demands of, and even humiliate his imperial bête noire, England's Football Association. In turn, Warner's prominent role in world soccer provided a platform for his assumption of ministerial posts in the national politics of Trinidad and Tobago.

Warner's maneuvering and unethical conduct, combined with his membership in several influential FIFA committees, was crucial, McCree argues, to the success of Trinidad and Tobago's bid to host FIFA's 2001 Under 17 World Cup in preference to seemingly stronger bids from Finland, Japan, Peru, and Scotland. Even worse, having secured the media rights for the tournament, Warner's close association with the Trinidad and Tobago government resulted in the awarding of contracts to build four new soccer stadiums to his own construction company, while family-owned businesses provided food and drinks inside them. For Warner, soccer-as-diplomacy gave him tremendous influence and substantial wealth, which he has been using to fight extradition to the United States.[29]

Assessing Soccer Diplomacy

The contributors establish that soccer diplomacy has been, and still is, pursued in a wide range of countries. Questions remain about the outcomes, performance, and effectiveness of soccer diplomacy, especially given the divergence of views in the literature. Generally speaking, the existing literature encourages us not to expect too much from soccer diplomacy in terms of place branding, reputation management, and policy impacts. Thus, Steven Jackson urges us to avoid overstating or understating sport's diplomatic potential. For McClory, "Soft power is notoriously difficult to deploy effectively, and despite its growth in profile, capability in its use is patchy."[30]

Areas for discussion, which make no claim to be all-embracing, include the following:

- How easy is it to measure any form of soft power, and especially its impact? Indeed, is it possible to do this? McClory, though producing annual soft power rankings, reminds us that "the difficulty of measuring soft power is well-documented," especially as soft power "is difficult to quantify." Notwithstanding his long-standing focus upon soft power as power, even Nye conceded the problem: "Power is also like love, easier to experience than to define or measure, but no less real for that."[31]
- Which criteria should be employed to evaluate soft power's performance in sport, especially soccer? For example, Pigman and Rofe advocate a unified approach based upon benchmarking, that is "identifying and disseminating standards of best practice." For Pigman, the "act of competing in sport internationally is at its

core about communicating to the public." From this perspective, soccer diplomacy, like any other form of public diplomacy, is all about communication, that is, making contact, engaging successfully with the target audience, and then transporting positive ideas and images from one mind into another. As Murray and Pigman observe, "If the diplomatic posture, image and message is thoughtfully crafted and aligned to positive sporting values, the perception of a foreign public can be significantly altered." Of course, throughout there is a risk that things could go very wrong, with negative politico-diplomatic impacts.[32]

- Illuminating varying levels of government control over and intervention in football, this book raises questions about the extent to which the state's participation in soccer's diplomatic networks affects the nature and effectiveness of soccer diplomacy. For example, how far does a heavy-handed government approach undermine soccer's soft power potential? Is it preferable for the government to stay, or at least appear to stay, in the background, focusing on infrastructural, visa, and other facilitating issues?
- How far is winning an essential requirement for successful soccer diplomacy? Or is style, fair play, dignity, and sportsmanship, especially in defeat, treated as possessing equal value diplomatically?
- How easy is it to link cause and effect in a meaningful manner? For example, sport diplomacy, pursued as one element of the anti-apartheid campaign, raised global consciousness and mobilized world opinion about the apartheid issue in South Africa, but its contribution to the eventual dismantling of apartheid remains highly debatable.[33]
- When assessing success, how easy is it to distinguish between ephemeral and long-lasting impacts, especially as soft power is normally considered to work over the long term?[34]

Contributors Address the Performance of Soccer Diplomacy

Apart from offering illuminating perspectives upon the above issues and perhaps raising as many questions as they answer, the contributors echo current thinking about the need for caution when assessing impact. They reaffirm the difficulty of linking cause and effect, particularly given the need to take into account the role played by other factors when evaluating the performance of soccer diplomacy. All the contributors emphasize the relevance of the historical and contemporary context.

For Dichter, Kioussis, and Nielsen, the Cold War provides an influential backdrop. Others emphasize alternative contextual factors. For Bolsmann, the fast-changing international politico-diplomatic context, combined with the intransigent stance of the South African apartheid government, was significant in explaining the suspension (1964) and the eventual expulsion (1976) of FASA from FIFA. In particular the growing momentum of the anti-apartheid movement across the world, the end of empire, and the increased voting power of newly independent states in international organizations and ISFs doomed South African soccer diplomacy aimed at the retention of FASA's FIFA membership to failure. For Dietschy, the decade following the First World War revealed an interesting mismatch between French politico-diplomatic hegemony and the disappointing performance of Les Bleus, the French national soccer team. Nor did soccer do much during the 1930s to help a France in decline counter the politico-diplomatic challenge launched by the Axis powers, Fascist Italy, and Nazi Germany.

Simón shows that Spain's links with the Axis powers influenced the nature and success of the Franco regime's soccer diplomacy, but he stresses the need to adopt a broad perspective that takes into account other factors. Simón acknowledges that it is difficult to credit soccer diplomacy, rather than some other factor, as prompting the post-1950 transformation in Spain's international position. Even so, it seems clear that football "serve[d] to enhance, improve and strengthen Francoism's diplomatic relations abroad," helping Franco's regime move on from the hostility and diplomatic isolation occasioned by its links with Hitler and Mussolini. However, Simón's claim that Real Madrid's European successes facilitated national cohesion requires qualification, given the omnipresent Catalan issue and Franco's repressive approach toward Catalan nationalism. For people living in Catalonia, regionalist passion subjugated a sense of Spanish identity, and FC Barcelona, not Real Madrid, represented their Catalan identity within and beyond Spain.[35]

At first sight, Kioussis's study of soccer exchanges conducted by Iceland and the United States during the mid-1950s furnishes perhaps the clearest example of successful soccer diplomacy. Soon after the Icelandic team returned from the United States, the American and Icelandic governments signed an agreement to extend the stay of the US Defense Force at Keflavik, the fundamental aim of the US State Department in sponsoring the national soccer team's tour to Iceland. The sequence of events—the United States–Iceland soccer exchanges occurred during 1955–1956 and the Keflavik agreement was signed in December 1956—might suggest that soccer diplomacy was responsible for the successful agreement, especially as positive media coverage and diplomatic feedback led the State Department to announce that it was "highly pleased" with the tour. The US Soccer Football Association (USSFA) president said the USSFA had "completed one of the greatest jobs they ever have on behalf of our country," claiming that soccer diplomacy had performed a critical Cold War role. Yet Kioussis, though acknowledging that the goodwill arising from the soccer exchanges made it easier for the Icelandic government to sell any deal to the people, concludes that in reality the outcome was largely the result of "hard power developments" centered on American financial support and Icelandic concern about the recent Soviet invasion of Hungary.[36]

From this same perspective, Nielsen's study of the Australian national team's visit to Vietnam in 1967 points to the blurred distinction between soccer diplomacy and soccer-as-diplomacy. Today there are—to quote Nielsen—"two partial understandings" of this episode. On the one hand, the adversarial autobiographical account advanced by Johnny Warren, the team's captain, presents the tour as basically an instrument of the Australian government's soccer diplomacy designed to win goodwill in "friendly" South Vietnam. For Warren, players were, in effect, soldiers placed in danger behind enemy lines, betrayed and let down by an uncaring government. On the other hand, Nielsen, making full use of the contemporary media and the partial archival record, advances a story of soccer-as-diplomacy, an episode that involved several actors, including the government and soccer authorities in South Vietnam as well as the Australian government, whose role was reactive, not proactive. Nielsen concedes that, regardless of the archival support underpinning his version, recent retellings of the story in the media and elsewhere have been influenced more by Warren's memoir than by his revisionist academic study.[37]

In a discussion of soccer diplomacy, it is easy to forget that the link between sport and diplomacy has both positive and negative dimensions. Football, like most sports, can be polarizing; Andrew Johns describes it as "parochial and universal, unifying and dividing."[38] Despite its value as a means of fostering positive images of a nation, bringing people together and so on, soccer diplomacy can go wrong, especially as, in practice, even those governments that claim to control sport within their respective boundaries possess limited influence and control over ISFs, teams, and individual players. Thus, as the contributors show, Franco's Spain, East Germany, the apartheid government in South Africa, and the Soviet Union controlled soccer to a substantial extent within their respective borders, but not outside, because they had to work within a global diplomatic framework defined largely by other governments and ISFs.

For most of the contributors, successful soccer diplomacy is treated as a function of results. Success on the soccer pitch is interpreted as the best form of soccer diplomacy. The central objective is to win, to defeat the team representing another country, an aspiration perhaps closer to the concept of hard power rather than of diplomacy. As a result, far from meeting its projected positive objectives, soccer diplomacy might unexpectedly prompt unfavorable negative images, such as through defeats or the misbehavior of players and supporters on and off the pitch. For example, Dietschy argues that Les Bleus did little to enhance images of French power and vitality—during the interwar period the team lost 70 out of its 118 games—even if any negative impressions were alleviated by occasional praise for its "good style."[39]

The US team's 1955 Icelandic tour exerted a similar impact. As mentioned above, both the State Department and the USSFA viewed the Icelandic tour as highly successful soccer diplomacy. And yet the US team lost all three matches. The United States' team did not win plaudits from the Icelandic media and people for its footballing prowess; rather, it won "victories by displaying the best in fair play and sportsmanship" in defeat. Kioussis also identifies a substantial unforeseen propaganda downside to these Iceland–United States soccer exchanges. The State Department hoped to use sport to promote the American way of life in the Cold War struggle for hearts and minds, but Kioussis raises questions about the impressions formed by visiting Icelandic footballers, officials, and media about the "vast wonderland" that was the United States, particularly regarding civil rights in everyday life and the militarism on view during their visit to the US Naval Academy: "While Washington could carefully construct the image that it projected abroad, it exerted far less control when it brought foreigners into the United States."[40]

Soccer mega-events, if hosted well, can yield mega propaganda benefits, but serious risks of mega negative impacts exist at every stage of the process, from bids to legacy. Dichter shows that in UEFA soccer tournaments held in

1961 and 1964, the East German question caused serious headaches for the host governments in the Netherlands and Portugal, as they were forced to balance the national interest in hosting a successful tournament against NATO obligations to veto East German participation. Elsey records how Chile used the 1962 World Cup finals to raise its profile on the world stage. The Chilean team gave a sterling performance, placing third overall. In retrospect, the tournament came to be perceived as a force for unparalleled national unity, the sense of political and social harmony accentuated over time by the discord of the ensuing Allende and Pinochet years. These positive outcomes were qualified by the negative commentaries about the country published by visiting Italian journalists, disappointing ticket sales, the small number of foreign spectators, and the lackluster defensive nature of the football on show. Nor were things helped by the marked disinterest in football reportedly displayed by President Jorge Alessandri.

By contrast, there is no doubt about the commitment of Brazilian presidents, especially Lula and his successor, Dilma Rousseff, to hosting a successful 2014 World Cup tournament. However, nationwide popular demonstrations against spending large sums on the World Cup rather than welfare benefits threatened to derail the whole project and delay essential infrastructure projects. The protests raised in an acute form the question of "World Cup for whom?" Subsequently Brazil's attempt to present itself as a modern, responsible, and stable country through mega-events was tarnished by revelations that bribery was used in contracts for staging the World Cup and the Olympics. Even worse, former president Lula, a prime mover in bidding for both events, was jailed for corruption in 2018.[41]

Assessing Soccer-as-Diplomacy

As Murray and Pigman point out, international sport has created a distinct type of specialized diplomacy: "In order for an international sporting competition to take place successfully, a whole category of multi-actor diplomatic representation and communication focused on negotiating the terms of and then producing the event must have occurred already."[42] Unsurprisingly, football's status as the world game means that, alongside the Olympics, it offers the best case studies for sport-as-diplomacy. However, in practice, it is not easy to evaluate the impact of soccer-as-diplomacy. It is more a specialized diplomatic process than a policy objective with targeted audience(s) and outcomes; and soccer-as-diplomacy networks serve basically as a means for pursuing soccer diplomacy.

Contributors Address the Performance of Soccer-As-Diplomacy

The contributors to this book show that soccer-as-diplomacy can confront governments and NGOs with serious challenges and difficult decisions, and may force organizations, like NATO, which do not claim interest or competence in such matters, to intervene in sport. Soccer-centered diplomatic networks vary in size, but Dichter shows that they can be quite extensive. In the ever-changing practice of diplomacy, soccer-as-diplomacy has introduced an additional mode of cultural diplomacy that involves soccer teams and ISFs. New non-state actors have emerged to work in a diplomatic framework linking soccer with governments, business, and the media.

Couto and Valente, whose chapter outlines the wide-ranging diplomatic network created through Brazil's hosting of the 2014 World Cup tournament, argue that the impact of soccer-as-diplomacy "may be even greater than of conventional diplomacy." Their claim, along with insights provided in other chapters, gives readers food for thought. Dietschy shows how the creation of a new diplomatic section within the French Ministry of Foreign Affairs led to a stronger focus on sport in diplomatic correspondence and the use of sport as a kind of barometer of France's international relationships. Murray and Pigman assert that "this specialized diplomacy that international sport spawns is arguably even more significant than the effects of international sport upon diplomatic relationships." For them, "the impact of this category on diplomacy is greater by virtue of its volume, frequency and ability to engage the hearts, minds and wallets of the global public."[43]

Looking Ahead

The growing academic focus on soccer diplomacy and soccer-as-diplomacy reflects in part the modernization of diplomacy, most notably the way in which it proves "innovative, effective and public." Soccer diplomacy and soccer-as-diplomacy are increasingly common features of the present-day world, particularly given the game's global popularity and perceived politico-diplomatic value in accessing large audiences. Dichter points out that the diverse worlds of sport and diplomacy have become increasingly and closely intertwined, and has noted elsewhere that "sport and diplomacy is a lively and growing subfield" of diplomatic and sports studies. Neither soccer diplomacy nor soccer-as-diplomacy figured in *Scoring for Britain: International Football and International Politics, 1900–1939*, my book published two decades ago. Then the prime focus was on politics and soccer, not diplomacy and soccer. In effect, diplomacy was subsumed within the term politics. Moreover, the Orwellian vision of international sporting realities as "war minus the shooting" loomed large in the contemporary sporting literature, an approach which proves—to quote Murray and Pigman—"the antithesis of diplomacy."[44]

By contrast, recent publications record a growing appreciation of the significance of the sport–diplomacy linkage. Murray and Pigman admit, "Today sport and diplomacy are no longer niche or backwater institutions but powerful foreign policy tools when working in tandem." This book, comprising a series of illuminating case studies of soccer diplomacy and soccer-as-diplomacy, establishes that cultural forms of diplomacy, especially those in the sphere of sport in general and soccer in particular, have played, still are playing, and will continue to play an increasingly influential role in international relations. Widespread public interest, support, and viewership are crucial to the success of any type of public diplomacy, a criterion that suggests the high potential impact of soccer diplomacy. In turn, the contributors show how diplomatization has emerged as yet another avenue for studying sport, especially in regard to international relations, public diplomacy, cultural diplomacy, and soft power.[45]

Reflecting a focus upon the politics of sport in general and the nation-state in particular, existing studies about sport and diplomacy have focused largely upon sport diplomacy, and especially the use of sport by governments to pursue their respective policy objectives in a fast-changing world. More recently, sport-as-diplomacy, although traditionally overlooked, has attracted increasing attention. Apart from recasting, indeed decentering, the nation and the state as well as stressing the role of non-state actors, this approach takes full account of participating domestic, international, and transnational actors, thereby allowing the emergence of a more nuanced appreciation regarding sport and diplomacy.[46] Against this background, the contributors provide an informed basis for further research on soccer diplomacy and soccer-as-diplomacy as well as upon sport diplomacy and sport-as-diplomacy in general.

Moreover, these studies prove timely, since soccer's proven ability to engage en masse means that it possesses massive public diplomacy potential in a fragmented world in which soft power assets, it is claimed, will become ever more valued, and sport, especially soccer, is represented as a "major asset in terms of soft power, not to be under-estimated." Lincoln Allison's comment that government policymakers are only too aware that "sport creates politically usable resources" has been widely quoted in the existing literature. This book establishes that soccer creates not only politically usable resources but also diplomatically usable resources. Generally speaking, hitherto the focus has been placed upon the positives. However, it is important also to appreciate its double-edged potential, that is possible negatives, most notably the challenge of translating soft power into policy, the risk of unforeseen consequences, and the fact that outsiders do not always respond to soccer diplomacy in the way expected. By implication the contributors, most notably McCree as well as Couto and Valente, point also to a worrying link between soccer diplomacy and unethical behavior.[47]

Finally, there are still serious questions about terminology in this emerging field of study. For Murray and Pigman as well as Rofe, terms like "sport diplomacy" seem "an odd hybrid," since "sport" and "diplomacy," when conflated, lose their uniqueness as distinct areas of study. Pointing to the differences between the diplomatic and sporting cultures, Rofe favors the use of "sport and diplomacy" in order to recognize both their links and independent nature. From this perspective, readers might consider it more illuminating to broaden the context by treating sport and diplomacy "as separate but equal realms rather as one subservient to the other."[48]

Notes

1. "Mercedes-Benz Triumphant: First and Second at Rheims," *Times*, July 5, 1954, 4; Diethelm Blecking, "Das 'Wunder von Bern' 1954—zur politischen Instrumentalisierung eines Mythos," *Historical Social Research* 40, no. 4 (2015): 200; Stefan Jordan, "Der deutsche Sieg bei der Weltmeisterschaft 1954: Mythos und Wunder oder historisches Ereignis?" *Historical Social Research* 30, no. 4 (2005): 263–287. This introductory section draws upon my forthcoming sequel to *Scoring for Britain: International Football and International Politics, 1900–1939* (1999) entitled *"Good Kicking" Is "Good Politics" and "Good Diplomacy" for Britain: International Football and International Politics, 1939–1958.*

2. "Politics in Football: Cup Hysteria in Germany," *Times*, July 10, 1954, 6; "President Heuss in Berlin," *Times*, July 17, 1954, 5; "President Heuss Re-Elected," *Times*, July 19, 1954, 6. The official FRG publication has a slightly different translation: "Not 'a German Football Wonder,'" *Bulletin* (Bonn), November 25, 1954, 6; *Deutschland Weltmeister im Fussball, 1954* (Frankfurt am Main: Wilhelm Limpert, 1954), 71.

3. Peco Bauwens,"Nur ein spiel," foreword to *Deutschland Weltmeister im Fussball, 1954*; "Politics in Football: Cup Hysteria in Germany," *Times*, July 10, 1954, 6; Blecking, "Das 'Wunder von Bern' 1954," 197–208.

4. Stuart Murray and Geoffrey A. Pigman, "Mapping the Relationship between International Sport and Diplomacy," *Sport in Society* 17, no. 9 (2014): 1098; J. Simon Rofe, "Sport and Diplomacy: A Global Diplomacy Framework," *Diplomacy & Statecraft* 27, no. 2 (2016): 215; J. Simon Rofe, "Introduction: Establishing the field of play," in *Sport and Diplomacy: Games within Games*, ed. J. Simon Rofe (Manchester; Manchester University Press, 2018), 1–7.

5. Nicholas J. Cull, *Public Diplomacy: Lessons for the Past* (Los Angeles: Figueroa, 2009), 17; Tim Adams, "Simon Anholt Interview: 'There Is Only One Global Superpower: Public Opinion'," *Observer*, November 30, 2014, https://www.theguardian.com/politics/2014/nov/30/simon-anholt-good-country-party-global-superpower-public-opinion (accessed August 1, 2017).

6. Report of the Advisory Committee on Cultural Diplomacy, *Cultural Diplomacy: The Linchpin of Public Diplomacy* (Washington, DC: US Department of State, 2005), 1; Jonathan McClory, *The Soft Power 30: A Global Ranking of Soft Power* (London: Portland, 2018), https://softpower30.com/wp-content/uploads/2018/07/The-Soft-Power-30-Report-2018.pdf; Anholt-GfK Nation Brands Index^{SM}, http://nation-brands.gfk.com/; Simon Anholt, "Beyond the Nation Brand: The Role of Image and Identity in International Relations," *Exchange: The Journal of Public Diplomacy* 2, no. 1 (2011): 1–2; Christopher Hill and Sarah Beadle, *The Art of Attraction: Soft Power and the UK's Role in the World* (London: British Academy, 2014), 6, 23.

7. Joseph S. Nye Jr., *Soft Power: The Means to Success in World Politics* (Cambridge, MA: Public Affairs, 2004), x, 1, 5; Joseph S. Nye Jr., "Public Diplomacy and Soft Power," *Annals of the American Academy of Political and Social Science* 616 (2008): 94–95; David Caute, *The Dancer Defects: The Struggle for Cultural Supremacy during the Cold War* (Oxford: Oxford University Press, 2003), 1–16; Peter J. Beck, "Britain and the Cold War's 'Cultural Olympics': Responding to the Political Drive of Soviet Sport, 1945–58," *Contemporary British History* 19, no. 2 (2005): 169–170. Unsurprisingly Nye's notion of soft power has changed over time in response to an ever-changing international political context: Melissa Nisbett, "Who Holds the Power in Soft Power?" *Arts and International Affairs*, March 13, 2016, https://theartsjournal.net/2016/03/13/nisbett/.

8. FCO memorandum, November 7, 1986, *House of Commons Foreign Affairs Committee, Fourth Report 1986–7: Cultural Diplomacy* (1987), 54; Jessica C. E.

Gienow-Hecht and Mark C. Donfried, "The Model of Cultural Diplomacy: Power, Distance, and the Promise of Civil Society," in *Searching for a Cultural Diplomacy*, ed. Jessica C. E. Gienow-Hecht and Mark C. Donfried (Oxford: Berghahn, 2010), 13–29; Joseph S. Nye Jr., "Soft Power and Cultural Diplomacy," *Public Diplomacy Magazine* 3 (2010): 120–124; Cull, *Public Diplomacy*, 19–20. Although sport is normally treated as one element of cultural diplomacy, there are exceptions, such as Phillip Blond, James Noyes, and Duncan Sim, *Britain's Global Future: Harnessing the Soft Power Capital of UK Institutions* (London: ResPublica, 2017). Michael Binyon and Marc Bennetts, "Books, Football and Gandalf Take Nation around the World," *Times*, August 5, 2017, https://www.thetimes.co.uk/article/the-british-council-formed-to-counter-nazi-influence-books-football-and-gandalf-take-nation-around-the-world-bqc9gxh5l (accessed August 5, 2017). Gandalf is a character in J. R. R. Tolkien's *Lord of the Rings*.

9. Speech by Nelson Mandela at the Inaugural Laureus Lifetime Achievement Award, Monaco, 2000, May 25, 2000, http://db.nelsonmandela.org/speeches/pub_view.asp?pg=item&ItemID=NMS1148 (accessed March 1, 2017); Sports Council Press Release, President Nelson Mandela: UK-South Africa Sports Initiative Reception, Lancaster House, London, July 11, 1996, quoted in Peter J. Beck, "'The Most Effective Means of Communication in the Modern World'?: British Sport and National Prestige," in *Sport and International Relations: An Emerging Relationship*, ed. Roger Levermore and Adrian Budd (London: Routledge, 2004), 77.

10. Murray and Pigman, "Mapping the Relationship," 1102; Dietschy; Simón.

11. Nye, *Soft Power: The Means to Success in World Politics*, 40, 47, 74, 76; Peter J. Beck, "Britain, Image-Building and the World Game: Sport's Potential as British Cultural Propaganda," in *The Image, the State and International Relations*, ed. Alan Chong and Jana Valencic (London: European Policy Unit, LSE, 2001), 58–66; Geoffrey A. Pigman, "International Sport and Diplomacy's Public Dimension: Governments, Sporting Federations and the Global Audience," *Diplomacy & Statecraft* 25, no. 2 (2014): 94–95.

12. Hill and Beadle, *The Art of Attraction*, 30; Nicholas Cull, *House of Commons Foreign Affairs Committee FCO Public Diplomacy: The Olympic and Paralympic Games 2012*, 2nd report, HC581, February 6, 2011, Ev36: https://www.publications.parliament.uk/pa/cm201011/cmselect/cmfaff/581/581.pdf; FIFA, "More Than Half the World Watched Record-Breaking 2018 World Cup," December 21, 2018, https://www.fifa.com/worldcup/news/more-than-half-the-world-watched-record-breaking-2018-world-cup (accessed March 14, 2019).

13. "Premier League Tops the British Icon Index II League Table," *Populus Insights*, July 2018, https://www.populus.co.uk/insights/2018/07/premier-league-tops-the-british-icon-index-ii-league-table/ (accessed May 12, 2019); *British Icon Index II: How Home-Grown Brands, Industries and Institutions Carry the Story of Modern Britain to the World* (London: Populus, 2018), 2–11, https://www.populus.co.uk/wp-content/uploads/2018/07/The-British-Icon-Index-II.pdf; Jonathan McClory,

"Soft Power and the World's Game: The Premier League in Asia," in McClory, *The Soft Power 30*, 143.

14. Murray and Pigman, "Mapping the Relationship," 1099; Eric Hobsbawm, *Nations and Nationalism since 1780: Programme, Myth, Reality* (Cambridge: Cambridge University Press, 1990), 143.

15. Dietschy. During the 1930s, British diplomats, who preferred cricket and rugby, were often reluctant to attend football matches as government representatives: Peter J. Beck, *Scoring for Britain: International Football and International Politics, 1900–1939* (London: Frank Cass, 1999), 40.

16. In 1980 I was able to interview Sir Stanley Rous (FIFA President: 1961–1974), whose responses have fed usefully into several of my publications.

17. Dietschy.

18. Simón. The author still remembers watching on television Real Madrid's impressive 7–3 win over Eintracht Frankfurt at Glasgow in 1960 played before 135,000 people.

19. Heather L. Dichter, "Sport History and Diplomatic History," *H-Diplo Essay no. 122,* December 17, 2014, https://networks.h-net.org/system/files/contributed-files/e122.pdf, 9.

20. Nielsen.

21. Couto and Valente.

22. Elsey.

23. Barbara J. Keys, *Globalizing Sport: National Rivalry and International Community in the 1930s* (Cambridge, MA: Harvard University Press, 2006), 2, 184; Murray and Pigman, "Mapping the Relationship," 1099, 1107, 1110.

24. Dietschy; Peter J. Beck, "Going to War, Peaceful Co-existence or Virtual Membership?: British Football and FIFA, 1928–46," *International Journal of the History of Sport* 17, no. 12 (2000): 113–134.

25. Dichter.

26. Beck, *Scoring for Britain*, 241–243. The British Council, created by the British government in 1934, possessed responsibility for British cultural propaganda.

27. McClory, "Soft Power and the World's Game," 140–143.

28. Lindsey C. Blom, Lawrence H. Gerstein, K. Stedman, L. Judge, A. Sink, and D. Pierce, "Soccer for Peace: Evaluation of In-Country Workshops with Jordanian Coaches," *Journal of Sport for Development* 3, no. 4 (2015): 1–12; Jacob W. Cooper, Lindsey C. Blom, Lawrence H. Gerstein, Dorice A. Hankemeier, and Tacianna P. Indovina, "Soccer for Peace in Jordan: A Qualitative Assessment of Program Impact on Coaches," *Journal of Sport for Development* 4, no. 6 (2016): 21–35; Lindsey C. Blom, Paz A. Magat, and Heather L. Dichter, "Grassroots diplomacy through coach education: Americans, Jordanians, and Tajiks," *Soccer & Society* 21 (2020), doi: 10.1080/14660970.2019.1689125.

29. Martyn Ziegler, "Warner: FIFA Officials Won't Change," *Times*, June 29, 2017, https://www.thetimes.co.uk/article/warner-fifa-officials-wont-change-r9jwrhm9x (accessed June 29, 2017).

30. Geoffrey A. Pigman and J. Simon Rofe, "Sport and Diplomacy: An Introduction," *Sport in Society* 17, no. 9 (2014): 1097; Steven Jackson, "The Contested Terrain of Sport Diplomacy in a Globalizing World," *International Area Studies Review* 16, no. 3 (2013): 276; McClory, *The Soft Power 30*, 16: https://softpower30.com/wp-content/uploads/2018/07/The_Soft_Power_30_Report_2016–1.pdf.

31. McClory, *The Soft Power 30*, 31, 96; Nye, *Soft Power: The Means to Success in World Politics*, 1.

32. Pigman and Rofe, "Sport and Diplomacy," 1097; Pigman, "International Sport," 96, 99; Alison Holmes with J. Simon Rofe, *Global Diplomacy: Theories, Types and Models* (Boulder, CO: Westview, 2016), 22; Murray and Pigman, "Mapping the Relationship," 1103.

33. See March Keech and Barrie Houlihan, "Sport and the End of Apartheid," *Round Table: The Commonwealth Journal of International Affairs* 88, 349 (1999): 109–121.

34. Pigman, "International Sport," 109–110.

35. Simón.

36. Kioussis.

37. Nielsen; Johnny Warren with Andy Harper and Josh Whittington, *Sheilas, Wogs, and Poofters: An Incomplete Biography of Johnny Warren and Soccer in Australia* (Sydney: Random House, 2002).

38. Andrew L. Johns, "Introduction. Competing in the Global Arena: Sport and Foreign Relations since 1945," in *Diplomatic Games: Sport, Statecraft, and International Relations since 1945*, ed. Heather L. Dichter and Andrew L. Johns (Lexington: University Press of Kentucky, 2014), 3.

39. Dietschy. For what one British diplomat described as "admirable examples of British [soccer] propaganda as it should not be" involving Chelsea and Arsenal, see Beck, *Scoring for Britain*, 225–226; Beck, "Britain and the Cold War's 'Cultural Olympics,'" 177–178. However, as one British Foreign Office minister conceded, it was difficult to control what happened on the pitch: "We can't control the footballers, I'm afraid." Beck, *Scoring for Britain*, 226.

40. Kioussis.

41. Couto and Valente; Jamil Chade, "Stadium Deals, Corruption and Bribery: The Questions at the Heart of Brazil's Olympic and World Cup 'Miracle'," *Observer*, April 23, 2017, https://www.theguardian.com/sport/2017/apr/23/brazil-olympic-world-cup-corruption-bribery (accessed May 31, 2017).

42. Murray and Pigman, "Mapping the Relationship," 1100.

43. Couto and Valente; Murray and Pigman, "Mapping the Relationship," 1099, 1107.

44. Dichter. On the development of academic study about sport and diplomacy, see Dichter, "Sport History and Diplomatic History"; Murray and Pigman, "Mapping the Relationship," 1104; Beck, *Scoring for Britain*, 37–38; Peter J. Beck, "'War Minus the Shooting': George Orwell on International Sport and the Olympics," *Sport in History* 33, no. 1 (2013): 72–94; Alan Tomlinson, "Diplomatic Actors in the

World of Football: Individuals, Institutions, Ideologies," in Rofe, *Sport and Diplomacy: Games within Games*, 47–50.

45. Murray and Pigman, "Mapping the Relationship," 1102, 1107.

46. Rofe, "Sport and Diplomacy," 218, 226.

47. Hill and Beadle, *The Art of Attraction*, 3, 6–7, 30, 45; Lincoln Allison, *The Politics of Sport* (Manchester: Manchester University Press, 1986), 12.

48. Murray and Pigman, "Mapping the Relationship," 1103; Rofe, "Sport and Diplomacy," 214–215.

Acknowledgments

Developing an edited volume is never an easy task, and selecting a topic with a global reach can make that process even more challenging. I am grateful to all of the authors who have contributed: Chris Bolsmann, Alan Castellano Valente, Euclides de Freitas Couto, Paul Dietschy, Brenda Elsey, George Kioussis, Roy McCree, Erik Nielsen, and Juan Antonio Simón. Some of these scholars previously knew me, while others graciously accepted the invitation to participate in this volume. Particular thanks go to Sarah Snyder and Peter Beck for their chapters, which involved reading all of the other contributions to identify themes that appear throughout the book. The work from this group of scholars—whose locations span the United States, Trinidad and Tobago, Brazil, the United Kingdom, France, Spain, and Australia—demonstrates the excellent international research being conducted in the field.

This book originated from a conversation with Michael J. McGandy of Cornell University Press in response to another project ultimately completed by J. Simon Rofe. Michael's encouragement and advice along the way have been valuable in shaping this book. Special thanks must of course be given to the editorial team at the University Press of Kentucky, including Melissa Hammer, who took on this project in one of her last acts at the Press, and Natalie O'Neal, as well as Studies in Conflict, Diplomacy, and Peace series editors Andy Johns, Kathryn Statler, and George Herring. Having previously coedited *Diplomatic Games: Sport, Statecraft and International Relations since 1945* with Andy, it was a delight to once again have an edited book on diplomacy and sport—this time just on soccer/football—with Kentucky. The anonymous reviewers also provided valuable feedback that greatly improved the book throughout the process.

Financial support for this book came from both the Leicester Castle Business School and Department of History at De Montfort University. As an academic working within two faculties, I greatly appreciate the support of both for research projects.

All of the book's contributors and the University Press of Kentucky staff were especially great in putting the final touches on the book in the middle of the COVID-19 pandemic. I cannot thank all of them enough for their efforts during this time.

Contributors

Peter J. Beck has a PhD from the London School of Economics and is emeritus professor of International History at Kingston University, Kingston upon Thames. The author of *Scoring for Britain: International Football and International Politics, 1900–1939,* he has published articles on the politics and diplomacy of sport in *International Affairs, Contemporary British History,* and *Historische Sozialforschung* as well as in the *Journal of Sport History, Sport in History,* and the *International Journal of the History of Sport.* His other books include *The War of the Worlds: From H. G. Wells to Orson Welles, Jeff Wayne, Steven Spielberg, and Beyond,* and *Presenting History: Past and Present.* Currently he is writing a sequel to *Scoring for Britain* covering 1939 to 1958.

Chris Bolsmann is a professor in the Department of Kinesiology at California State University, Northridge. He previously worked in higher education in Britain and South Africa. He has published a range of journal articles and coedited two books on South African sports history. He recently coauthored *English Gentlemen and World Soccer: Corinthians, Amateurism, and the Global Game.*

Euclides de Freitas Couto is a professor of the Postgraduate Program in History at the Federal University of São João del-Rei in Minas Gerais, Brazil. He researches sports matters in the Laboratory of History of Sport and Leisure at the Federal University of Rio de Janeiro (Brazil). He has published articles in the *International Journal of History of Sport* and *Recorde: Revista de História do Esporte, Aletria.*

Heather L. Dichter is associate professor of Sport Management and Sport History at De Montfort University as well as a member of the International

Centre for Sports History and Culture. She previously coedited *Diplomatic Games: Sport, Statecraft, and International Relations since 1945* with Andrew Johns and *Olympic Reform Ten Years Later* with Bruce Kidd, and she has published articles in *International Journal of the History of Sport, Diplomacy & Statecraft, Sport in History,* and *History of Education.* Her research and publications focus on sport in occupied Germany, sport in the Cold War, international sport, and Olympic bids and corruption.

Paul Dietschy is professor of Contemporary History at the Franche-Comté University and director of the Lucien Febvre Center (Besançon, France). He specializes in sport and soccer history. His recent publications include *Origin and Birth of "the Europe of Football," Histoire du Football, Le sport et la Grande Guerre,* and with Stefano Pivato, *Storia dello sport in Italia.*

Brenda Elsey is associate professor of History at Hofstra University in New York with a specialism in gender, politics, and popular culture in Latin America. She is the author of *Citizens and Sportsmen: Fútbol and Politics in Twentieth-Century Chile* and coauthor with Joshua Nadel of *Futbolera: A History of Women's Sport in Latin America.* She has also written for mainstream outlets such as the *Guardian, New Republic,* and *Sports Illustrated.* She is the cohost of the weekly sport and feminism podcast, Burn It All Down.

George N. Kioussis is an assistant professor in the Department of Kinesiology at California State University, Northridge. His primary research centers around sport governance and globalization, with an emphasis on (trans) nationalism, exceptionalism, and cultural flows. He has published articles in the *Journal of Sport History, Sport in History,* and the *International Review for the Sociology of Sport.*

Roy McCree is a sociologist and senior research fellow at the Sir Arthur Lewis Institute of Social and Economic Studies (SALISES) at the University of West Indies, St. Augustine campus. His main research interests relate to sport, youth, community development, and social capital. He has published previously in the *International Journal of the History of Sport, Sport in Society, Journal of Sport and Social Issues,* and the *International Review for the Sociology of Sport.*

Erik Nielsen is a research officer at Macquarie University, Sydney, Australia. His main area of research is the history of Australian sport's relationship with the British Empire and Asian region. His book *Sport and the British World, 1900–1930: Amateurism and National Identity in Australasia and Beyond* won the 2015 Australian Society for Sports History Book Prize.

Juan Antonio Simón has a PhD from Carlos III University of Madrid. He is currently head of the Department of Sport Science and teaches Sport History at the Universidad Europea of Madrid. His work focuses principally on the history of sport in Spain, the links between football and international relations, and the history of sports mega-events like the FIFA World Cup and the Olympic Games. He has published in Spanish and English, including a chapter in *Beyond Boycotts: National, Continental, and Transcontinental Sporting Relations during the Cold War,* edited by Philippe Vonnard, Nicola Sbetti, and Grégory Quin, and a recent article on Real Madrid FC in the *International Journal of the History of Sport.*

Sarah B. Snyder teaches at American University's School of International Service. She is the author of two award-winning books, *From Selma to Moscow: How Human Rights Activists Transformed U.S. Foreign Policy,* which won the 2019 Robert H. Ferrell Book Prize, and *Human Rights Activism and the End of the Cold War: A Transnational History of the Helsinki Network,* which was awarded the 2012 Stuart Bernath Book Prize and the 2012 Myrna F. Bernath Book Award. In addition to authoring several chapters in edited collections, she has also published articles in *Diplomatic History, Cold War History, Human Rights Quarterly, Diplomacy & Statecraft, Journal of Transatlantic Studies, European Journal of Human Rights,* and *Journal of American Studies.*

Alan Castellano Valente received his MA in English Literature from the Universidade Federal de Minas Gerais. He has been an adjunct professor of Portuguese Writing and Philosophy at Centro Universitário Una and at Universidade do Estado de Minas Gerais (UEMG) in Belo Horizonte, Minas Gerais, Brazil. He coauthored the Pitágoras English Collection for High School and has published articles in *Aletria Special Edition on Football.* He also worked as the technical editor for *Revista de Estudos da Linguagem, Revista Brasileira de Linguística Aplicada, Revista Pós,* and *Revista Brasileira da Educação Básica.*

Index

Studies in Conflict, Diplomacy, and Peace

Series Editors: George C. Herring, Andrew L. Johns, and Kathryn C. Statler

This series focuses on key moments of conflict, diplomacy, and peace from the eighteenth century to the present to explore their wider significance in the development of U.S. foreign relations. The series editors welcome new research in the form of original monographs, interpretive studies, biographies, and anthologies from historians, political scientists, journalists, and policymakers. A primary goal of the series is to examine the United States' engagement with the world, its evolving role in the international arena, and the ways in which the state, nonstate actors, individuals, and ideas have shaped and continue to influence history, both at home and abroad.

Advisory Board Members

Books in the Series

Truman, Congress, and Korea: The Politics of America's First Undeclared War
Larry Blomstedt

The Legacy of J. William Fulbright: Policy, Power, and Ideology
Edited by Alessandro Brogi, Giles Scott-Smith, and David J. Snyder

The Gulf: The Bush Presidencies and the Middle East
Michael F. Cairo

Reagan and the World: Leadership and National Security, 1981–1989
Edited by Bradley Lynn Coleman and Kyle Longley

American Justice in Taiwan: The 1957 Riots and Cold War Foreign Policy
Stephen G. Craft

Diplomatic Games: Sport, Statecraft, and International Relations since 1945
Edited by Heather L. Dichter and Andrew L. Johns

Soccer Diplomacy: International Relations and Football since 1914
Edited by Heather L. Dichter

Nothing Less Than War: A New History of America's Entry into World War I
Justus D. Doenecke

Aid under Fire: Nation Building and the Vietnam War
Jessica Elkind

Enemies to Allies: Cold War Germany and American Memory
Brian C. Etheridge

Grounded: The Case for Abolishing the United States Air Force
Robert M. Farley

Foreign Friends: Syngman Rhee, American Exceptionalism, and the Division of Korea
David P. Fields

The Myth of Triumphalism: Rethinking President Reagan's Cold War Legacy
Beth A. Fischer

The American South and the Vietnam War: Belligerence, Protest, and Agony in Dixie
Joseph A. Fry

Lincoln, Seward, and US Foreign Relations in the Civil War Era
Joseph A. Fry

The Turkish Arms Embargo: Drugs, Ethnic Lobbies, and US Domestic Politics
James F. Goode

Obama at War: Congress and the Imperial Presidency
Ryan C. Hendrickson

The Cold War at Home and Abroad: Domestic Politics and US Foreign Policy since 1945
Edited by Andrew L. Johns and Mitchell B. Lerner

US Presidential Elections and Foreign Policy: Candidates, Campaigns, and Global Politics from FDR to Bill Clinton
Edited by Andrew Johnstone and Andrew Priest

Paving the Way for Reagan: The Influence of Conservative Media on US Foreign Policy
Laurence R. Jurdem

The Conversion of Senator Arthur H. Vandenberg: From Isolation to International Engagement
Lawrence S. Kaplan

Harold Stassen: Eisenhower, the Cold War, and the Pursuit of Nuclear Disarmament
Lawrence S. Kaplan

America's Israel: The US Congress and American-Israeli Relations, 1967–1975
Kenneth Kolander

JFK and de Gaulle: How America and France Failed in Vietnam, 1961–1963
Sean J. McLaughlin

Nixon's Back Channel to Moscow: Confidential Diplomacy and Détente
Richard A. Moss

Breaking Protocol: America's First Female Ambassadors, 1933–1964
Philip Nash

Peacemakers: American Leadership and the End of Genocide in the Balkans
James W. Pardew

The Currents of War: A New History of American-Japanese Relations, 1899–1941
Sidney Pash

Eisenhower and Cambodia: Diplomacy, Covert Action, and the Origins of the Second Indochina War
William J. Rust

So Much to Lose: John F. Kennedy and American Policy in Laos
William J. Rust

Foreign Policy at the Periphery: The Shifting Margins of US International Relations since World War II
Edited by Bevan Sewell and Maria Ryan

Lincoln Gordon: Architect of Cold War Foreign Policy
Bruce L. R. Smith

Thomas C. Mann: President Johnson, the Cold War, and the Restructuring of Latin American Foreign Policy
Thomas Tunstall Allcock

www.ingramcontent.com/pod-product-compliance
Lightning Source LLC
Chambersburg PA
CBHW031545260326
41914CB00002B/278

* 9 7 8 0 8 1 3 1 7 9 5 1 3 *